EXPLORATIONS IN PEER TUTORING

Edited by
**Sinclair Goodlad and
Beverley Hirst**

BLACKWELL EDUCATION

Sponsored by GE Foundation Inc

© Basil Blackwell Ltd 1990
First published 1990

Published by
Basil Blackwell Ltd
108 Cowley Road
Oxford OX4 1JF
England

British Library Cataloguing in Publication Data
Explorations in peer tutoring
  1. Peer teaching
  I. Goodlad, Sinclair *1938–*.   II. Hirst, Beverley
  371.3

ISBN 0–631–17518–0
ISBN 0–631–17519–9 pbk

Typeset in 10/12pt Bembo
by Times Graphics of Singapore
Printed in Great Britain
by T. J. PRESS LTD, PADSTOW, CORNWALL

Contents

Preface and acknowledgements

It is a pleasure to acknowledge the help of those whose efforts made this book possible.

Our principal and most immediate debt is to the GE Foundation Inc of the United States, for their generous benefaction.

The conference from which the papers in the book derive was generously supported with grants, and benefactions in kind, from: the Anglo-Israeli Foundation; British Gas; British Petroleum; British Telecom; the Department of Education and Science; Esso; ICI; Olivetti; Pilkington; Rank Xerox; and Shell. Their support (which covered many of the overheads costs of the conference so that the fee could be set at a level that teachers could afford) ensured a good attendance at the conference and lively discussion.

The staff work behind the conference was secured by a special initiatives grant of the (then) University Grants Committee of the United Kingdom. It was fitting, and a privilege to all present, that Sir Peter Swinnerton-Dyer spoke at the conference dinner, which was presided over by Professor Bryan Coles, Pro-Rector of Imperial College.

The contributors helped greatly by getting in quickly such changes to their papers as we requested, and James Nash and Marion Casey of Basil Blackwell were most courteous and helpful throughout.

We are grateful to the publishers (Carfax) of the journal *Educational Psychology* for permission to reprint 'Peer Tutored Paired Reading: outcome data from ten projects' by Keith Topping, which first appeared in 1987, and to the publishers of the journal *Remedial and Special Education* for permission to publish 'Special education students as tutors: a review and analysis' by Russell Osguthorpe and Thomas Scruggs, which first appeared in 1986.

Much of the administration of the conference was carried out by Joy Hill. John Milne assisted with graphics work. The Imperial College Conference Office and Refectory helped to ensure that all went smoothly.

Our spouses, (and Emily Goodlad), inevitably, put up with a great deal. To all these people we give our thanks – and exonerate them from any responsibility for imperfections which remain in the text.

Sinclair Goodlad and Beverley Hirst
Imperial College of Science,
Technology and Medicine
July 1989

1 Explorations in peer tutoring

Sinclair Goodlad and Beverley Hirst

Definition

Peer tutoring is the system of instruction in which learners help each other and learn by teaching.

Invented in the late 18th century by Joseph Lancaster and Andrew Bell, the technique has been re-discovered in recent years and put to use in a wide variety of projects which *inter alia:* enable students to teach students; students to teach children; children to teach children; non-professional adults to teach other adults: and even learning-disabled children to help other children. In this book, the common phrase 'peer tutoring' is used to describe all of these schemes – 'peer' being defined as someone belonging to the same group in society where membership is defined by status. In this case, the status is that of being a fellow-learner and not a professional teacher.

Object of the book

The object of this book is to stimulate interest in an important and under-used resource by making available to educational researchers, educational administrators, trainers of teachers and practising teachers in primary, secondary, and tertiary (higher) education a set of case studies in the theory and practice of peer tutoring. The introductory and review chapters set these case studies within the context of the international literature on the subject.

Although the book is aimed primarily at practitioners, it is suitable also for researchers interested in the underlying social and psychological processes involved in peer tutoring. Classroom practitioners will find that the emphasis throughout is on what has been done and with what effect – on the assumption that readers will feel more confident in carrying out their own explorations in peer tutoring if they have to hand records of the work of others who have entered what may seem to be unfamiliar territory. To appeal to researchers, there is a strong emphasis on those explorations in Peer Tutoring which have tried to relate specific practice to learning theory in systematic ways.

Origin of the book

In 1987, the (then) University Grants Committee of the United Kingdom provided Dr Sinclair Goodlad with a two-year grant for a project on students as tutors in science, engineering, and mathematics. (At that time the Committee had launched a special initiatives scheme to stimulate the flow into teaching of graduates in science, mathematics, and engineering.) The objects of the project were to disseminate information about a scheme known as 'The Pimlico Connection'. Since 1975 some 800 students from Imperial College have been involved in the scheme aiming to help teachers in local schools by tutoring some 9000 pupils; to establish similar projects elsewhere; and to promote tutoring more widely. One effect of 'The Pimlico Connection' has been to attract students of mathematics, science, and engineering into teaching as a career.

The centrepiece of the project was an international conference on peer tutoring held at Imperial College in April 1989. In preparation for the conference, Sinclair Goodlad and Beverley Hirst wrote *Peer Tutoring: A guide to learning by teaching* (Goodlad and Hirst, 1989) which should be read in conjunction with *Explorations in Peer Tutoring*. The pre-conference book, Peer Tutoring, is a sort of 'cognitive map' or basic introduction to the field. It offers a description of some early experiments; an analysis of expected benefits (corresponding to a list of pedagogic aims); a review of research on some of the effects of tutoring on participants, and a guide to how to start a tutoring scheme. *Explorations in Peer Tutoring*, which is built around representative papers from the Imperial College conference, examines selected topics in more detail. It is, in effect, a detailed examination of some of the terrain sketched in the 'cognitive map'.

Overview of the content

The sections which follow highlight some of the key issues from the papers and set them in the context of the educational issues they seek to address and the research in the various sub-fields.

One of the most striking features of the field is the great variety of permutations and combinations of educational levels and subjects in which peer tutoring is used. Table 1.1 will help readers find the themes most closely related to their specific interests, chapters are identified by number (from the table of contents) and by the first-named author.

How peer tutoring works

Peer tutoring as a relief of stress for teachers
In recent years, teachers at all levels of the education system have been put under increasing pressure; large classes, reductions in 'non-contact' time and major changes to examination systems have significantly increased their workload. New assessment procedures have placed more demands on their time, not only by increasing the amount of institution-based assessment, but also by putting more emphasis on individualised work schemes and the continuous monitoring of student progress. In many schools which no longer stream pupils, and where mixed-ability grouping or 'broad bands' are the norm, providing individualised instruction to meet the needs of the wide range of abilities within a class is not merely preferable, but essential. Unfortunately, extra funding has not been provided to reduce the pupil:teacher ratio to a level at which pupils can receive the one-to-one instruction they need. Given this situation, some strategy is needed which permits individualised instruction to be provided at minimal cost. Peer tutoring offers a possible solution to the problem.

There is, of course, a cost element involved in developing a peer tutoring scheme. As with all innovations, someone has to devote time to the initial planning and subsequent implementation of a programme. However, most of those who have used tutoring schemes report that, once they are established, the time-commitment necessary to organise follow-on programmes is significantly reduced. Moreover, when tutoring is under way, teachers are freed from routine tasks within the classroom and can devote themselves to the higher-level skills of teaching: directing instruction; facilitating learning; and subsequently evaluating that learning. Time spent on planning *before* a tutoring lesson is more than repaid *within* it.

As with most schemes additional to conventional classroom teaching, peer tutoring does incur expenses (although these are generally on a small scale). Nowadays, however, any financial outlay by educational institutions, no matter how small, has to be justified. It is no longer sufficient for a teaching innovation to be proved effective; it must also be proved 'cost-effective'. Educational administrators, local education authorities, directors of study, headteachers, school governors, and parent teacher associations all balance improved outcomes against financial outlay. It is worthy of note, therefore, that in a recent 'cost-effectiveness' study to assist decision-makers in considering different approaches to facilitating the learning of elementary-school children, Levin, Glass and Meister (1987) found peer tutoring to be more cost-effective than computer-assisted

Table 1.1 Outline coverage by level, mode, and subject

	Primary	Secondary	Tertiary	Cross-age	Same-age	Reading	Maths	Science
1 GOODLAD (a)	✓	✓	✓	✓	✓	✓	✓	✓
2 FITZ-GIBBON	✓	✓		✓			✓	
3 KENNEDY (a)	✓			✓	✓	✓	✓	
4 FRESKO	✓	✓	✓	✓		✓	✓	
5 BEARDON	✓	✓	✓	✓			✓	✓
6 JONES	✓	✓	✓	✓				✓
7 BUTTON			✓	✓				✓
8 FALCHIKOV			✓		✓			✓
9 ARBLASTER	✓				✓	✓		
10 TOPPING	✓	✓		✓	✓	✓		
11 KENNEDY (b)		✓		✓		✓		
12 OSGUTHORPE	✓	✓		✓	✓	✓	✓	
13 QUIN				✓	✓			✓
14 KELLETT	✓				✓			
15 WINTER	✓				✓	✓		
16 GOODLAD (b)	✓	✓	✓	✓	✓	✓	✓	✓

instruction (CAI), and both of these were more cost-effective than reducing class size or increasing the length of the school day.

Educationalists taking on more and more contractual responsibilities will not be willing to organise new projects and schemes unless they are convinced of some positive outcome. Peer tutoring sounds like a 'nice idea' in that learners help one another to learn; but practitioners have to be convinced that this learning actually does take place before being prepared to devote time and energy to implementing a scheme. There is now a wealth of literature (mostly published since the 1960s) attesting to the efficacy of peer tutoring schemes in facilitating learning. In 1975, Wilkes reported 268 publications on the subject; in 1989 we found that over 1000 further papers had been published since then.

Despite the large number of publications in the field, however, there is still some difficulty in forming a cohesive body of knowledge about peer tutoring. To date, those implementing schemes have employed a wide variety of methods, adopted different objectives, and used different evaluation criteria. Indeed, this very flexibility is one of the main attractions of peer tutoring. Schemes vary in the characteristics of their participants (achievement, gender, race, social class, age) or the specific characteristics of the programme (number of participants, subject-matter, tutor-training, duration of programme). Such variations have resulted in diverse findings by those researching the effects of tutoring. Nevertheless, although opinion may differ on, for example, the optimum length of a programme, the effect of sex-pairings on the dyad, or the necessary degree of structure to incorporate, the research evidence is clear: *peer tutoring can improve the attainment of both tutor and tutee* in the content area being tutored. In addition, many studies report affective gains for participants.

Benefits to participants of taking part in peer tutoring schemes
A recent meta-analysis to assess the educational outcomes of tutoring (Cohen, Kulik and Kulik, 1982), examined the cognitive and affective effects of 65 school-tutoring programmes. Only those studies which took place in actual elementary or secondary school classrooms are reported, and quantitatively-measured outcomes for tutored pupils and control groups are included in the analysis. Of the studies which examined the effects on academic achievement of tutors (n = 38) and tutees (n = 52), the majority indicated that the participants in the tutoring schemes out-performed controls on examinations in the subject being taught. (Over a third of these studies demonstrated effects which reached statistical significance.) Results from studies which examined affective changes were not so consistent; but indications are that benefits are possible in this area for both tutors and tutees.

Very similar findings were reported by Cook et al (1986) who conducted a meta-analysis on available research documenting the effectiveness of handicapped students as tutors of others. All of the 19 articles reviewed employed learning-disabled, intellectually-handicapped or behaviourally-disordered students as tutors in an academic subject. Data from these studies indicated that being involved in a tutoring scheme raised the performance-level of the tutors and tutees above that of the controls, with tutees generally achieving greater academic gains than tutors. Again, changes in self-concept and sociometric measures were negligible for both tutors and tutees, although behaviour ratings of tutors were perceived to change more than those of tutees. Both tutors and tutees seemed to have improved their attitudes towards school or the subject-area being tutored.

Cognitive gains for tutors
Many of the research articles on peer tutoring have placed more emphasis on predicting and explaining the effects on tutors than on examining the effects on tutees. Several theories have been proposed as to why cognitive and affective gains should accrue to tutors (Goodlad and Hirst, 1989; Malamuth and Fitz-Gibbon, 1978). In summary advocates of the efficacy of peer tutoring for improving the performance of tutors claim that tutors learn by reviewing, and finding meaningful use of, subject-matter, filling in gaps in their own education, consolidating learning, or learning through a process of reformulation. In addition, it is suggested that once students find a meaningful use for their knowledge, it becomes of more interest to them: they assimilate it more readily, and so they become interested in acquiring more of that knowledge - so improving their motivation and attitude to the subject-area being tutored.

Accelerated learning has been reported, particularly for under-achieving pupils who have served as tutors to younger children. Tutoring schemes involving these students have been employed predominantly in reading, probably, as has been previously suggested (Goodlad and Hirst, 1989:61), because such programmes provide a face-saving way of enabling adolescents to study reading material several years below their expected achievement level. For example, Rosner (1970) reported average gains of 17 months on the comprehension test of a basic skills reading subscale by remedial 10 and 11 year olds after a 10 week intervention in which they tutored 7 and 8 year olds. Other researchers have found significantly greater gains on reading, vocabulary and comprehension tests for low-achieving tutors (Liette, 1970; Lakin, 1972; Shisler et al, 1986), whilst their tutees gained as well. Pupils have also been shown to make academic gains when they tutor in mathematics (Rust, 1970; Mohan, 1972; Roach et al, 1983).

In Chapter 2 of this book, Carol Fitz-Gibbon suggests that low-achieving students might, in fact, be more effective tutors for tutees than very able pupils. They are used to going over work more slowly and laboriously and they thus may present new work to younger pupils at a more realistic pace, allowing plenty of opportunity for repetition of the subject-matter. To date, few studies have examined this issue in detail, although Sharpley et al (1983) and Ackerman (1970) found that the achievement level of tutors had negligible effects on the achievement gains of tutees in mathematics.

Gains for tutors are not only typical of 'low-achieving' tutors, however; those who show grade-appropriate ability on pre-tests have also gained from the experience (see, for example, Cloward, 1967; Morgan and Toy, 1970; and King, 1982, in reading, and Guarnaccia, 1973; Morgan and Toy, 1972; and Maheady, 1987b, in mathematics).

Cognitive gains for tutees
Although tutoring has clearly been shown to offer benefits to those who tutor (regardless of their ability) most educationalists would feel unhappy about implementing a strategy which benefits one group of students at the expense of another. It is gratifying, therefore, that those who are tutored can similarly benefit from the experience. By participating in a tutoring scheme, tutees receive individual attention, more of that attention, and the systematic feedback that they require if they are to make real advances in the subject-area being studied. Substantial improvements in reading grade-equivalent for underachieving tutees, following tutoring interventions of relatively short duration, have been reported (eg Cloward, 1967; Rogers, 1970a; Morgan and Toy, 1970; Stander, 1972; and Hendrickson, 1982). Pupils have also shown marked improvements after involvement in mathematics-tutoring programmes, (see Mohan, 1972; Levine, 1976; Bar-Eli and Raviv, 1982; Sharpley et al, 1983).

Although the studies cited above all relate to tutoring in reading and mathematics, the strategy has not been employed exclusively in these areas. In a recent review paper, Sharpley and Sharpley (1981) located tutoring programmes incorporating tasks and activities drawn from 18 different subject areas. The cross-age tutoring programmes described by Toni Beardon and John Jones (Chapters 5 and 6 of this book) modelled on 'The Pimlico Connection' (Goodlad and Hirst, 1989: Chapter 5) concentrate on providing a tutorial service within science lessons. It is interesting that such schemes, which employ undergradutates as tutors to school children of all abilities, also indicate that acting as a tutor offers academic benefits. A significant proportion of the undergraduate tutors involved in these schemes feel that tutoring in schools reinforces their knowledge of some aspect of their subject; tutees also feel that they learn more.

These findings should be of interest to those working in higher education. Whilst it would seem likely that, if tutors and tutees are reasonably close in age and knowledge, the process of thinking through material to teach it will help the tutor to master it, this effect might not have been anticipated with such a substantial age/experience differential. It is perhaps worth noting here that little systematic evidence is available concerning the optimal age difference between tutor and tutee, although Sharpley and Sharpley (1981) cite several studies which consistently showed that children were no less effective than adults in enhancing the achievement of child-tutees. Indeed, the optimal age difference may vary as educators balance the needs of tutor and tutee, depending upon the objectives of the scheme.

Same-age or cross-age tutoring?

Opinion differs as to whether same-age or cross-age programmes are the most desirable. Carol Fitz-Gibbon (1980:18) concludes, from a study of peer tutoring in inner-city secondary-schools, that cross-age tutoring is more promising than same-age. She suggests that an age difference of between two and four years between tutor and tutee is preferable. Of the five controlled studies to which Fitz-Gibbon refers (in Chapter 2 of this book), the two which involved same-age tutoring were considered unsuccessful. Sharpley and Sharpley (1981) also indicate that many advocates of peer tutoring claim that it has a better chance of long-term success because a minimum differential of two years lessens the tendency towards resentment or personality-clashes. However, logistical arrangements also have to be taken into account; teachers may consider cross-age tutoring most beneficial to their pupils, preferring an age-gap between tutor and tutee, but choose to employ same-age tutoring because of the relative ease of implementation. As Topping (1988) points out, any cross-age tutoring arrangement will almost inevitably create difficulties of matching timetables and organising the movement of pupils.

Affective gains for tutors and tutees

As was suggested by the meta-analyses described above (Cohen, Kulik and Kulik, 1982; Cook et al, 1986), although cognitive gains as a consequence of a tutoring intervention are well-documented, there is less strong evidence for affective gains. This is perhaps one of the most bewildering findings for those synthesising research on tutoring. Numerous papers which provide more subjective, qualitative reports of tutoring interventions testify to the success of schemes in improving the attitude, behaviour and self-esteem of tutors. These reports, however, are not supported by more quantitative, psychometric studies.

There are, however, good reasons for those implementing schemes to anticipate improvements in the affective domain for all pupils. Tutors are given trust and responsibility which one would expect to improve their self-confidence and so self-esteem (this would only apply, of course, if they were also provided with the necessary support and training to ensure that they were effective tutors). By being given the role of teacher, it is anticipated that they will adopt behaviours consistent with that role and, as a consequence, will exhibit inappropriate (disruptive) behaviours less often. Additionally, tutors are given responsibility for the learning of others, a nurturing role which could influence their attitude towards their class-mates, shifting the classroom atmosphere away from one of competition towards one of cooperation. Indeed, as Carol Fitz-Gibbon indicates in Chapter 2, tutoring may be invaluable in a classroom where pupil cooperation is problematic.

Tutees also have much to gain; they are provided with a companion involved in their learning who shows interest in their work and is more available to praise their successes. As Topping (1988) has suggested, children are very important to children, increasingly so as they get older and withdraw more from parental influence. Peer tutoring has few of the institutional and authoritarian overtones of relationships between professional teachers and students, so the distance between teacher and learner is reduced, and may indeed be replaced by a genuine affection. On the basis of these suppositions, it is surprising that reports of changes in the affective domain for tutor and tutee have not been more strongly validated by psychometric research.

Despite the lack of consensus in this area, individual studies have reported encouraging findings. For example, Moon and Wilson (1970) found that 10-year-old children who had previously been labelled as discipline problems showed marked improvements in classroom behaviour after participating in a six month programme in which they tutored younger children in reading, and that the classroom atmosphere became much more cooperative. Bremmer (1972) used socially-disadvantaged 12 to 13 year olds as tutors to elementary school children and found that school attendance improved for 60% of the tutors, although no significant changes in attitude were found. Some studies have reported statistically significant effects. Maher (1982) found that adolescents with conduct problems who worked as cross-age tutors for elementary school mentally-retarded students not only improved significantly on social science and language arts grades, but also had significantly reduced rates of absenteeism and disciplinary referrals. Lazerson (1980) employed aggressive and withdrawn children as tutors of peers having similar behavioural problems; after five weeks of participation in the programme, all children (tutors and tutees) had made higher self-concept gains and greater improvements in behaviour than controls (although these did not reach statistical significance).

Affective gains have not been limited to those pupils who have previously displayed learning difficulties or behaviour problems. Roberston (1971) studied the effects of tutoring on the self-concepts of ten year-old pupils who tutored six year olds in sight-reading. A semantic-differential test revealed that the tutors developed significantly different and more positive self-concepts than those in the control group. Mainiero et al (1971) reported that children who tutored in the Ontario-Montclair tutoring scheme improved their self-concept, as did the nine-, ten- and eleven year old tutees. Systematic differences in classroom behaviour between tutors and controls were also found.

Given these findings, it is difficult to understand why reports of affective gains are not more prevalent. It has been suggested (Goodlad and Hirst,

1989) that attitudes and behaviour may change only while the intervention is taking place and that these changes are not transferred to other settings. Meyer (1972) proposes that attitudes are more resistant to change than achievement; as tutoring schemes are typically of short duration, attitude changes are not given time to develop. Bar-Eli and Raviv (1982) draw a similar conclusion after an intervention in which 10 to 11 year-old students who were weak in mathematics tutored similar seven year olds but failed to show any changes in attitude.

It could be that as tutoring generally occurs for only a relatively small part of the school day, and an even smaller proportion of the school year, global effects on attitude and self-concept will be minimal. For the rest of the time, pupils are assigned the role of learner in the conventional classroom setting. Alternatively, it is possible that test instruments to measure self-concept and attitude changes are insufficiently sensitive to detect positive changes which are taking place within students, and that teachers themselves are more responsive to these changes. Equally, it could be that these changes do not really take place, but that teachers and researchers are so enthusiastic about the strategy that they attribute merits to it for which there is no psychometric evidence. It should be added as a practical aside, however, that struggling teachers are unlikely to advocate an intervention which causes more classroom disruption. The fact that so many teachers strongly recommend peer tutoring indicates that, even if behavioural and motivational changes are not long-term, temporary improvements do occur whilst tutoring is actually taking place.

Explaining the mechanisms of peer tutoring
Although theories have been proposed to explain why peer tutoring should work, no-one has yet conducted experiments to specifically test the appropriateness of any theory for explaining the changes which clearly do take place in both tutors and tutees. It is this issue which Mary Kennedy addresses in Chapter 3 of this book. Kennedy argues that although global theories can predict the phenomena associated with tutoring, such as 'learning by teaching', they could just as readily predict their absence. She suggests that the application of theory to explain 'learning by teaching' is somewhat premature since the phenomenon has never been demonstrated to result from tutoring as opposed to a confounding factor such as tutor-training (see also Levine, 1976) or time-on-task.

It is true that many tutoring schemes, particularly those initiated in the 1960s, such as the *Homework Helper Programme* (Deering, 1975) provided a tutorial service which was additional to normal class teaching. Similarly, many Paired Reading programmes involving parents (Topping, 1986c: 146) have involved children in extra hours of reading practice. However, other researchers have implemented programmes which have replaced conventional classroom teaching, attempting to keep instructional time constant. Even so, because in a tutoring situation pupils receive immediate responses and so can progress through work schemes more quickly (see Arblaster et al in Chapter 9), it may be difficult to isolate the cause of the observed effect. Although tutoring interventions may occupy the same amount of classroom time, the time-on-task, or engaged time, is very much increased.

There is no simple way of controlling for time-on-task. Teachers have tried numerous methods to keep pupils 'on task' in the classroom. One would not wish to cut down on this in the tutoring situation by discouraging those involved in tutoring from engaging fully in their work. It is plausible, therefore, that as Fitz-Gibbon (1977:22) and Mary Kennedy (Chapter 3 below) suggest, peer tutoring is only successful in raising the achievement of tutees because it increases pupils' time-on-task. The fact that fellow-pupils are doing the teaching may be incidental and have no positive impact on learning gains. However, even if this is the case, it does not negate the usefulness of peer tutoring schemes in raising the attainment levels of students. It is unlikely that, without the use of peer tutoring, state education will ever produce a system whereby each child can be guaranteed at least 30 minutes of individual attention in one day. It is, of course, desirable that researchers design experiments to deduce what it is about peer tutoring which makes it so effective; but for the present, suffice to say that whatever the mechanism, peer tutoring seems to offer learning possibilities which cannot easily be achieved by other means.

Peer tutoring involving higher education students

Students as tutors in schools
Many western societies are currently experiencing a significant demographic phenomenon: a drop in the age-cohort of 18 to 22 year olds. The predicted consequence of this is that there will be substantial shortages of people qualified for many occupations (a problem of which industry is only too acutely aware). This demographic decline is not only causing competitiveness between employers in trade and industry to escalate, but higher education establishments are also now competing for a smaller number of 18 to 22 year olds.

The response of institutions to this problem has been two-fold. First, academic staff and administrators have had to publicise the merits of their own institutions to teenagers. They have consequently raised their profile in schools by participating in, among other things, presentations to sixth-form students, career fairs, college-based workshops and summer-schools. Second, they have had to address the issue of access to higher education, encouraging those students who have traditionally sought employment at 18 to consider higher education as a viable alternative. This has meant not only reconsidering entry qualifications to higher education, but also identifying and targeting for advice pupils who may not be aware of the opportunities available to them. This aim has been so specific, that some establishments have adopted programmes which have linked them with local schools in which they have identified such students early on in their 'A' level courses and nurtured them for higher education.

The demographic decline, however, is not the only factor which has led to increased liaison between schools and higher education establishments; those in higher eduation have become increasingly aware of the public perception of their institutions. Too often, these are seen as catering only for the academically elite, having little accountability to the rest of society. Recognising that such feelings harbour resentment which can only hinder recruitment to higher education, there has been a move towards involving staff and students in useful work and projects which encourage positive links between members of the community and the college population. Possible ways in which higher education students can make positive contributions to the community, in a context in which they feel at ease, include: the peer tutoring schemes described by Toni Beardon (Chapter 5) and John Jones (Chapter 6), in which undergraduate students visit local schools to work alongside school teachers in science, maths and CDT, and that described by Barbara Fresko and Amos Carmeli (in Chapter 4) which enables students to provide an out-of-school tutorial service for socially-disadvantaged Israeli children.

Undergraduate tutors in the Cambridge STIMULUS (Chapter 5) are not paid for their services; however, in Israel, where the ever-rising costs of higher education have necessitated students supplementing their funds by carrying out paid work while they study, tutoring has offered a possible solution. In Israel, although the PERACH tutoring scheme is voluntary, tutors receive a rebate of approximately 40% of their tuition fees in return for tutoring services, so enabling more students to meet the costs of higher education. The development of peer tutoring schemes such as this, which offer some reimbursement to students in return for teaching others, could provide a means of helping students in other countries to supplement ever-dwindling grants. In this way, students would be able to provide a service to other learners, in a context congenial to themselves, whilst financing their own learning.

Students tutoring students
Many higher education institutions have adapted their entry requirements in recent years, be it in response to the decline in the 18–22 age cohort or for more idealistic reasons. Such changes have led to a widening of the spread of achievement of students at entry. Higher education teachers can no longer assume a uniformity of knowledge and experience amongst a new student intake. Given the large number of undergraduates who enter higher education each year, it is impossible for lecturers to assume that each student has the necessary background, knowledge and understanding for subsequent study in a particular area. Some mitigation of the situation could

be achieved, however, by assigning each student a tutor (or proctor) from the remainder of the student population. Proctors are fellow-students, usually slightly more advanced in their study, who help other students by asking and answering questions about their work, giving guidance and making recommendations for further study. Additionally, they often have a responsibility for providing feedback to the course instructor on the general progress of students and their reactions to the content of the course. In this way, peer tutoring helps academics to monitor more effectively the progress of students; they no longer have to rely solely on the 'often-too-late' end-of-year exam or course work. It is one of the simplest ways in which course instructors can facilitate individual instruction for all students.

Benefits to students of taking part in tutoring

We have outlined several reasons why peer tutoring schemes are desirable both within higher education establishments and linking institutions with schools. However, overriding these is the social satisfaction which under-graduates gain by being assigned the role of tutor to others. Students in higher education can often feel quite isolated in their studies, seeming always to be absorbing information from their seniors and having little opportunity for interaction during the learning process. As we have suggested elsewhere (Goodlad and Hirst, 1989:16), if education is to be adequate preparation for life it must be simultaneously intellectually enriching and humanly rewarding. Peer tutoring can transform learning from a private to a social activity. This is becoming increasingly important as changes in higher education (such as the growth in the number of part-time and mature students, the closure of smaller colleges in favour of large institutions, and increased pressure on colleges to offer only those courses which will be heavily subscribed and result in undergraduates being taught 'en masse'), are leading to a loss of 'collegiality' among the student population. To perceive the fundamental purpose of a social institution, and thereby perhaps identify with it, the individual must be given an opportunity to share in the process by which the institution defines itself; peer tutoring is attractive in drawing the maximum possible number of people into the process of sharing knowledge.

Peer tutoring can be incorporated into higher education as one form of Study Service, itself a subvariant of experiential learning, in which students learn by doing. Study Service involves students in study which leads them to an academic qualification whilst carrying out some form of direct practical service to the community. Students in Study Service do not compete with paid professionals, but rather do work which could not otherwise have been done (ie providing extra support to pupils by working *alongside* the professional teacher). In particular, peer tutoring is an attractive type of Study Service in that it is relatively simple to set up, being within the capacity of institutions in terms of personnel and resources. (For more information on peer tutoring as a form of Study Service see Goodlad and Hirst, 1989, Chapter 6).

Some uses of peer tutoring within higher education institutions

As is indicated by the range of activities described in Chapters 4–8 of this book, peer tutoring has many points of application in higher education, both within higher education institutions and between institutions. Most peer tutoring schemes operating within institutions approximate to one of the following categories outlined by Cornwall (1979): teacherless groups; co-tutoring; proctoring; and surrogate teaching.

In the UK, *teacherless groups* are probably the most widely employed form of peer tutoring within higher education at present. These are usually peer-led project or discussion groups which meet without a teacher and require students to take on more responsibility for their own learning by becoming more personally involved and self-directed in their work (see, for example, Goodlad, 1977). Collier (1980) gives a comprehensive review of this teaching strategy.

Co-tutoring (or reciprocal peer tutoring) occurs when students take responsibility for the learning of their peers, usually those at a similar point of study to themselves. This could be in the form of one-to-one peer tutoring such as that described by Goldschmid (1970a, 1970b). In Goldschmid's 'learning cells', students in one class are paired to work together. Following a period of independent study, they take turns in questioning one another on the subject-matter of their study during class time.

An interesting form of co-tutoring has been devised by Selig and Perlstadt (1985) at the University of Michigan, Flint. The course leaders for the medical sociology course, which comprises health-care students and sociology students, pair students from the different categories to work together on assignments. In this way it is intended that students will perceive a clear link between the concepts of medical sociology and health-care practice, and recognise the strengths and limitations of their different backgrounds.

Another form of reciprocal peer tutoring can occur when one student instructs a small group of students. One such example is that used by Hendelman and Boss in the Gross Anatomy Laboratory at the University of Ottawa, Canada (Hendelman and Boss, 1986). In this programme, medical undergraduates give 15–20 minute presentations to their peers in place of demonstrations by the faculty.

As Nancy Falchikov shows (in Chapter 8 of this book), if co-tutoring or reciprocal peer tutoring is employed with students of similar age and/or at a similar stage of study, some sensitivity needs to be exercised when assigning the role of tutor or tutee. When implementing a scheme in which tutor and tutee were students in higher education of the same age,

Falchikov found that although tutees found the scheme beneficial, they did so to a lesser extent than did tutors. In the initial intervention, some tutees expressed a lack of confidence in their tutor, although this concern was not manifest in a follow-up programme for the same tutor/tutee dyads. However, this could clearly be a problem if tutees feel that their tutors are less able than themselves.

Although there seems to be little research examining this issue in higher education, Bierman and Furman (1981) examined the role of contextual factors, such as assignment rationale, on the attitudinal effects of peer tutoring on elementary-school pupils. Overall, children enacting tutor roles tended to form more positive attitudes than children in tutee roles. Bierman and Furman suggest that the positive effects of peer tutoring on the tutor may, to some extent, be counterbalanced by less desirable effects on the tutee. An emphasis on the competence of the tutor resulted in positive attitudes for the tutor; but the tutees tended to have more negative attitudes than when a rationale of chance assignment was used (when all pupils were told that they were of equal competence and that their role had been decided by the toss of a coin). Bierman and Furman suggest that one solution to the dilemma is to structure programmes so that children switch roles periodically. This was the method employed by Hendrickson (1982) when a peer tutoring scheme was employed to help 5/14-year-old underachievers in reading and maths. At the start of the programme Hendrickson trained all the pupils in peer tutoring techniques so that, although pupils were initially assigned the role of tutor or tutee, these roles could be swapped every two or three sessions. The programme seemed to have remarkable success in raising the achievement level of the children. There are indications that a systematic alternating of roles will have similarly beneficial effects in higher education.

The term *proctoring* has perhaps been most frequently associated with Keller-plan, PSI (Personal System of Instruction) courses in which proctors facilitate mastery by other students in units of study (see, for example, Keller, 1968; Keller and Sherman, 1974; Bridge, 1975; Hill and Helburn, 1981). However, proctoring can also take the form described by Button, Sims, and White (in Chapter 7 of this book). In this programme at Trent Polytechnic, final-year students of Mechanical Engineering lead a small group of first-year students in an Engineering Design project. Button, Sims, and White highlight how, as with other types of peer tutoring, proctoring gives students the opportunity to use and develop their communication skills in a friendly and supportive environment. At the same time the proctored students gain from the experiential knowledge of the proctors. In addition, the activity allows more opportunities for subject-intergration between different years of the course.

An interesting type of proctoring scheme, although not described as such by the instigators, is that employed in a teacher-training course at the University of North Carolina (Riley and Huffman, 1980). Senior-level students of the course who have already completed teaching practice are assigned as 'peer support persons' to other students just entering their teaching practice. The responsibilities of the peer-support students are to watch their 'tutees' teach on six occasions throughout the teaching practice, to share ideas, insights and experiences with them, and to keep them informed of events happening on campus. The course leaders feel that there is much to be gained by the proctor from this type of scheme: many students feel frustrated on returning to university after successfully completing teaching practice and are eager to start work; this type of programme helps them to keep in touch with school life. Proctors also have the opportunity to see other teaching techniques and resources which have not been used in their own teaching-practice school.

Surrogate teaching involves the delegation of some of the responsibilities of the academic staff to selected students, usually those at postgraduate level. These surrogate teachers can help with such things as marking and grading, leading small-group discussion, demonstrating in the laboratory and possibly teaching of large classes. An example of a surrogate teaching programme is that described by Carsrud (1984). In this scheme, graduate psychology students are invited to submit proposals for research experiments suitable for undergraduate study. If the proposal is accepted, and a student opts to work on the project, the postgraduate is then assigned to be supervisor of the work. The programme is mutually beneficial to the two parties involved: it offers undergraduate students the opportunity to carry out a piece of original research and so acquire an appreciation of what psychological research involves; postgraduates are enabled to supervise novel work and to pursue wider research interests and opportunities in their specific fields than would otherwise be possible.

Uses of tutoring between higher education institutions and schools
Scheme 'S' was developed by Queen Mary College, University of London. It includes a surrogate teaching component in that postgraduate students have taken over some of the responsibility for working with sixth-formers in the Tower Hamlets area. In this scheme, pupils are given advice about the opportunities available to them in higher education, are visited by academics in their sixth-form centre, and are invited to visit Queen Mary College. Much of this work has now been delegated to postgraduates under the supervision of academic staff. (Pindar, 1988)

As reported by Toni Beardon and John Jones (Chapters 5 and 6 below) and Goodlad and Hirst (1989:99) tutoring schemes in which college students work with schoolchildren are able to provide pupils with the extra help and support they need with their academic work and, in addition, information about higher education: what university life involves; how to get there, etc. Schoolchildren will often discuss the possibility of higher education in far more depth with a tutor than with a teacher, particularly if they doubt their own capabilities and are unsure of the teacher's response (exactly the kind of pupils that colleges are trying to attract). Tutoring schemes such as this not only offer the cognitive and affective gains for tutees previously outlined, they also provide a form of career guidance, a heightened awareness of possibilities.

By participating in this type of scheme, tutors can test a possible vocation for teaching. By serving as tutors, they get insight into the teaching/learning process, are required to develop their communication skills and to reflect on how others perceive their subject (skills which are not only important for those considering a teaching career, but also for students who subsequently enter industry, management or personnel-related work). As Toni Beardon indicates in Chapter 5, as a result of tutoring many students come to view teaching as a challenging career. This is particularly important at a time when may people in the teaching profession are demoralised and many teachers feel that the public have little respect for their profession and fail to recognise the demands which it places upon them. Although undergraduates who have continued in school for as long as possible are likely to appreciate the complexities of the occupation, they need to work *alongside* teachers before they can recognise teaching as the multi-faceted role it is. This recognition could have important consequences.

The demographic decline aside, there are already shortages of teachers in some subjects, and an obvious need to recruit good-quality graduates into teaching in these areas. Peer tutoring schemes such as those described by Fresko and Carmeli, Beardon, and Jones (Chapters 4, 5 and 6) offer the possibility of attracting more students in these shortage areas into teaching. Many students in the 'Pimlico Connection' have already used the opportunity to tutor as a 'test-bed' for a career in teaching (Goodlad and Hirst, 1989:107). As a result, some undergraduates have been attracted to a career in teaching; others (a somewhat lesser number) have been deterred. Those students who have tried peer tutoring and are still keen (or more keen) to teach, have a realistic idea of what teaching will involve before they commit themselves to a Postgraduate Certificate of Education course. Those who are less keen are dissuaded from teacher-training while there is still time to think about some other career, instead of finding out midway through their course that they are not suited to being teachers. (This clearly has substantial savings for themselves and the tax-payer).

Another benefit which this type of scheme offers is that of keeping students up-to-date with developments in education. Education in the United Kingdom has undergone major changes in the past few years. For example, science is now rarely taught as three discrete units, a coordinated or integrated approach being more commonly adopted. For student tutors, this has necessitated reviewing subjects that they themselves did at 'O' level but pursued no further. They begin to appreciate the difficulties that many teachers who graduated in a single-subject discipline may be facing when expected to teach a combination of the three sciences. Indeed, many teachers could benefit greatly from being assigned a science tutor trained in a different discipline to themselves. In 'The Pimlico Connection' (Goodlad and Hirst, 1989, Chapter 5) science tutors have been invaluable in primary schools, not only as helpers in the classroom, but also for providing suggestions for science experiments and projects; no doubt they will become increasingly so with the advent of the National Curriculum.

Another important side-effect of such schemes is that many of the students who have tutored but do not pursue a career in teaching, but who subsequently go on to work in industry start to think seriously about education. Many of them would probably not otherwise reflect on changes in education until they had children of school-age themselves. As many of the large industrial companies are now involved in some form of school liaison, it can only be of benefit to these people to be aware of what is happening within schools. Evidence from the 'Pimlico Connection' (Goodlad and Hirst, 1989:111) shows that some tutors who go on to work in industry become actively involved in school liaison projects as a consequence of their tutoring experiences.

The evaluation of tutoring with higher education students
With all peer tutoring schemes which expand to incorporate more schools, and involve more teachers and more students, evaluation becomes increasingly difficult. For example, the High School Homework Helper Programme was carefully evaluated by Cloward in the early stages (Cloward, 1967) and produced encouraging findings. This was one of the first research studies to highlight the 'learning by teaching' effect. Unfortunately, once the programme expanded, detailed research was no longer carried out. It is, therefore, unclear if the benefits to tutors and tutees were maintained once the preliminary project became an institutionalised programme under the auspices of the New York City Board of Education. The PERACH team, likewise, have had particular difficulties in evaluating their scheme; the main impediment to clear-cut evaluation lies in the fact that the project goals are neither specific nor sharply-defined (see Chapter 4). As a result, tutor/tutee dyads engage in a wide range of activities during the tutoring sessions. With the large number of tutor/tutee pairs involved (approximately 12000), it has been impossible for the research team to take account of this in their evaluation. Clearly the more sharply-defined the objectives, and the smaller the number of tutor/tutee pairs involved, the more readily can the success of the project be evaluated.

The more variety that is incorporated in a tutoring scheme, the more difficult psychometric evaluation becomes. Although 'The Pimlico Connection' is evaluated annually, as the scheme has expanded it has no longer been feasible to carry out the rigorous evaluation performed in the earlier stages. The flexibility of the scheme, which enabled students to work alongside different teachers, in different schools, with pupils of a wide variety of ages and abilities, following different syllabuses, made it almost impossible to match tutored groups with controls and psychometric research was deemed no longer suitable.

A major problem, of course, in evaluating all schemes of this nature is that where there are children who need help (the ones who could possibly form a control group), tutors who are willing to give it, and suitable physical conditions, then help is given where needed in preference to controlling for the outcome of that help. For these reasons, large-scale peer tutoring schemes created to meet situations of real need can rarely be evaluated by rigorous psychometric methods. Such projects are much more amenable to qualitative, 'case study' or 'illuminative' evaluation. It is possible that findings from studies evaluated in this way are not as reliable as those from smaller, more tightly-controlled studies incorporating a greater degree of objectivity. Equally it should be kept in mind that because of the degree of control exerted the findings of small pilot-projects may not transfer well to the typical classroom situation.

In Chapter 2 Carol Fitz-Gibbon suggests that the outcomes of a project can be very much affected by the presence of researchers working to implement it. Once they withdraw their efforts, either because the project has been well developed and so adopted by the institution, or because funding has been withdrawn, reported findings may no longer be sustained. Isaacs and Stennet (1979) identified this as a problem in a school-based tutoring intervention when they replicated a Master's study by Travoto (1978). The original study had indicated very large reading gains for pupils reading at below grade-level following a five-month tutoring intervention. Isaacs and Stennet found that without a full-time researcher working on the project, although the children all made gains in reading, these were not as large as those in Travoto's study. They conclude that without constant attention, the gains which are possible through tutoring can be lost through seemingly minor deviations from the programme.

Peer tutoring involving school pupils

Enhancing the professional role of teachers
Peer tutoring is a classroom strategy which enhances the professional role of teachers, freeing them from routine direct instruction to concentrate on more complex issues, such as the management of learning-conditions and the planning of the curriculum. Teachers often comment that they feel many areas of study covered by their teacher training courses (child psychology, sociology, philosophy of education, innovative learning techniques, etc), become redundant once they begin full class teaching. They find that there is little time to reflect on these issues, since they are constantly inundated with routine questions or required to deal with classroom organisation and discipline problems (which often make teaching simply a matter of survival). However, if teachers were to employ a peer

tutoring programme they would have more control over the learning situation, and be freed to plan the overall strategy of the lesson.

As indicated above, the most badly-behaved of pupils are reported to have participated well in peer tutoring schemes, even coming to sympathise with the teacher's role! Ill-disciplined children often cause disruption in the classroom by drawing attention to themselves; indeed, this attention-seeking is one of the main factors which diverts the teacher from a well-structured lesson plan. By being given a working partner, these children get all the attention they need and spend less time distracting the teacher. Other problems can arise when children have to wait for a long time to have a question answered because the teacher is engaged elsewhere. Often these questions could be dealt with by a fellow pupil, leaving the teacher free to spend more time on the more difficult conceptual problems. These are just two ways in which peer tutoring offers a possibility of reducing discipline problems in the classroom.

As many schools now employ mixed-ability grouping, in the typical classroom pupils are either working on different exercises or are doing the same exercises but working through them at very different rates. Using a strategy which enables pupils to work together, means that the teacher can arrange for pupils to help one another to complete the tasks, consulting the teacher only in the case of real difficulties. Pupils who are very able can be paired together to do extension work and stretch one another's capabilities while the rest of the class are able to complete their assignments. Equally, pupils who are falling behind with the work, or who lack confidence, can be assigned a tutor to help them, instead of the teacher having to spend large proportions of a lesson with one pupil. Tutoring can help teachers to ensure some uniformity of subject-coverage with a mixed-ability class (an issue which is of grave concern to many teachers finding that some children have finished a unit of work before others are 'off the starting blocks').

This is not to say that peer tutoring is a panacea for the problems of modern teaching, although it may solve some of them. Rather it should be seen as another addition to the teaching repertoire, along with field-trips, project-work, library-research etc. Tutoring is a technique to be employed as, and when, teachers feel it is appropriate (perhaps as Carol Fitz-Gibbon suggests in Chapter 2, as a relief for pupils who are bored with more conventional classroom strategies). Not all activities lend themselves equally well to tutoring; it is most suitable for exercises which necessitate pupils getting practice in using standard techniques, work which requires repetition such as drill-exercises, mathematics problem-sheets, or reading practice. More complex conceptual explanations are, on the whole, best left to the teacher. In this way the professional role of the teacher is enhanced, with teachers freed from the more mundane and repetitive work to concentrate on complex teaching-tasks in which training is needed. Far from replacing teachers, peer tutoring emphasises their unique professional role.

'Mainstreaming' handicapped and learning-disabled pupils through tutoring
Recently, peer tutoring has been seen as an aid to helping the integration of learning-disabled and handicapped pupils into the regular school classroom. Despite significant efforts to 'mainstream' handicapped pupils into local secondary schools, these pupils are still experiencing problems of social rejection and academic deficiency. It has been found that simply initiating contact between the handicapped and non-handicapped does not necessarily reduce the negative perceptions which are held of the handicapped. Interventions are needed which will facilitate their acceptance.

One of the potential benefits of peer tutoring schemes is that tutor and tutee can interact in a socially-structured setting. Tutoring programmes have, therefore, been introduced to instigate interactions between handicapped and non-handicapped peers. Such projects have fallen into two categories: those in which the non-handicapped students tutor their handicapped peers and those in which the handicapped students tutor non-handicapped students (schemes often described as reverse-role).

Those interested in peer tutoring as a means of easing the mainstreaming problems of the handicapped tend to favour reverse-role tutoring as a strategy. This type of scheme places handicapped students in a position where they will be viewed as competent teachers holding skills valued by the non-handicapped - so increasing their social acceptance. Fenrick and Peterson (1984) found that when 11-year-old non-handicapped pupils tutored moderately- and severely-handicapped students, the tutors found them to be more capable than did the control group and expressed more willingness to be involved with the handicapped in school and social settings. In addition, one of the primary problems of these pupils may be their academic capabilities. Given that tutoring has been shown to facilitate accelerated learning-gains for the tutors, they could reap both academic and social benefits from such a programme. In Chapter 12 of this book, Osguthorpe and Scruggs synthesise the results of investigations using special-education students as tutors, emphasising the effects of tutoring on the academic and personal/social skills of both tutors and tutees.

Some uses of peer tutoring with children
Peer tutoring has been shown to be effective with children as young as six acting as tutors. Arblaster et al (see Chapter 9) found children of six and seven to be proficient at carrying out tutoring duties in a reciprocal same-age tutoring programme, whilst Topping (Chapter 10) found that eight year olds could function well as tutors in the Paired Reading technique. Moreover, these pupils enjoyed the experience of tutoring, so much so that in the programme described by Arblaster et al, they rated it equally as popular as playtime! Perhaps the satisfaction that all pupils felt at taking part in the scheme can be attributed to the fact that they all had a turn at being the tutor. Although several studies have been conducted in which young children have been tutees, few have employed them as tutors

- yet Chapters 9 and 10 indicate that if tutors are given adequate training they can execute tutoring techniques very effectively.

Many research studies have highlighted the importance of tutor-training in making peer tutoring schemes effective. Training does not have to be complex; it can consist of coaching in a few elementary procedures which tutors need practice in employing. Shaver and Nuhn (1968) showed that when more detailed training was given to tutors, this did little to influence the effectiveness of the tutoring intervention. It is preferable that pupils are told the simple procedures to use whilst tutoring, and are also given a chance to practise them before the intervention begins. Niedermeyer (1970) showed that tutors who had been trained in a few basic tutoring techniques related to structured-tutoring schemes subsequently employed the behaviours, whereas those who had not been trained did not. As Arblaster et al explain in Chapter 9, training sessions need not take long. Winter (1986), likewise, indicates that the highly-structured Paired Reading techniques can be taught to children as young as 10 or 11 years old in two short sessions. Those considering when training or tutoring could be timetabled, might refer to the programme implemented by Mary Kennedy (see Chapter 11 in which tutoring took place in morning registration-periods a time which many secondary school teachers are desperately searching for useful ways to fill!).

The peer tutoring schemes described in Chapter 9 (Companion Reading) and Chapter 10 (Paired Reading) are highly-structured and require specific responses from the tutors. The degree of structure which those implement-ing peer tutoring will wish to include in programmes is probably dependent upon the relative importance placed upon benefits to tutors and tutees. Tutors seem to gain more from unstructured (or semi-structured) tutoring schemes which require them to reformulate and reflect on the work to be taught, thus allowing more opportunity for concepts to be integrated within their conceptual framework. However, evidence indicates that more-structured schemes produce greater gains for tutees (Harris, 1968; Ellson et al, 1968). Practitioners need to balance out benefits to tutors and tutees before deciding upon the degree of structure to incorporate in a programme. It is worth noting that tutors are likely to find tutoring socially satisfying in both structured and unstructured programmes; the personal satisfaction to be derived from tutoring does not depend upon a completely spontaneous relationship between tutor and tutee. Of course, if teachers choose to use structured schemes, then materials have to be collected for inclusion in the programme. For reading, commercial programmes are available; however, teachers of other subjects may have to develop materials for themselves. This can be time-consuming, as Maheady et al have shown (Maheady et al, 1987a, 1987b, 1988a, 1988b). One solution to this problem could be to involve the tutors in the production of the teaching materials under the professional guidance of the teacher. In this way, the tutors reap some of the benefits of an unstructured programme by formulating the programme of work, but also learn about the teaching procedures to be used in lessons, which is of benefit to tutees.

Involving parents in tutoring schemes

Tutoring schemes obviously have huge potential for involving parents in their chidren's education. Most structured materials could be used by parents at home with their children, in addition to the tutoring which takes place in schools. Schemes which encourage the involvement of parents in reading could be of enormous benefit to pupils; research has shown that whether parents hear their children read at home is a major factor in reading development irrespective of other factors such as socio-economic status (Tizard et al, 1982). Recently, many parents have become involved in Paired Reading schemes and so facilitated accelerated reading gains for their children (Miller et al, 1986; Topping 1986b:148). Travoto (1978) showed that although all under-achieving tutees in a school-based five-month peer tutoring scheme showed improved reading gains, those who were in the school-tutored-plus-home-reinforcement groups (parents also hearing their children read) experienced gains statistically higher than those of the children who took part only in the school-based tutoring. The possibility of encouraging more parents to take an active role in their children's academic development by employing tutoring schemes could make peer tutoring particularly attractive for support by parent-teacher associations. Given that the costs of implementing peer tutoring within a school are not great (money being needed mainly for resource materials), such schemes could be proposed as suitable for sponsorship by the school's PTA.

The concept of peer tutoring as one of very wide applicability

We have illustrated how peer tutoring provides a means of enabling professional teachers to multiply their effects. This model could, however, be applied equally well to other contexts outside formal education. Examples of different ways in which tutoring on a voluntary basis has been employed for the benefit of others are described by Goodlad and Hirst (1989:148). These include: para-professionals carrying out routine health work and health education work; law students giving legal advice when a fully-trained lawyer is not essential; trainee social workers giving child-care advice. In advocating the extension of the tutoring model to other occupations, we are not suggesting a need for fewer professionals; rather, we are recognising that, given the current demographic trends, essential services may be cut through lack of people to carry out necessary work, not all of which requires the immediate attention of a professional. What is being suggested is for professionals to supervise the work of others (as the teacher supervises the tutors) - to be *managers* rather than direct operators.

The tutoring model is currently being implemented in novel situations, as Melanie Quin illustrates in Chapter 13 of this book. A wide variety of people have offered their services as volunteer interpreters in interactive-science centres; people of all ages and experience derive a great deal of pleasure from sharing knowledge and ideas with others. Moreover, while volunteer guides are advising the public and entertaining them with exhibits, curators are freed to spend more time in planning and developing new additions to the centre. For the past 17 years, school pupils have fulfilled the role of interpreter at the Exploratorium in San Francisco. The benefits of this scheme have been two-fold. First, the students serve the museum by providing help for visitors and much-needed staff support in areas of maintenance and security. Second, the scheme has been found to influence teenagers' interest in learning in general and in the learning of science in particular; it has been a major influence in stimulating some explainers to go to college, and served as a career-start for others (Diamond et al, 1987). When applied to different situations, the tutoring model appears to be mutually beneficial to the volunteers and to those they serve.

Opportunities for research

Research findings about peer tutoring are diverse because of the wide varieties of schemes employed. That is not to say that schemes should be limited in scope, or that evaluation should cease. Rather, it suggests that the more evaluation that is carried out on a multitude of programmes, the greater the likelihood of success in developing a body of theory which can be applied to tutoring whatever the context.

Wherever practitioners' interests in educational research lie, they will no doubt wish to incorporate some evaluation into their programmes (if only to convince themselves that their efforts have been worthwhile). However, understandably, the degree of control which can be exercised in the everyday classroom context will differ from that exerted in more tightly-controlled studies. This does not negate the usefulness of evaluation of the former; many of those who wish to employ tutoring want effectiveness in the classroom and may feel more convinced of the worth of the strategy if gains have been shown for schoolchildren working *in their normal environment*.

Meanwhile, as Kennedy suggests in Chapter 3, the researcher has different responsibilities - primarily to define as rigorously as possible the relationship between a teaching strategy and its outcome. If the researcher can ascertain this, then the information can be communicated to the practitioner and schemes can be devised which capitalise on the findings.

In Chapter 14 David Kellett indicates that if specific mechanisms can be shown to be respoonsible for the tutoring effect, then a potentially profitable contribution to education has been made because the mechanisms can be included as component processes within styles of peer interaction. Researchers may find evidence, for example, that tutoring is successful merely because it increases time-on-task or is a novelty; if this is the case then teachers can make use of this knowledge. The Hawthorne experiments (where people's behaviour changed in the hoped-for direction simply because they were favoured by being subjects of experiments) are well known; if this phenomenon applies to peer tutoring programmes, then teachers can exploit the effect by restricting the length of interventions and reintroducing them at appropriate points in the academic year. Winter suggests, in Chapter 15, that it may not be the specific techniques of an intervention which account for improved achievement of participants but organisational and social-psychological factors, the outcome being dependent on how all participants respond to being included in the project.

Concluding observations

In summary, the range of applications of peer tutoring included in this volume indicates the potential of the strategy as a teaching aid at all educational levels. Without doubt, many questions regarding tutoring remain unanswered and there is a need for careful evaluation to enable researchers to identify the mechanism by which effects are seen to occur. However, research which has already been carried out shows tutoring to be effective at producing both cognitive and affective gains for tutors and tutees in very many contexts. We hope, therefore, that readers will find the following studies inspirational, that they will be encouraged to try out some of the tutoring strategies described, and perhaps help to answer some of the questions raised.

2 Success and failure in peer tutoring experiments

Carol Taylor Fitz-Gibbon

Five controlled field-experiments were conducted. Two of these involved same-age rather than cross-age tutoring and neither was considered successful. The other three experiments were successful in a variety of ways; tutors generally learned more than equivalent pupils spending the same time on the content, and tutees showed significant learning gains. Two of the experiments are considered in detail, one being a replication in the UK of an experiment originally conducted in the US.

These two experiments, conducted in inner-city schools, involved 14 year olds tutoring 9 year olds in fractions. Cognitive benefits to tutors were significant in five out of six classes involved in the experiments but various confounding factors led to a cautious interpretation: at least tutors could spend considerable amounts of time helping others without falling behind in their own work.

In cross-age learning-by-tutoring projects, certain non-cognitive effects are fairly reliably present. These are the 'responsibility' effect; the 'insight-into-learning' effect; the 'teacher-empathy' effect; the 'relief-of-boredom' effect and the 'peer-tutoring-appreciation' effect.

There are many accounts of successful experiments in peer tutoring, but accounts of failures are understandably more rare. Nevertheless, if we are to understand *how* peer tutoring creates better learning and other positive benefits, and if research is to guide practice, then it is just as important to study projects which failed as it is to examine projects which have succeeded.

Of course, the dichotomy 'failure or success' is too crude. The outcomes of tutoring are multi-faceted, and there may be aspects of 'success' and aspects of 'failure' within a single project. In the main, we shall be concerned with two broad categories of outcomes: the learning of both tutors and tutees (cognitive outcomes) and their attitudes (affective outcomes).

The tutoring projects considered here are listed in Table 2.1. Some selected aspects of the Los Angeles Fractions project are summarised because, although a full account is available elsewhere (Fitz-Gibbon, 1975), this account is not readily accessible. Moreover, the method and results are needed here since the first of the projects undertaken in England ('UK Project I') was designed to replicate the major features of the Los Angeles project.

UK Project I is reported in some detail, using both qualitative and quantitative data. The purpose of this detailed examination is to cast light on *how* peer tutoring works. UK Project II has been reported elsewhere (Fitz-Gibbon and Reay, 1982) and is included here only as another example of a 'successful' cross-age project from the same research programme. UK Projects III and IV represent rather clear failures. Both were 'same-age' rather than 'cross-age' projects. An account of these projects is available in Fitz-Gibbon, 1981.

All the projects were 'learning-by-tutoring' projects in which both tutors and tutees were expected to learn the topics under study. None was a 'tutorial service' project in which tutors were providing a service to 'tutees'. In these projects, therefore, tutoring was used as a teaching strategy and pupils' participation was no more voluntary than in any other classroom activity.

The Los Angeles Fractions Project

The experiment was conducted in an inner-city junior high-school in California. The school's population was approximately 90 per cent black and 10 per cent Hispanic-American.

Tutors were 40 ninth-grade students (14 year olds) randomly selected from four low-achieving mathematics classes. Tutees were 68 nine year olds randomly selected from the fourth-grade classrooms at an adjoining elementary school. Tutoring was conducted for a three-week period and aimed at 11 objectives concerned with the addition of fractions. Immediate post-tests and questionnaires were administered, followed three months later by retention tests. The cognitive tests contained five items measuring each of the 11 objectives.

The initial training of tutors was brief and concentrated primarily on the content to be tutored: fractions. It consisted of three class periods during which the addition of fractions was explained, methods of teaching the meaning of fractions were demonstrated, and some use was made of role-play. In three of the four ninth-grade classes, tutors and non-tutors received this initial instruction together. In these three classes, the non-tutors then worked with their regular teacher on the 11 objectives throughout the next three weeks; tutors spent the same three weeks

Table 2.1 Summary of the tutoring projects

Title	Type	Topic	Tutors	Tutees	Age difference	Main design (a)
US Project (Los Angeles)	Cross-age	Fractions	9th Grade (14 yrs +) Lower half in ability	4th Grade (9 yrs +) Mixed ability	5 yrs	R O X O R O O
UK Project I (replication of US project)	Cross-age	Fractions	Drawn from two 4th form CSE Classes (14+ years old)	Two mixed-ability classes of 9 and 10 years olds	4 or 5 yrs	R O X O R O O
UK Project II	Cross-age	French: weather, numbers etc	All pupils in the lower of two 4th form French classes	All pupils in a 1st form introductory class	3 yrs	O X O O O
UK Project III	Same-age	Maths: area, bar graphs, networks, probability	Four 4th form lowest stream maths classes		0 yrs	R O X$_1$ O R O X$_2$ O R O O
UK Project IV	Same-age	Maths: solving equations	Two 4th form lowest stream maths classes		0 yrs	R X$_1$ O R X$_2$ O R X$_n$ O

(a) Notation follows Campbell and Stanley (1966)

teaching the objectives to the nine year olds under the supervision of the experimenter. Non-tutors in those three classes thus constituted a competing-treatment control group: they received classroom instruction whereas the experimental group participated in supervised tutoring. The time allocated to supervised tutoring was either 30, 40, 60, 65 or 80 minutes per day and tutors worked with either one, two or four tutees.

In another class, the teacher had already 'done' fractions, so tutors were simply taken out of the class for initial instruction and for the three weeks of tutoring, during which time the class continued with its ninth-grade general maths programme. Since no effort was made to have the class work on the 11 objectives, students in this classroom formed a no-treatment or baseline control group.

At pre-test, in all four classes, there were no significant differences (even at the .25 level), but on the immediate post-test there were differences between tutors and non-tutors in favour of tutors (Figure 2.1). These differences remained on the retention test given three months later. The major effect seems to have been the better learning experienced by tutors in

Figure 2.1 Results of the LA Project by classroom

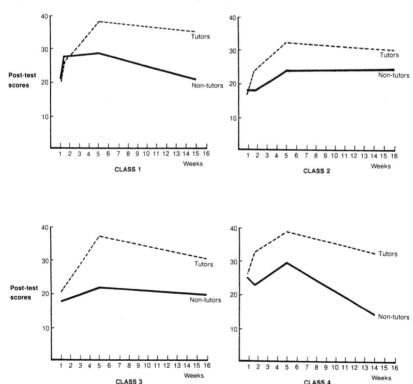

the course of the tutoring project (between pre- and post-test) rather than any differential retention; the eroding effects of forgetting seemed to apply to all groups.

The net result, however, was that three months after the intervention, at 'retention-test' those who had tutored knew significantly more about fractions than they had before the project; those who had not tutored had often sunk back to their pre-test levels of performance, having a set of scores on the retention-test not significantly different from their scores on the pretest. The almost total lack of retained progress seen in the non-tutor group must have occurred routinely every year, since every year fractions were dealt with in maths classes and every year, with lower-achieving pupils, teachers found it necessary to re-teach from scratch. Tutoring appeared to have broken this depressing pattern.

The mean score obtained by students in the no-treatment control group was approximately 22; the mean for the competing-treatment control group was 27. The groups consisting of tutors obtained means ranging from 33 to 43. Using Tukey's HSD, a contrast of the competing-treatment control group with the tutoring groups was significant (t = 3.02, df = 65, p = .004). Tutors who had spent three weeks teaching fourth graders about fractions had themselves learned more about fractions than had equivalent students practising fractions in their maths classes.

Means and 95 per cent confidence limits for ninth-graders on the immediate post-test are displayed in Figure 2.2.

The effectiveness of low-achieving students as tutors

Had these low-achieving students been effective in teaching the fourth-graders? All fourth-graders took a post-test covering the 11 objectives but employing smaller numbers than involved on the ninth-grade test.

On this fourth-grade test, the items were randomly ordered rather than occurring in groups of five as had been the case in the ninth-grade test. This randomly-ordered test was called the 'Scrambled Fractions' test. Means and 95 percent confidence limits on the means are displayed in Figure 2.3 for the non-tutees ('0 minutes time allocated') and for tutees who had received 20, 30 or 40 minutes per day. A one-way, fixed-effects, analysis of variance on the post-test scores indicated significant effects ($F_{(3,90)}$ = p < .001). Tutees had clearly learned from the tutoring provided by the ninth-graders.

Many practitioners with experience of running tutoring programmes in schools maintain that less-able students make better tutors, perhaps because they are patient and tolerant of repetition. To examine the relative effectiveness of the tutors in this study, tutee residual-gains were computed by regression of post-test scores on three variables: amount-of-tutoring

Figure 2.2 Ninth grade post-test results:
Post-test means and 95% confidence limits for ninth graders in the
seven conditions.

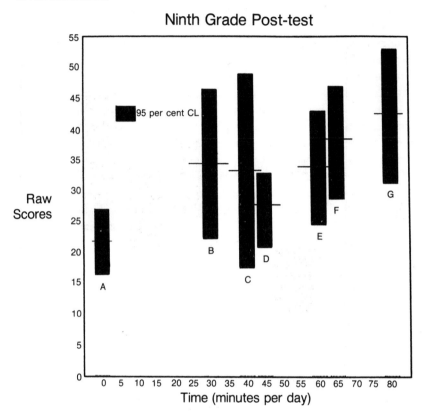

Notes: A = no treatment control group
       B = competing treatment control group
       C, D, E, F, G = tutoring groups

actually received (in minutes); tutee-ability; and tutee's 'effort' characteristics. ('Effort' was a rating by the student's teacher of the student's usual
level of academic effort in the regular classroom.) For each tutor, the
average residual gain of his or her tutee was then computed. What kinds
of tutors produced the highest achievement in tutees when time, ability,
and effort were controlled? As a first indication it can be noted that tutees'
average residual gains were not significantly correlated with tutor-ability
(r = −.09), pre-test (r = −.14) or post-test (r = −.15). The correlation
between tutee residual gains and tutors' retention test scores was -.28,
significant at the .05 level and there was a significant negative correlation
between average tutee residual-gains and tutors'-effort ratings (r = -.30,

Figure 2.3 Fourth grade post test-results:
Post-test means and 95% confidence limits for fourth graders allocated
zero, 20, 30 or 40 minutes of tutoring daily.

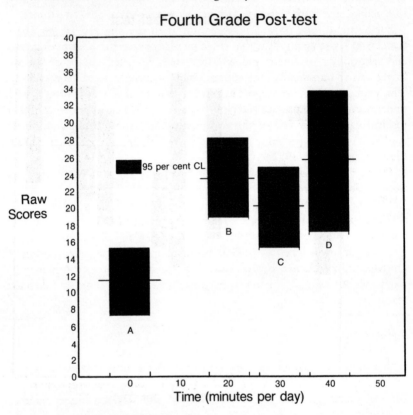

Notes: A = no treatment control group
     B, C, D = tutored groups (tutees)

$p = .03$, $n = 39$). These trends indicated that low-effort, low-achieving
students were slightly more effective as tutors than were high-effort,
high-achieving students. The tendency was not a strong one but *was*
sufficient to refute any suggestion of a tendency in the opposite direction
for this group of students (a group, it must be remembered, of generally
low achievement). These findings are consistent with the observations of
many practitioners: poor students are frequently relatively effective tutors.

How can persons less competent in the subject be as effective as, or more
effective than, more competent persons when acting as tutors? In considering answers, it must first be recalled that *tutoring is not teaching*. Tutoring
means explaining a limited, usually prescribed, set of concepts; very often
it is performed following training. Had tutors had responsibility for

selecting the curriculum, analysing it, and organising it into clear objectives, then one might expect subject-matter competence to become important, if not crucial, to success. But in the context of clearly-delimited instruction, and with training, low-achievers can make effective tutors.

Furthermore, one possible explanation as to the slightly greater effectiveness of less-able pupils is that these pupils covered the objectives slowly and laboriously – which helped the tutees to learn. In other words, lower-ability tutors avoid the mistake of presenting material too quickly. This explanation found support in another finding of this study: tutors who underestimated the amount their tutees had learned had tutees with higher residual-gains (a reversal of the commonly-cited, though not empirically well-supported, expectancy effect, cf Rosenthal and Jacobsen, 1968; Elashoff and Snow, 1971).

Another indication of how less-able tutors may be particularly effective may be deduced from reports such as those by Stallings and Kaskowitz (1974) and Soar (1972). They presented evidence from large-scale analyses that teacher's use of open-ended questions, ie questions high in the Bloom taxonomy (Bloom, 1956), was negatively related to achievement. Direct questions at lower levels of the Bloom taxonomy facilitated acquisition of knowledge by students. Lower-achieving or less-competent tutors may be likely to ask simple, direct questions rather than indirect, abstract, reasoning-type questions.

Retention tests
Tests three months after the brief tutoring experiment showed tutors still with a significant advantage over non-tutors. Non-tutors, in fact, had sunk back to a mean score not significantly higher than their pre-test score. Among fourth-graders, tutees still showed significantly higher average scores than non-tutees (t = 2.68, p<.05. Effect size = .81).

Summary

In summary, as far as cognitive outcomes were concerned, the results of this experiment conducted in a school setting indicated that after 14-year-old pupils had received initial instruction, acting as a tutor produced significantly higher achievement than did classroom-instruction. Nine-year-old tutees made significant gains as a result of receiving tutoring and both tutors and non-tutors still showed significant advantages over equivalent control groups three months after the three-week experiment. There was a slight tendency for low-effort, low-achieving students to have been the more effective tutors.

The LA project had the following characteristics:

- Cross-age with an age-gap of five years (14-year-old pupils tutoring 9-year-old pupils).

- Cross-school: tutors left their secondary school to tutor in a primary school.
- A structured set of objectives which tutors were assigned to teach, in the area of fractions.
- Tutors were low achieving: tutees a complete range of the school's intake.
- Initial training consisted of three days in the regular classroom, tutors along with non-tutors, explaining the objectives and including some role-playing of tutoring: these lessons conducted by the researcher.
- The tutoring sessions were supervised by the researcher; the normal classroom-lessons were conducted by the regular teachers who, because of the removal of half of the class for tutoring, benefited from a reduced class-size.

The last-named characteristic represented a flaw in the design, the kind of flaw which one must often accept due to practical problems involved in setting up field experiments. The effects of tutoring could have been attributed to the effect of the supervising teacher. Efforts were made in the replication study to aviod this confounding of teacher with treatment.

UK Project I Cross-age (Fractions)

This was the project which most closely resembled the inner-city LA project.

Participants

A secondary school was located which had a primary school nearby. It was a comprehensive school serving pupils in a lower socioeconomic status area in north-east England. With the agreement of the teachers of the classes involved, the Head of Mathematics chose two classes in the fourth form to participate in the project. These classes were randomly divided into tutors and non-tutors; they will be referred to as class S1 and class S2 (secondary 1 and secondary 2). The two classes were at the second level in a four-level stream and were preparing for CSE examinations. For comparison purposes, two classes from the level below the experimental classes (S3 and S4) were also given the pre-and post-tests.

At the primary school, two classes of nine- and ten-year-old children represented the entire range of ability for the school's intake. Since the number of tutees needed was almost equal to the number of pupils in these classes, there was no control group for the tutees. The class containing children of ten years and older will be referred to as P1; the class with children of 9 years and older as class P2.

Design

The project was designed to examine two major effects: the effect on secondary pupils of being assigned a tutoring role as opposed to remaining in a regular classroom situation; and the effect on tutors of tutoring one tutee for 30 minutes as opposed to two tutees consecutively for 15 minutes each. In other words, there were two manipulated variables in the design: tutoring vs not-tutoring and, within the tutoring condition, having one as opposed to two tutees. The latter planned variation would also allow tutees to receive different amounts of the treatment in so far as some tutees received 15 minutes of instruction on each occasion whereas others received 30 minutes. The design was implemented as a pre-test post-test 'true' experiment (Campbell and Stanley, 1966) with secondary pupils assigned randomly to the tutoring- or no-tutoring condition, and the tutors then randomly assigned one or two tutees. The assignment of the tutees to the tutors was based on the rank-ordering of both groups on the pre-test, with higher-scoring tutors assigned higher-scoring tutees. Such a procedure was considered necessary to avoid the unsatisfactory situation of a tutee knowing more than a tutor. Despite the age difference of about 5 years, it was apparent from pre-test distributions that this situation could easily have arisen: 16 of the 44 primary children tested fell within the range of the tutors' scores (see Figure 2.4). It must be noted that the tutees covered the

Figure 2.4 Distribution of scores on the fractions pre-test

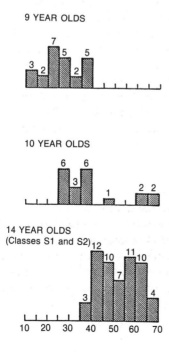

entire ability range for the school's intake, whereas tutors did not include any pupils from the top stream.

Procedures

The timetables at the two schools dictated the extent to which tutoring could be implemented. For one experimental class (S1), tutoring could occur during two out of the three weekly one-hour lessons, making a total of six tutoring sessions in the three weeks of the project. For the other experimental class at the secondary school (S2), scheduled activities at the primary school (such as radio broadcasts, visits to the swimming-baths) meant that tutoring could only occur on one of the three lessons per week, yielding therefore only three tutoring sessions during the three weeks of the project.

A major problem in the design of the LA experiment had been the confounding of supervision with experimental condition – the researcher supervised the tutors throughout the experiment, and some of the strong positive effects could have been attributed to the effect of the supervising teacher rather than just to the effect of tutoring. It was possible for class S1 in this experiment to control more effectively for the supervising teacher effect: the Researcher Associate and the S1 teacher alternated between taking the normal class instruction and supervising the tutoring. Unfortunately this balance was not achieved in S2, in which the regular teacher supervised only one of the three tutoring sessions and the Research Associate worked with the tutors the rest of the time.

During lessons when tutoring was scheduled, the non-tutors worked in a normal classroom fashion consisting of demonstration of the problems on the board, discussion and exercises. For tutors, the procedure was first to assemble and walk across to the primary school (this took about ten minutes). At the primary school a room was ready with tables-for-two placed irregularly throughout the space available. Tutees were brought in for tutoring for 30 minutes, the remainder of the one hour period being taken up with completing 'Tutor Record Sheets' and returning to the secondary school. On the 'Tutor Record Sheets', tutors were to tick off which objectives they had worked on and write comments on how the session had gone.

Instruments

The objectives to be covered during the planned three weeks of the project were agreed upon by the teachers and the Research Associate. A fractions test was constructed, with five items per objective and this was administered in the primary and secondary classrooms two or three weeks before the project started. The Standard Progressive Matrices (SPM) test (Raven, 1958) was also administered to all classes by the Research Associate. Due to the danger of a ceiling effect on the fractions test, (some had scored as high as 70/72 ie 97%), a more difficult test was constructed for the post-test. A questionnaire was administered to tutors at the end of the project.

Table 2.2 shows reliabilities for the pre- and post-tests used in this project with internal consistency measures ranging from .71 to .91.

Table 2.3 summarises the experimental conditions and the pre-test scores. As would be expected from the random assignment procedure, tutor and non-tutor groups were equivalent on the Standard Progressive Matrices and on the fractions test. Differences were not even statistically significant at the .20 level.

Table 2.2 Reliabilities of the Objectives Based Test

Sample	n	Internal Pre-test	Consistency[a] Post-test	Test-retest r	p
Tutees	39	.87	.91	.85	<.001
Tutors	25	.73	.71	.37[b]	.04
Non-tutor	63	.74	.86	.65	<.001
All tested	127	na	na	.81	<.001

Notes: (a) Cronbach's alpha
(b) The low test-retest correlation for tutors suggested that tutors' rank orders changed considerably from the pretest. For class S1 the test-retest correlation was .72 whereas for S2 it was .42. This suggests the re-ordering of ranks was primarily in class S2. This re-ordering appparently brought achievement more in line with ability since the correlation with the SPM increased from .41 to .66. In class S1 correlation with ability changed only marginally, from the surprisingly low values of .16 to .10.

Implementation and pupil response

In the following paragraphs, comments from pupils and teachers are used to illustrate both how the project was implemented and how pupils responded to it.

Attendance
Attendance was good, as is often the case in the first term of a school year. There were no substantial or significant differences between the attendance of tutors (average of 93%) and non-tutors (average of 90%) as measured by their presence in maths classes.

Teachers' reports
Teachers were asked to record their impressions of the project in writing. The Head of the primary school, where the tutoring actually took place, wrote:

Table 2.3 Experimental conditions and pre-testing results

Class[a]	Stream	Experimental condition	Periods allocated			n	SPM		Fractions Pre-test	
			To Tutoring	Tutor Preparation	Normal Classwork		$\overline{X}$	SD	$\overline{X}$	SD
S1	2	Tutors	6	3	0	13	45	6.3	53	8.3
		Tutor control	0	0	9	14	45	8.3	54	10.1
S2	2	Tutors	3	6	0	13	45	4.9	52	8.9
		Tutor control	0	0	9	15	43	7.0	54	8.1
S3	3	Comparison Gp.	0	0	9	18	43	6.8	45	8.9
S4	3	Comparison Gp.	0	0	9	17	41	8.7	48	5.8
			Tutoring time allocated							
P1	Mixed ability	Tutees (10 yrs +)	Either 3 × 15 mins = 45 or 3 × 30 mins = 90			20	38	10.5	42	14.0
P2	Mixed ability	Tutees (9 yrs +)	or 6 × 15 mins = 90 or 6 × 30 mins = 180			24	35	8.0	26	8.2

(a) S = Secondary   P = Primary

When I had the opportunity to visit the library where the children were working, I was most impressed by the quiet, controlled working atmosphere. The junior children treated the older girls and boys with respect (and most of them referred to the secondary school children as 'students') and the secondary children were patient and pleasant with them.

One of the two secondary teachers involved observed:

Attitude and interest of tutors seem to be generally positive (varying in enthusiasm from pupil to pupil of course). Tutees, in general, seem to be keen and more than happy at being taught in this way.

(Teacher of class S1)

The other teacher wrote:

The tutors responded in a very adult and responsible way. They worked hard in class and on their files, were concerned with their tutees' progress as well their own, and have shown considerable subsequent interest in the exercise.

(Teacher of class S2)

Pupil reports
The written comments from pupils provided a glimpse of their attitudes to, and perceptions of, the project. Some provided accounts of what happened between tutor and tutees.

Written comments are a very difficult kind of data to handle. Inevitably, a certain amount of 'exampling' is used: one makes a point and selects a quotation which illustrates it. This is, of course, highly-selective use of the raw data.

In trying to move towards some summary of this kind of data, one strategy is to form categories and count the occurrence of comments which fall into these categories, preferably checking reliability by having the assignment to categories cross-validated by other raters. But breaking up of a set of comments from one person often loses what might be termed the 'clinical-insight' which is gained by considering all the comments from one 'case' together, as a miniature case-study.

The problem is illustrated by the case shown in Figure 2.5. Tension and ambivalence are discernible, pervading a stressful experience of tutoring for a not-very-able pupil. This pupil, incidentally, made an above average residual gain during the project.

Using categories, this pupil would have contributed counts to such categories as: 'being influenced towards teaching' (lines 19, 20) 'being influenced away from teaching' (lines 5, 6), 'thinking the project was good' (lines 13, 14, 16, 17, 18) 'liking it' (line 5) and 'hating it' (lines 4 and 11). The approach of counting categories was not used.

Figure 2.5 One tutor's comments

Time comment was written	Comment	Line No
Prior to tutoring:	I'm looking forward to it bit nervus	1
After tutoring on	He no's about fraction's. did not	2
Day 1	have very long. Bite nervise	3
	A bite slow	4
Day 2	I like it. Got to know him a bit more.	5
	I would not wan't to become a teacher.	6
Day 3	I need to work on my fractions. Any	7
	tutor has to work on his fractions.	8
Day 4	I like it but getting a bit sick of it.	9
	I know him much more.	10
Day 6	I enjoyed today because it was the last	11
	one. I am sick of keep coming over	12
	here. It help't me to do fractions	13
	much better than before. He nows more	14
	than he started with I think.	15
	It would be good if we could do this	16
	again in the 5 year to help us to	17
	revise for are exams.	18
	I would like to teach children between	19
	9–11.	20

Tutees' comments

In reporting the comments from tutees, an indication will be given of the characteristics of the pupil who made the comment. 'Relative gain', one of the characteristics to be reported, comes from 'residual gain analysis'. In a residual gain analysis, the pupil's post-test performance is interpreted in the light of the score which would have been expected from that pupil, knowing his or her pre-test score, Standard Progressive Matrics' (SPM) score, and the general gain made by the class as a whole. Thus the residual gain score shows the learning gain made by the pupil *relative* to other similar pupils in his or her class. These relative gains were classified from high to low in five groups, the terms used for reporting the gains being those shown in Table 2.4.

In the presentation of comments below, tutees are described by five pieces of information:

Class	Age-group of class	Sex	Entry level	Relative gain

Table 2.4 Categories used for reporting relative gains made during the project

Standardised residual gain score (Relative gain)	Descriptive term applied
Over 1.5	very good
0.5 to 1.5	good
-0.5 to 0.5	average
-0.5 to -1.5	below average
below -1.5	poor

The 'entry level' was a composite standardised score for each class, based on the fractions pre-test and the SPM score. As with relative gain, pupils' relative standing in their class has been expressed on a five-point scale, this time using the descriptive categories A, B, C, D and E. An 'A' indicates a pupil at the top of his or her class.

Take, for example, this pupil:

P2: 9 years, Female, C, average gain

This pupil was in class P2 (Primary 2), of nine years olds. She was about average for her class ('C') and made gains during the project which were about average for pupils with similar scores on the fractions pre-test and on the SPM.

Here, from the pens of tutees, are some descriptions of tutor behaviours:

I thought my teacher was very nice. She understood when I needed help. She was also very patient, she also explained everything very clearly. The things I did I thought were *just* a bit hard, and when I forgot to cancel the fractions down she just told me I'd forgotten and said remember next time.

(P1: 10 years, Female, C, Good gain)

My teacher was nice. He told me to ask him if I was stuck and he said 'Here's a ruler and rubber'. He explained all right but he said 'do it my way' and I did not understand his way so I got them wrong. I think the work was hard because I could not understand the sums.

(P2: 9 years, Female, C, Good gain)

I think my teacher was very nice. I think the scheme was a good idea, because when we get to the secondary school it will save the teachers a lot of time teaching us how to do it (the fractions). She explained things very well and she was very understanding. Some of the fractions I already knew but some of them I didn't know. Most of them were very simple. I enjoyed it a lot.

(P1: 10 years, Female, C, Good gain)

I like my teacher very much, she helped me and I think I knew a lot more about fractions when I finished than when I started. She was very good at teaching but she was a little bit impatient and she told me to hurry up. When I had just started, she said "Are you finished yet" but she was funny. She did some sums for me. And she said she didn't like doing fractions very much but she wanted to be a teacher. I thought the work was just right.

(P2: 9 years, Female, C, Average gain)

Some of the younger tutees in particular found the work hard and thought the tutors spoke too quickly.

I thought my teacher was kind. But she said the words too fast.

(P2: 9 years, Male, B, Average gain)

I thought my teacher was talking a little too fast. She didn't explain properly and she kept making mistakes herself. She was very nice though. She helped me as much as she could and she did some sums for me. I thought the work was a little hard for me. I didn't learn anything because it was too hard. I thought the idea was a very good idea even though I didn't learn anything. I think it might have been easier for the teacher because she didn't have as many children in the class when we went for fractions.

(P2: 9 years, Female, C, Poor gain)

I thought that my teacher was a bit too fast. When I was doing a sum which was hard he said "hurry up, you're taking a long time." He taught me for a half hour. When I was there for a while I started to do fractions OK.

(P2: 9 years, Female, C, Average gain)

My teacher was a bit too quick because she told me the answer when I could have got it if I was given a minute.

(P2: Male, B, Average gain)

As might be expected, since tutees were drawn from a full ability-range across two age-groups, there were also tutees who found the work easy. Apparently they enjoyed the experience nevertheless:

The teacher was nice. It was a good idea. I liked it. It was organised well. I had a patient teacher. I didn't learn anything but it was good practice.

(P1: 10 years, Male, A, Good gain)

It was good and the kids that taught us didn't rush us. The sums were dead easy and simple. We did those sums last year.

(P1: 10 years, Male, B, Average gain)

My teacher was very nice. When I got there each day we used to have sweets. We had to hide them from [the Research Associate] because you are not allowed to eat sweets. If he had found out that we had sweets we would have to chuck them in the bin. I liked my work I was doing. I thought it was easy work and he was always telling me the answers and I got all of them right.

(P2: 9 years, Male, D, Scored zero on post-test)

[Perhaps always telling a tutee the answer was not good tutoring. But for this below-average nine year old the post-test was too difficult, so interpretation is problematic.]

Tutees had opinions about the factors influencing tutors' effectiveness as teachers.

My teacher was a good one because he did one thing at a time.

(P2: 9 years, Male, B, Average gain)

Many tutees expressed the thought that it was a good idea to have pupils as tutors:

I think it was good because they were younger than other teachers and I think they understood you better.

(P2: 9 years, Male, B, Average gain)

Tutors' comments

Turning from tutee reports to tutor reports, a further impression of the process of tutoring was gained from examination of tutor record sheets. Below, comments from the tutors have been grouped into postulated 'effects'. In the writer's experience, most cross-age tutoring projects yield anecdotal evidence of these effects and while it is unlikely that fundamental or substantial readjustments in attitudes could be expected from a few brief experiences of being a tutor, one might wonder what the cumulative effect would be of regular use of periods of cross-age tutoring.

Tutors are described by five pieces of information:

Class	Sex	Entry level	Relative gain	Tutee's relative gain

It will be recalled that some tutors had two tutees.

The responsibility effect
Teachers often comment with pleasure and surprise at the effort tutors make, the responsibility they seem to feel towards their tutees. One aspect of this effect was the attitude revealed when, before the first tutoring-session, those who were to be tutors were asked to write down what they thought of the idea. Their comments frequently reflected anxiety as to whether they would be able to tutor well.

I feel a bit worried in case I get the fractions wrong, but other wise I am quite looking forward to it.

(S1 Female, C, Below average gain. Tutee gain: good)

I'm looking forward to it but nervous.

(S1 Male, D, Good gain. Tutee gain: good)

It might be very embarrassing for you if you forget how to do the sums yourself.

(S1 Male, B, Below average gain. Tutee gain: below average)

In low achieving secondary school mathematics classes, it is sometimes quite difficult to induce in pupils any sense of *needing* to learn mathematics. Prim references to later employability or examination success mean little to restless teenagers. The comments just cited indicated the way in which the tutoring project provided tutors with an *immediate* need to know the work.

Tutors' daily records often reflected their concern and the efforts they were making to get tutees to understand.

. . . at times it could be frustrating when they did not understand the work.

(S1 Female, B, Below-average gain. Tutee-gain: below average)

And the elation clearly felt by one tutor after the tutoring session:

Success! Claire has worked hard this morning and got the hang of No. 9 straight away.

(S1 Female, D, Average-gain. Tutee-gain: average)

I sometimes feel terrible when he is just sitting there and I think he's stuck so I go to help him and he says "I know" and carries on.
(S1 Female, C, Good-gain. Gain made by tutee referred to: average.

Other tutee: good)

The insight-into-learning effect

Early proselytisers of peer tutoring claimed that tutoring would cause pupils to 'learn how to learn'. (Gartner, Kohler and Riessman, 1971). Whilst no empirical evidence for this effect appears to have been presented, it remains an interesting hypothesis. The hypothesis receives some support from comments like that below:

I think that this project has been quite useful to me. It has helped me notice how much you must concentrate and listen to the teacher's explanations of how to do the sums and how important it is to ask if you get stuck.

(S1 Female, B, Below average gain. Tutee gain: below average)

Teacher empathy effect

Being cast in the role of tutor could be expected to induce some understanding of teachers' roles.

I think I have learnt how to teach and I found out how hard it is for a teacher to teach 30 kids never mind 1 or 2.
(S1 Male, B, Below average gain. Tutee gain: average)

I didn't really learn anything apart from teachers must have a hard job.
(S1 Male, C, Below average gain. Tutee gain: below average)

The relief of boredom effect
Tutoring was a valuable experience if only in that it was a change from routine; the boredom that is too often felt at school was held at bay. It must be stressed that this relief was not gained at the expense of basic cognitive instruction. Tutors *were* working on fractions but some nevertheless regarded the project as a relief from normal schooling.

It makes a change from being in the same classroom and being taught by the same old teacher.
(S1 Male, B, Below average gain. Tutee-gain: below average)

A tutor, one of whose tutees showed one of the lowest residual gains, wrote in clear, neat handwriting prior to tutoring:

I am looking forward to teaching these children as it means getting out of the classroom as I do not like maths but I will like teaching these children.
(S1 Male, C, Average gain. Tutees' gains: poor and below average)

Another, more effective, tutor wrote

It has been great not just because missing maths in school, it is very exciting.
(S2 Male, C, Average-gain. Tutees' gains: very good and average)

The peer tutoring appreciation effect
Both tutors and tutees perceived some benefits from their being more close in age to each other than are regular teachers and pupils:

Also tutees you teach might feel better with their own generation teaching them.
(S2 Male, C, Good gain. Tutees' gains: average and poor)

Some tutors appeared to be aware of the idea that a reason for teaching work might be to assist their own learning. Thus one comment was:

It would be worth continuing because it saves some teachers a lot of time explaining when they already know.
(S2 Male, C, Average gain. Tutees' gains: very good and average)

and an unintentionally humorous comment:

It helps the tutee to learn as well as teaching your self. This could be improved but it is a very useful way of teaching young kids of 9 and 10. Instead of having fully growning adults doing it . . .
(S2 Male, C, Good gain. Tutees' gains: average and poor)

Cognitive outcomes

Did tutoring have a positive effect on the achievement of tutors? A no-treatment control group was provided by the pupils in classes S3 and S4, the undisturbed other two fourth-year groups, with a correction applied for different initial levels of performance. The results of this comparison, not surprisingly, showed statistically significant effects ($p < .001$) in favour of tutors. Tutors scored on average 46 on the fractions post-test, as against an average of 29. Adjusted for differences in initial level, the mean would be 44 as opposed to 31, still a difference of 0.98 of a standard deviation. That is to say, the effect size for a comparison with a no-treatment group was 0.98. The comparison of tutors with no-treatment control classes only answered the question; 'Did tutors gain from the tutoring project?' They did. But the more important question is whether tutors gained more from tutoring than they would have gained by spending the same time on the same topics in the regular classroom. For this question, the appropriate comparison was with the pupils in classes S1 and S2 who did not tutor but who worked on the same topics. This 'competing-treatment' control group will be referred to as the 'non-tutors'.

A straightforward initial test, pooling results from classes S1 and S2 is shown in Table 2.5.

Table 2.5 Simple comparison of tutors vs non-tutors on the immediate post-test

Group	n	x̄	SD	t	p (one tail)	Effect size
Tutors	25	46 (67%)	8.6			
				1.08	.14	0.25
Non-tutors	30	43 (62%)	13.9			

Although the tutor average was slightly higher than that of the non-tutors, it did not look as though the strong effects found in the Los Angeles experiment had been replicated. A difference significant at the .04 level could be shown, however, if simple gain scores (post-test minus pre-test) were used. This was due to the fact that the random selection had by chance favoured the non-tutors (cf table 2.3). Both these results were sufficiently positive to maintain that the tutors, who had spent from three to six hours (out of nine hours of maths lessons) on helping primary school pupils had done at least as well on the post-test as an equivalent group of pupils remaining in a regular classroom situation. *Tutors had not provided tutoring at the expense of their own learning.* Furthermore, it must be remembered that the class size in the regular classroom situation was reduced by about 50% due to the withdrawal of the tutors. For non-tutors the pupil-teacher ratio was 1:13 and 1:18 in S1 and S2 respectively, whereas it was 1:26 in the tutoring sessions when the tutees were being supervised as well as the tutors.

To some extent, effects weaker than those found in the LA experiment had been expected for a number of reasons. There was a tighter design: the confounding of tutoring with supervision by an outside person had been removed in one experimental class (S1). There was also a considerably smaller amount of 'treatment': the amount of actual tutoring had been only either 180 minutes (class S1) or 90 minutes (class S2) in the three week period, whereas the amount had ranged from 280 to 1120 minutes in the Los Angeles experiment. Third, there was a different context: it was felt that the regular classroom (the control group condition) was more effective in this school than in the stressed conditions of a Los Angeles 'ghetto' school. Thus the difference between the effectiveness of tutoring in comparison with the control condition would be expected to be less, since the 'control' was more effective.

Given that tutors did not apparently show any decrement in achievement, and did enjoy and possibly benefit in other ways from the experience, it might be argued that this was sufficient evidence to justify continuing to recommend cross-age tutoring as an instructional procedure. But such a position might fail to take sufficient account of the fact that organising cross-age tutoring requires a considerable amount of extra work from teachers. One would much prefer to see cognitive as well as non-cognitive benefits. Further analyses of the data were undertaken in an attempt to elucidate the conditions under which tutoring seems to be beneficial for the tutors.

The graphs in Figure 2.6, overleaf, show the post-test scores separately for classes S1 and S2 and for boys and girls in those classes. Only for females in class S1 was the mean score for non-tutors higher than that for tutors. Separate analyses (Table 2.6) showed that the differences due to tutoring/non-tutoring in class S1 were not statistically significant, whereas those in class S2 were, at the .02 level, one-tail. Thus having been picked by the random-assignment process to tutor resulted on average in no significant difference in class S1 but significantly better performance in class S2.

Clearly it is important to consider the characteristics of the two classes and differences in the way the project was implemented. These contextual factors are summarised in Table 2.7 on page 49, along with some cognitive and non-cognitive outcomes.

Figure 2.6 Post-test scores for S1 and S2

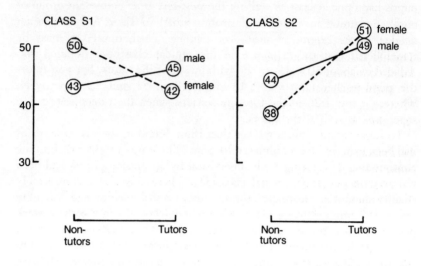

Table 2.6 ANCOVAs for post-test scores

Class	Source	df	MS	F	P
S1	Sex (S)	1	7.68	0.121	0.73
	Tutoring (T)	1	35.24	0.553	0.47
	S x T	1	4.42	0.069	0.79
	Covariates:				
	SPM	1	0.91	0.014	0.91
	Fractions	1	1220.09	19.154	0.01
	Residual	17	63.70		
	Total	22	108.79		
S2	Sex (S)	1	129.74	1.608	0.06
	Tutoring (T)	1	376.79	4.670	0.04
	S x T	1	39.06	0.484	0.49
	Covariates:				
	SPM	1	1097.85	13.607	0.01
	Fractions	1	85.66	1.062	0.31
	Residual	21	80.68		
	Total	26			

Table 2.7 Summary of Project I cross-age (Fractions)

	Class S1	Class S2
Characteristics of class		
Teacher attitude to tutoring	doubtful	neutral to positive
Pupil co-operation level in normal classes	high	not as high
SPM achievement correlation	.16 (n = 23)	.46 (n = 27)
sex achievement correlation	.001	.13
Implementation		
Supervision of tutors by research associate	5/9 periods	8/9 periods
Time allocated to objectives:		
Tutors	9 lessons	9 lessons
Non-tutors	about 7 lessons	9 lessons
Number of tutoring sessions	6	33
Number of sessions:		
before tutoring	1	1
preparation during tutoring	3	6
Class size for supervision:		
tutors and tutees (a)	average of 22	average of 17
non-tutors	13	18
Cognitive outcomes		
Post-test: tutors	62%	72%
non-tutors	65%	59%
Retention test: tutors	68%	57%
non-tutors	68%	54%
Tutor attitudes		
Per cent positive response to 'Would you like to have tutoring as a term's course?'	62%	100%[b] or 85%
'Would you like your whole maths class to go regularly to tutor?'	38%	82%

(a) Class size for supervision was 26 when tutors were tutoring tutees, 13 where preparing for tutoring. The averages arise from different proportions of tutoring and preparation.
(b) Only 11 of the 13 tutors answered the questionnaire.

Complexities in a seemingly simple experiment

Teacher attitude

There is a school of thought which claims that the outcome of any innovation depends crucially on the attitudes of the teacher who implements it. It would be fair to report that the teacher of class S1 was less enthusiastic about tutoring than the Research Associate or indeed than the teacher of class S2. He said, for example, 'I wouldn't want it to be thought they learned more by going and tutoring than by being in my class'. His somewhat negative view of tutoring was one possible factor in the differences in outcomes. However, there were many other factors and this one should not be given undue weight. There is no systematic evidence regarding teacher effects on the outcomes of experimental implementations (trials) of innovations, effects which would surely depend in any case on the extent to which teacher actions affected the particular innovation. In the present case, it was felt that the experiment was given a fair chance in both classes concerned and that differences in the attitudes of the teachers should not be seen as a major explanation of the cognitive outcomes, although teachers' attitudes may have influenced tutors' attitudes.

Pupil co-operation level

If, as is often claimed, tutoring wins co-operation from pupils who are otherwise poorly motivated and indifferent or even antagonistic to work in regular classrooms, then it follows logically that the beneficial effects of tutoring when compared with regular classwork would be greater the more difficult the pupils. This hypothesis could be invoked to explain the different effects in classes S1 and S2 and also the lesser effects in this project when compared with the LA project in which general classroom conditions were much worse.

Correlations

The correlations of SPM and of sex with achievement are listed for interest and future reference rather than because their interpretation is yet clear. The lack of correlation between sex and achievement suggested that in each class boys and girls were achieving equally. This was not the case in all classes. The class of ten years olds in the primary school had a correlation of $-.45$ (females were achieving somewhat less well in fractions than males) and the secondary school class S3 showed a correlation of .33, a weak trend in the opposite direction. The correlation of .46 ($P < .05$) in class S2 between achievement and the SPM, a measure of aptitude, is difficult to interpret; but this correlation may be an indicator of classroom processes, one of the possible statistical indicators about which more research is needed (Lohnes, 1972). However, not for nothing have correlation coefficients been called the slippery statistics, the *difference* between the correlation in class S1 and that in class S2 was not statistically significant ($z = 1.11$, $p = .28$).

Supervision

Supervision was balanced in class S1 between the Research Associate and the teacher, whereas in class S2 the Research Associate supervised the tutors for eight of the nine mathematics lessons. Attempting to control for the effects of a supervising teacher is one of the major problems facing experimentation in schools, since teacher effects might not themselves be stable and might vary with the situation. Certainly, however, the alternation of supervision achieved in S1 was a tighter design than the confounding of supervision with treatment that occurred in Class S2. Consequently it must be noted that some of the positive effects of tutoring found in class S2 might have been due to the supervision of tutors by the Research Associate.

However, this finding is not without quite positive implications for tutoring as a technique. As in the LA experiment, we have the situation of a stranger coming into a fairly difficult situation and getting a high level of co-operation and hard work from the pupils. Would the same level of co-operation have been afforded a stranger who came in to continue regular classwork? Supply teaching in the inner city is not known to be an easy assignment for a teacher, even in the UK. In Los Angeles, it was perceived as inviting disaster unless you were an intimidating male of the husky footballer variety: yet a small female with a foreign accent (ie English) was able to run a three-week tutoring project with no trouble. In short *tutoring may be valuable in situations where pupil co-operation is a problem.*

Time allocated to objectives

Under this heading, note has been taken of the fact that the non-tutors in class S1 finished the objectives before the end of the project and moved on to other work. This could represent a cost of tutoring projects: they may slow down coverage of the curriculum topics. Again, this reinforces the concern to make sure that tutoring projects are run as effectively as possible, as far as cognitive learning is concerned. If topics are covered more slowly, they must be learned more thoroughly – if, that is, we judge the value of a project by what is learned academically. It could be argued that teaching fewer topics in a way which might promote co-operation and caring would be better than getting through the syllabus regardless of pupils' attitudes to others.

Number of tutoring sessions and training sessions

As already noted, class S1 had six periods in which they could tutor whereas class S2 had only three. Because class S2 could not tutor so often, they had more time to prepare for tutoring during the project (two lessons of preparation to one lesson of tutoring per week). This 'mix' might be another factor which led to the greater success of tutoring in Class 2. Again, we confront one of the complexities of classroom experimentation: a treatment must be evaluated not as an isolated event but also as an event in a sequence of events. The effectiveness of the procedure might depend upon events immediately preceding or following the procedure, the 'mix' of experiences. The importance of a mix of procedures can be inferred from another controlled experiment in classroom settings. Chalip and Chalip (1978), ran a five-week experiment in which three sets of pupils were assigned to work in three different ways:

(1)   Co-operatively in small groups
(2)   Individually
(3)   In an alternating fashion, cooperatively one day and individually the next.

No affective measures or sociometric choice measures showed significant differences, but on a test based on the learning objectives (noun and verb identification), the mixed condition produced significantly higher achievement (F(2.29) = 12.50, p< .001). Interestingly, however, better achievement for the mixed-treatment groups did not occur in a similar experiment in which the mix of co-operative and individual working conditions was achieved by a switch half-way through the experimental period, rather than by daily alternation (French et al 1977). These results seem to tell us that not only is variety the spice of life, but it should be peppered in, not introduced in lumps. As for tutoring, careful consideration must be given to the balance between tutoring and preparation for it during a project. It must be mentioned in this connection that the Research Associate reported that the tutors themselves were disgruntled at having to spend time preparing for tutoring when they would have preferred to be tutoring. Teachers may have to schedule the preparation lessons needed, ignoring opposition from tutors (to be realistic, however, the balance may well be determined, as it was here, by the timetable rather than by educational judgements).

Class size
The effect of class size, or the pupil-teacher ratio, during the project has already been mentioned; the point made was that it favoured the non-tutors, thus providing an even more stringent test of the effectiveness of tutoring.

Summary
The two classes differed in the effects of the tutoring project. In one class, achievement as measured by the post-test showed no significant differences, while in the other, tutors achieved more highly. These differences in outcomes could be attributed to differences in implementation procedures

and/or to contextual effects such as teacher attitudes. Only further experimentation will elucidate the effects of tutoring. At least tutors did not suffer any immediate or long-term decline in achievement as a result of spending some time helping primary pupils.

One or two tutees?

It will be recalled that some tutors, randomly selected, were assigned one tutee to whom to provide 30 minutes of tutoring; others were assigned two tutees whom they tutored for 15 minutes each, consecutively.

What might one expect? That longer tuition would lead to higher tutee-gains perhaps? Or would the same amount of instruction merely expand to fill the time available? Tutors might cover the same ground more slowly, leading to better retention or they might socialise a little – leading, perhaps, to the more positive effect associated with longer sessions. Or might tutors run out of work and feel embarrassed? Would tutors themselves benefit from repeating the lesson to a second tutee?

It was fairly clear from reading their comments about tutoring that many tutors who had been assigned two tutees had not found the short 15-minute sessions satisfactory:

> The first tutee got on very well with his starting out his shapes but there is one thing: that is you don't get long enough with your tutees. When you have two kids to teach it is difficult to get all of the things you would like to do in the small amount of time.

This less satisfactory experience had perhaps slightly affected their attitudes, as shown on a questionnaire. There was a tendency for tutors who had been assigned two tutees to show less enthusiasm towards the idea of regularly tutoring in mathematics classes than tutors who had had one tutee.

Even tutors with only one tutee found the time short:

> "I think we should be given more than half an hour"
> (S2 -12: Female, B, Average gain. Tutee missed post-test)

> "The project could be improved by having more time with the child. . . ."
> (S2 Female, C, good gain. Tutee gain average)

One tutor who felt 15 minute sessions were too short for the tutees seemed to have formed the hypothesis that since having two tutees meant teaching each objective twice, this might enhance the tutor's learning:

> "It would be much better if we just had one pupil each because with two pupils you can not get on, but it helps yourself to learn more about fractions".
> (S1 Male, D, Average-gain. Tutee-gain: one absent, one poor)

However, comparison of post-test and retention test scores did not yield much support for the hypothesis of better tutor learning with two tutees. Post-test means were 46.7 for the 11 tutors with one tutee and 45.5 for the 14 tutors with two tutees, an entirely non-significant difference (p = .84). However, one might expect that the repetition of the tutoring might have led to better long-term retention of the topic. Retention tests given 14 weeks after the end of the project did show that tutors in each class who had had two tutees scored higher than tutors who had had only one tutee. Again, however, the effects were weak and not statistically significant (in class S1, 59% as opposed to 56%; in S2, 55% as opposed to 45%- $F(1,24) = .52$ p = .46)

Cognitive effects, then, were lacking, but written comments from several tutors indicated that they preferred longer tutoring sessions and therefore one, rather than two, tutees. On the Tutor Questionnaire, those with two tutees, while not reporting that they themselves found the sessions too short, tended to think their tutee found the session 'short' whereas the average response from tutors with one tutee indicated that the tutee found the sessions 'OK', a difference which was statistically significant (t = 2.04 p = .05). However, overall, the shorter sessions seemed to have had no effect on tutors' reports of their own or their tutees' enjoyment of the project nor on the amount of preparation for tutoring sessions they reported having done at home.

Long-term effects

Cognitive

The fractions post-test was re-administered as a retention-test some three months later. As reported in Table 2.7, scores at this time showed that in each class tutors and non-tutors were indistinguishable; but class S2 showed more decline than class S1, perhaps due to differences in work covered between the two tests. So we are confronted with evidence that, unlike the LA project in which cognitive benefits from having been a tutor were still in evidence three months after the project, in this project the most positive comment that can be made is that tutors did not seem to have suffered from having spent time helping younger pupils. Taking time out to tutor younger pupils might have been a positive experience as far as enjoyment and attitudes were concerned and it had not detracted from the tutors' own learning.

However, the retention test was a measure of achievement *in the topics which were involved in the tutoring project*. How about achievement in other parts of the mathematics syllabus? Were there any unanticipated effects there? The following report from the teacher of S2 was disturbing:

Many of the tutors were placed in the bottom half of the class on the after-Christmas exam – quite a proportion of which was based on the exercise material. I'm not sure of the significance of this at this stage.

Following this report, the school exam papers were borrowed for analysis. This revealed that the difference between tutors and non-tutors would not normally count as 'statistically significant', reaching only the .20 level. Nevertheless, there was a difference of 10 points between the means on a test of about 60 items and this was a cause for concern. It seemed possible that there was an effect which might be termed a 'post-Hawthorne depression'.

Following the interesting and novel experience of tutoring, the regular classwork might have seemed dull in comparison and have been less well attended to. If this had been the case, the school tests referred to above in the teacher's report should have shown tutors doing less well on the work which was covered in class but the same or better on work covered in the tutoring project. Analysis of the test items revealed that this was indeed the case. The entire difference was accounted for by the difference on items which had been covered in class, not in the tutoring project.

The observations here are not conclusive enough to suggest that there was definitely a post-Hawthorne depression leading to lower achievement on other parts of the curriculum; but it does raise an interesting issue in evaluation : How would we value a project that was so pleasant that it made regular classwork particularly unappealing by contrast? One response would be to recommend that the project be continued, replacing regular classwork.

However, perhaps the solution lies in the notion of variety referred to earlier. Continued longer, tutoring too could satiate and regular classwork become the welcome change. Regular breaks from tutoring to renew enthusiasm for it have been strongly recommended (Fitz-Gibbon, 1978: 39) and a meta-analysis of 65 projects indicated maximum cognitive benefits had been derived from projects lasting four weeks or less (Cohen, Kulik and Kulik, 1982).

Non-cognitive effects
The same teacher who reported the problem with the school-test scores continued:

> Nevertheless, I hasten to recommend the exercise because I feel the benefits far outweight the disadvantages.

And in the same report he recorded his perception of the benefits:

> Most of the children have matured because of the experience and have a more realistic attitude to learning and a more sympathetic attitude to teachers. They have a confidence in themselves – having been teachers – but tend to recognise their own difficulties in learning. Of course there are exceptions to this.

In responding to the Teacher Questionnaire item: 'Were there any pupils for whom you felt tutoring was particularly useful? If so what kind of pupil and why?' The teacher wrote

> For a term or so the lads who used to cause trouble or be lazy and truant.

These perceptions of some of the longer-term effects of a tutoring project, added to the evidence for non-cognitive benefits presented earlier, leave the impression that positive effects on various tutors' attitudes are fairly reliably produced and are perceived both by tutors and by teachers. These attitudinal effects are often highly valued and perhaps account for the great enthusiasm for tutoring shown by many practitioners. Experimentation, however, suggests that claims regarding *cognitive* benefits need careful scrutiny. Perhaps the greater ease of measuring cognitive gains makes our standards of evaluation in this area very much more strict; but it might equally be the case that cognitive benefits are not as stable an effect of tutoring as are the immediately visible effects of the change of role. Indeed, in general, given equal opportunities to learn, classroom processes may have more effect on pupils' attitudes than on pupils' cognitive achievements. This may well be true of tutoring: it may have more effect on pupils' attitudes than on their learning.

Conclusion

In this chapter, controlled field experiments have been reported from four inner-city Los Angeles classes and two inner-city classes in north-east England. All experiments involved low-achieving 14 year olds tutoring nine or ten year olds in fractions.

The method of the controlled experiment was chosen in order to obtain stronger inferences than would be possible with less rigorous methods. However, while the interpretations of controlled experiments are far less fraught with uncertainties and ambiguities than are interpretations of 'passive observational' studies (Cook and Campbell, 1979), nevertheless results never determine the conclusions which can be drawn. They only *put constraints* on those conclusions.

These constraints are often sobering for any claimed 'better method'. Experiments keep researchers from believing their own sincere rhetoric. In the present instance, as mentioned briefly at the beginning of this paper, two *same-age* projects were not successful. In the *cross-age* projects, the significant gains demonstrable in the four LA classes were only replicated in one of the two UK classes, and even there the advantage to tutors was no longer detectable on a retention test 14 weeks later, whereas in LA the benefits had apparently been retained. Many possible explanations can be considered for the difference between the US and UK results. In particular, one suspects that normal classroom instruction – the control group's treatment – was more effective in the UK. Also, perhaps, one must consider the much shorter experimental period in the UK and the fewer resources committed. The LA project ran for three weeks and employed a room for tutoring with special booths and practical equipment such as Cuisennaire rods, circles of paper, scissors etc, whereas the UK project was run for only two weeks in a spare classroom in which tutoring pairs sometimes tended to distract each other.

On the other hand, considering other kinds of learning than academic learning, confidence has been increased that the *cross-age* tutoring role will evoke in tutors strong feelings of responsibility towards tutees, insights into the learning process, expressions of empathy with teachers, relief-from-boredom, a recognition that peer tutors may be able to assist learning and, very importantly, high levels of co-operation with their own teacher or with a stranger.

These are valuable effects and their value will become even more appreciated if schools come to face the kinds of social adjustment problems experienced in inner-city Los Angeles schools. New ways become more valuable when traditional ways no longer work.

Acknowledgements
The support of the Social Science Research Council (now the Economic and Social Research Council) is gratefully acknowledged. The author also wishes to record appreciation for the energy and skills which David Reay brought to the UK projects.

Correspondence
Dr C Fitz-Gibbon, School of Education, University of Newcastle-upon-Tyne, St Thomas Street, Newcastle-upon-Tyne, NEI 7RU.

3 Controlled evaluation of the effects of peer tutoring on the tutors: are the 'learning by teaching' theories viable?

Mary Kennedy

This chapter presents the findings of several studies in which the effects of peer tutoring on the tutor have been evaluated. Some of these studies have found significant attainment gains amongst tutors. The methodology rests on random allocation between experimental and control groups; there are experimental controls for the effects of several factors (eg exposure to the subject matter tutored; gender pairing; gender; tutor-tutee age differential).

Most of the experimental work described in this chapter concerns an evaluation of the effects of twice-weekly tutoring sessions over an eight-week period. The evaluation of the effects on the tutor was based on data for 62 pupils aged between eight and ten years. Attainment gains amongst some groups of tutors were significantly greater than those made by various control groups.

Follow-up studies and attempts to replicate the findings are also discussed.

The experimental work followed a review of previous empirical studies and of theoretical explanations for the phenomena observed. At that time theoretical explanations rested on the premise that attainment gains and other changes among tutors were caused by acting as a tutor. The empirical work described in this paper demonstrates that this premise may be inadequate. Some groups of tutors attain more than non-tutors and others do not; in the studies presented in this chapter these differences were not accounted for by 'time spent tutoring' or 'exposure to the subject-matter tutored'. Other factors, such as gender pairing, were found to be important.

The chapter also examines methodological and theoretical issues arising from the research.

Background

Theory is fundamental to the progress of science as described in Kuhn's (1970) *Structure of Scientific Revolutions*. It can be used to direct research by suggesting important questions to be asked and encouraging a cohesive body of experimental data. Best (1970) writes that 'a theory establishes a cause-effect relationship between variables with the purpose of explaining and predicting phenomena'. Some workers (eg Verma and Beard, 1981), however, dispute the appropriateness of this definition in social sciences such as education, in which cause and effect relationships are notoriously difficult to establish. Nevertheless, theoretical prediction and explanation abound in the educational press and in academic journals of educational research. Reports about peer and cross-age tutoring schemes in which students are taught by students, for example, often include references to psychological theories. When appraising new educational initiatives, such as tutoring schemes, Malamuth and Fitzgibbon (1978) state that 'One is more easily persuaded of the likelihood of success of a project if strong theoretical reasons can be adduced as to why it should succeed'. Encouraging the application of theory into research in this field, Feldman, Devin-Sheehan and Allen (1976) argue that:

> *Unless researchers in this area make a stronger attempt to draw more directly upon the mainstream of psychological and educational theory, it is likely that research on tutoring will be rather fragmented, inconclusive and non-cumulative. The wider use of systematic theory should lead to the formation of research problems of greater sophistication and significance and thereby contribute directly to the numerous practical problems encountered in devising tutoring schemes for children.*

In this chapter, the application of psychological theory to tutoring research is reviewed and its value assessed. Conclusions have ramifications in many branches of applied social science. Subsequently, an example of a controlled experiment designed to test the appropriateness of a given theory is presented.

Application of psychological theory to tutoring research

Theories used to predict that the tutor will benefit from peer and cross-age tutoring include : *role theory* (Malamuth and Fitzgibbon, 1978; Goodlad, 1979; Sarbin, 1976 and Allen 1976); the theories of *the bases of social influence, de-individuation, cognitive dissonance* and *attribution* (Malamuth and Fitzgibbon, 1978), *Gestalt theory* (Goodlad, 1979), *ethology* (Hartup, 1976) and *social skills theory* (Argyle, 1976). These analyses range from general interpretations (eg Goodlad and Hirst, 1989) to the precise definition of specific relationships (eg Sarbin, 1976). There have also been a few experimental studies designed to test hypotheses arising from particular theories eg Garbarino 1975 (attribution theory) and Wood 1976 (role theory).

These theories are useful in that they point to the mechanisms that might produce beneficial changes in the tutor. Their application does, however, have limitations:

1   The same theories can sometimes be used to predict a failure to produce beneficial outcomes.
2   The theories sometimes involve hypothetical constructs that cannot be evaluated.
3   The theories are sometimes based on empirical studies involving extreme and artificial situations and may, therefore, not generalise to peer tutoring.

Examples of theories that can predict both the presence and the absence of beneficial changes in the tutor include role theory and cognitive dissonance theory (see, for example, Malamuth and Fitzgibbon 1978).

Using role theory as a basis, it has been predicted that, through taking the role of teachers, tutors increase their empathy with teachers and their understanding of the difficulties under which teachers operate. This proposition is quite plausible. Nevertheless, within the role-theory framework, it is also possible to hypothesise that if the tutors feel that they have been more successful than the regular teacher, a reduction in empathy and understanding will occur.

Cognitive dissonance theory has been used to predict that pupils with poor behaviour and/or attainment will have to make some change to reduce the dissonance between their own attributions and their role as tutors. Within this framework, it is suggested that the greatest change will be observed amongst those who perceive themselves as being least suitable for the role. This notion is also appealing. Unfortunately, using the same theoretical premise, it may be predicted that those who perceive themselves as being least suitable for the role of tutor will reduce the dissonance between their attributions and their role by failing to adopt the appropriate behaviour or, perhaps, behaving in a manner that is calculated to get them discharged from their duties.

Examples of theories that have been used to predict beneficial effects on the tutor and involve hypothetical constructs which cannot be evaluated include: a model of social identity which is based on role theory (Sarbin, 1976) and cognitive dissonance theory (eg Malamuth and Fitzgibbon, 1978).

The most important variable in Sarbin's role theory is 'status'. This ranges along a dimension from ascribed (eg granted by birth or mother) to achieved (eg occupation). Sarbin proposes that there is relatively less freedom to disengage from ascribed roles and that these are usually rewarded affectively with, for example, respect and caring; achieved roles differ in that they are generally rewarded with tokens of esteem such as money. Sarbin proposes that peer-tutoring schemes foster affective roles amongst children and that the affective rewards contribute to improvement in tasks related to the focus of tutoring. He suggests that children may be less responsive to tokens of esteem (eg marks) which are, traditionally, used in school. The value of the theory is limited because the extent to which the 'status' dimension is ascribed or achieved cannot be evaluated; the tutor might, for example, think that being given the role of tutor was a token of esteem, ie that the role of tutor was achieved rather than ascribed.

The predictions of cognitive dissonance theory relate to the pupil's perception of her/himself as suitable for the role of tutor. These predictions cannot be tested without a valid and reliable measure of self-perceptions; such measures are unlikely to be developed.

Examples of theories that are based on extreme and artificial situations (which may not generalise to the tutoring situation) include some forms of role theory (eg Sherif and Sherif 1969) and de-individuation theory (eg Diener, Fraser, Beamer and Kelem, 1976). Extrapolations from ethological studies also fall into this category (eg Hartup 1976).

Various methods of enhancing the benefits of tutoring have been suggested. These methods sometimes draw from a particular theory. It has, for example, been suggested that tutors should be given badges stating their job title (role theory – Allen 1976). It has also been suggested that benefits to tutors will be improved if they are given little financial reward, are helped to feel personally responsible for what they do and to believe that their actions have significant consequences (see the extrapolation of the discussion of Collins and Hoyt (1972) of forced compliance effects in Malamuth and Fitzgibbon 1978).

Implications for the use of theory

Discussion of the application of psychological theory to research into tutoring schemes must be prefaced by the observation that the theories have been applied to phenomena that may not be produced by tutoring but by an associated factor such as 'novelty' or 'training-to-tutor' (Feldman et al, 1976; Kennedy, 1985). Mouly (1978) contends that

> Premature attempts to reach a formalised theoretical position are likely not only to delimit the areas explored but also to lead to the investigation of the more trivial aspects of science (eg rote memory) simply because they are easier to investigate. The result is a neglect of

the more theoretically complex but also more scientifically significant aspects of a problem.

The application of theory described in the previous section may indeed be premature and, if used as a basis of research, could unjustifiably delimit the areas explored by particular research teams. Furthermore, the enormous diversity of tutoring projects and attempts to evaluate them (see Wilke 1975; Feldman et al 1976) provides no evidence that the constraints imposed by the psychological theories described in the previous section have improved the cohesion of the area through delimiting the areas investigated. It seems that there is a persistent tendency among some educationalists, education policy makers, and researchers to believe that if a desired effect can be predicted by an established body of theory, the probability that it will occur is increased.

It is essential that researchers draw a distinction between (i) 'theories' which generate testable hypotheses and are designed to be modified as hypotheses based on these are accepted or rejected, and (ii) 'theoretical frameworks', such as 'role theory' 'attribution theory' and 'reinforcement theory' that are designed to explain and/or predict a multitude of human behaviours far wider than the sub-group of behaviours desired by the educationalist. Such established 'theoretical frameworks' can predict the presence of beneficial changes amongst peer tutors. More importantly, however, they can predict the *absence* of beneficial changes in a number of ways. For example:

- the persistence of attributions awarded outside the tutoring session (attribution theory);
- the legitimate or referent power of pre-tutoring relationships (the theory of the bases of human influence – Raven, 1965);
- the role of tutor being essentially the same as informal helping practices occurring outside tutoring sessions with friends and siblings (role theory);
- the 'status' of tutor being perceived as primarily ascribed (Sarbin's (1976) model of social identity).

A related point concerns the selection of dependent and independent variables: if experimental hypotheses do not involve variables that can, validly, be empirically evaluated, results will always be open to criticism and will not be widely accepted as a basis for further research. This is a particular problem in the investigation of 'social-psychological variables' (Klaus, 1975) such as self-perception (an essential dimension in attribution theory) and is relevant to work concerning many other theoretical social-psychological constructs (eg de-individuation). Whether the aims of a research project in education are primarily practical (such as comparison of the *effects* of two methods of teaching) or primarily theoretical (such as investigating the *mechanism* through which a method is effective), researchers should try to conduct empirical studies using measures with a relatively high intrinsic validity (such as attendance, attainment, 'time-on-task' and frequency of social initiatives). These measures are preferable to controversially-defined social-psychological constructs of contentious relevance. Experimental hypotheses will be untestable and, therefore, incapable of providing a basis for a scientifically-established theory if they involve social-psychological variables that may not be viable constructs and for which no valid measures exist.

Conclusions from analysis of theory

Loose general references to complete theoretical frameworks within psychology (eg Gestalt theory) are unlikely to aid the production of a cohesive body of information or assist the discovery of cause and effect relationships concerning educational phenomena. This is because, in general, such frameworks can produce theoretical mechanisms that account for both the presence and the absence of the phenomenon studied. An alternative course for educational researchers is to

1   Construct hypotheses about tutoring outcomes based on their own theory regarding the cause of the phenomenon. (Frequent communication between researchers in the field is important, thus enabling researchers to formulate hypotheses from as comprehensive a data-base as possible.)
2   *Test that theory through experiment.*
3   Reject, modify, retest and review the theory or support it.

This methodological approach should produce a more useful and cohesive body of knowledge than that achieved through experiments that are not logically developed from each other. A logical progression through a series of experiments supplemented by good qualitative studies will provide more valuable insight into the educational phenomenon studied than tenuous links with psychological theory. Whilst it might be useful for researchers of educational phenomena to draw analogies from psychological theories and empirical work, neither psychological nor educational research has a sufficiently well-established body of 'fundamental laws' to justify direct generalisation.

Implications for practitioners and researchers

The foregoing discussion will have demonstrated to the practitioner that the theoretical descriptions of the tutoring process are not a sufficient justification for starting a tutoring scheme. Nevertheless, for teaching practitioners, there are several benefits from peer tutoring programmes:

- they offer participants experience that cannot easily be obtained in any other way;
- they need not be costly;
- there is a vast amount of anecdotal evidence that they are effective and that the participants enjoy what they are doing;
- there is some experimentally-controlled evidence that the schemes are effective for some participants.

The researcher, however, has different priorities and responsibilities. It is the researcher's job to define, as rigorously as possible, the relationship between teaching methods and their outcomes. Where possible, the evaluation should be structured in a way that will allow different methods and/or groups of participants to be compared. The information obtained should be fed back to practitioners to help them develop schemes that are likely to meet their objectives. For the researcher, it is important to know whether any benefits from tutoring arise from factors that are unique to the tutoring situation or from associated, but confounding, factors such as novelty or exposure to the subject-matter. This information should be fed back into the wider body of educational research.

The following controlled experiment illustrates the feasibility of executing complex experimental designs that can point to causal relationships in peer tutoring. This type of design can be used to test theoretical explanations of the causes of changes associated with peer tutoring.

An experimental evaluation of the effects of peer tutoring on the tutor

The phenomenon of 'learning-by-teaching' is widely reported and has been the basis of numerous peer- and cross-age tutoring schemes (Thelen, 1969; Gartner, Kohler and Riessman, 1971; Wilkes, 1975; Allen, 1976; Center for the Study of Evaluation, Los Angeles, California, 1978; Goodlad, 1979; Cohen, Kulik and Kulik, 1982). As outlined in previous sections, the phenomenon of 'learning-by-teaching' has been explained by recourse to various psychological theories (see, for example, Malamuth and Fitzgibbon, 1978; Goodlad and Hirst, 1989). Such theorising may, however, be premature as previous studies have tended to lack the necessary controls to delineate the variables responsible. In the study described here, an attempt was made to provide a more objective foundation for theoretical interpretations of reported learning gains through peer tutoring.

The majority of controlled studies into the effect of tutoring reading on the reading attainment of tutors have found that tutors attain more than non-tutors (Cloward, 1967; Morgan and Toy, 1970; Duff and Swick, 1974; Conrad, 1976; Strodtbeck, Ronchi and Hansell, 1976; King, 1982). Although some studies have reported no treatment-effect (Page, 1975; Ramig and Ramig, 1976; Wood, 1976), these studies have usually differed from the former in using a control group who did the tutoring task (reading) by themselves, ie they controlled for exposure to text. In the present study, the text-exposure factor was controlled for by ensuring that all groups of tutors and non-tutors spent the same time studying the tutoring material.

The relationship of attainment gains amongst tutors and the subject-matter that they teach has not, hitherto, been systematically investigated; it has not been established whether reading attainment gains are confined to tutors of reading or whether equivalent reading attainment gains could be produced by tutoring other types of material. In the present study, the 'teacher' components of the role of 'reading tutor' were investigated by comparing the attainment scores of 'reading tutors' with those of 'mathematics tutors'. The effects of tutoring on 'self-concept of ability' (as measured by the Boersma and Chapman *Students' Perception of Ability Scale*) were also assessed.

The mixed-sex, mixed-ability environment in most British primary schools produces individual differences between randomly-allocated pairs. This variation could mask significant effects on subgroups of participants in a tutoring programme. In the present study, the influence of eight pupil-factors was evaluated in an attempt to detect any systematic effects of these factors.

The aim of the study was to provide a preliminary investigation of the following questions:

1 Does 'learning-by-teaching' occur?
2 Does 'learning-by-teaching' occur because of exposure to the subject matter in which attainment gains are made?
3 Does 'learning-by-teaching' occur because the tutor teaches the subject-matter in which attainment gains are made?
4 Does 'learning-by-teaching' occur in only some groups of tutors, and, if so, what characteristics of the tutors and/or tutoring situation define these groups?

Additionally, the effect on the attainment of tutees was evaluated and an informal appraisal of the difficulties faced by teachers and researchers running this type of programme was made.

Participants

108 pupils (51 male, 57 female) attended all experimental sessions as either tutors, tutees or controls. This sample (with a further 37 who had been

absent at some stage in the programme) comprised all the second- and third-year pupils (aged 8 years 3 months to 10 years 3 months) and randomly-selected first-year pupils (aged 7 years 3 months to 8 years 3 months) from two state-operated Merseyside junior schools whose catchment area included a wide range of social classes.

Tutees were either first-year pupils (aged 7 years 3 months to 8 years 3 months) or those second- and third-year pupils whose reading accuracy score (Neale, 1966) ranked in the bottom 2/7th of their class; the resulting sample was 46 pupils (22 male, 24 female).

Tutors were second- and third-year junior pupils whose reading accuracy scores ranked in the upper 5/7th of their school class: 62 pupils (29 male, 33 female).

Design and measures used

The study may be thought of as a set of sub-experiments on the same group of pupils. For each sub-experiment, pupils were randomly allocated into the same three groups:

Tutor reading
Tutor mathematics
Study reading and mathematics alone; do not tutor.

This random allocation is fundamental to the experimental design. Tutors were not systematically differentiated from non-tutors by their behaviour, personality or whether they had volunteered to tutor.

Sub-experiments differ from each other in the sub-group formed within each group of tutors. In each sub-experiment each group of tutors was divided into two groups according to one of eight criteria:

1 Sex pairing in the tutorial dyad: 'same sexes', 'opposite sexes';

2 Sex: 'male', 'female';

3 School class pairing in the tutoring dyad: 'same school class', 'tutee from a younger class';

4 Scores on both dimensions of the *Junior Eysenck personality inventory* (Eysenck, 1965): 'above median', 'below median';

5 Scores on each scale of the *Student perception of ability scale* (Boersma and Chapman, 1979): 'above median', 'below median';

6 Pre-test reading accuracy score on *Neale analysis of reading ability* (Neale, 1966): 'above median', 'below median';

7 Extent of tutee reading improvement on NARA (Neale, 1966): 'above median', 'below median';

8 The differential in the Reading-accuracy scores of the tutor and tutee (NARA; Neale, 1966): 'above median', 'below median'.

'Reading attainment', and 'self-concept of ability' were measured before and after the series of tutoring sessions. Reading attainment was measured using parallel forms (A and B) of the *Neale Analysis of Reading Ability* (NARA; Neale, 1966) which simultaneously evaluates accuracy and comprehension.

Self-concept of ability was measured using the *Students' Perception of Ability Scale* (SPAS; Boersma and Chapman, 1979) modified slightly to reform the North American vocabulary (eg 'smart' was changed to 'clever'). Unlike most other available measures of self-concept (eg Cooper-smith, 1967), this test is designed for use with children in this age group and provides a profile on six subscales of self-concept of ability as well as an 'overall score'.

After all the tutoring sessions were finished, 'preferences for tutoring again' were assessed by asking participants the following questions:

1 *Would you like to be a tutor/tutee again?*
2 *Would you like to do it with the same person or change to a different one?*
3 *Would you like to do reading/maths again or change to maths/reading?*

Procedure for tutoring sessions

'Reading' and 'mathematics' tutoring sessions lasting 20 minutes were held twice a week for eight weeks. Reading-tutoring sessions were scheduled to coincide with a time when the tutors, tutees and control group pupils not involved in the session would be reading, by themselves, in class. Similarly, mathematics-tutoring sessions coincided with a time when those pupils not involved in the session would be working from a workbook of pre-set mathematics exercises by themselves. All pupils had their reading and mathematics material selected for them by their class teacher from a wide range available. Instructions to participants were brief. Tutors and tutees were introduced to the partner to whom they had been randomly allocated. Tutees were told to bring their maths/reading book to each session where their tutor would help them. Tutors were told that, during session, they were their tutees' 'teacher' and that they were to help them with the work that was brought. The status of tutors was emphasised by a badge saying 'TEACHER' (after Allen, 1976). Intervention by the experimenter was kept to an absolute minimum - to prevent gross breaches of discipline and to stop tutors and tutees from swapping roles. The control group pupils who studied alone throughout tutoring sessions were told that there had not been enough children needing help to let them be tutors on this occasion but that 'next time' they would be chosen.

Tutors: analysis and results

Differences between non-tutors and the each of four groups of tutors were evaluated in a two-factor mixed-design ANOVA: groups (5 independent levels) x test session (two related levels). Since this design could not evaluate the effects of the interaction between the subject matter tutored (reading or mathematics) and any of the secondary independent variables, (eg sex pairing - same sexes or opposite sexes), a three-factor mixed design excluding the control group who studied alone was also used: subject matter tutored (two independent levels) x secondary independent variable eg sex-pairing (two independent levels) x test session (two related levels). The unweighted means solution of the ANOVA was used in each case, as absenteeism during the programme (for reasons unrelated to the treatment) had resulted in unequal group sizes (Keppel 1973). Group-differences in 'preferences-for-tutoring-again' were evaluated using Chi square.

In both the two-factor and the three-factor ANOVAs, the overall performance of the groups was different ($F = 2.33$ df $= 4,57$ p <0.05 and $F = 7.99$ df $= 1,45$ p <0.01 respectively). A checking ANOVA confirmed that there had been no difference between the groups before the experiment had begun. Further analysis revealed that the only group of tutors whose reading-accuracy score increased significantly more than that of non-tutors was the group that tutored reading to the opposite sex: an average gain of approximately 11 points in this group compared with approximately 4 points amongst the non-tutors ($F = 5.76$ df $= 4,57$ p <0.025). Further planned comparisons revealed that the increase in reading-accuracy of the group that tutored reading to the opposite sex exceeded that of pupils who tutored reading to their own sex ($F = 6.98$ df $= 1,45$ p <0.025) or mathematics to the opposite sex ($F = 11.18$ df $= 1,45$ p <0.01). The tutors of mathematics to their own sex also gained less than tutors of reading to the opposite sex, but there is a probability of between 0.05 and 0.1 that this difference arose by chance ($F = 3.2$ df $= 1,45$). Mean scores are detailed in Table 3.1.

There was no evidence that the effect of gender-pairing differed for boys and girls, but these comparisons were not very powerful as the groups involved were quite small.

Table 3.1 Mean raw scores on the reading accuracy scale of the NARA amongst tutors and controls

Subject area tutored	Sex pairing of tutor and tutee	No. of pupils	Name	Pre-test mean	Post-test mean
Reading	Same	10	TRS	68.60	72.00
Reading	Opposite	15	TRO	66.66	77.87
Maths	Same	10	TMS	70.10	76.40
Maths	Opposite	14	TMO	58.71	60.93
None	N/A	13	SA	58.23	62.35

There was no evidence that any of the other factors (2-8) listed on page 66 above had any effect on reading accuracy. Reading comprehension (as measured by the NARA) did not differentiate groups; this may have been because of limitations on the sensitivity and validity of the test (Kennedy 1985).

Analysis of the 'self-concept of ability' scores revealed no differences between sub-groups of tutors and non-tutors. (It also failed to discriminate between groups of tutees.)

Of the tutors, 91.3% wanted to tutor again; there was no significant difference in the numbers of reading and mathematics tutors who wanted to change partners: 77% wanted to tutor the same subject area again. It was interesting, however, that significantly more tutors of the opposite sex wanted to change their tutees than tutors of their own sex: 52.6% of tutors of their own sex compared to 93% of tutors of the opposite sex (χ^2 = 10.64; d.f. = 1; p <0.005).

Tutees: analysis and results

The reading attainment of pupils tutored in reading improved significantly more than those tutored in mathematics who read by themselves for the duration of the tutoring programme (Table 3.2 summarises the 2 factor/mixed ANOVA of the data).

Tutee groups did not significantly differ in attainment level prior to the experiment. Further analysis revealed that tutee reading-attainment was not affected by whether their tutor was of the same or the opposite sex, whether the tutor was from the same school-class or an older one or whether the tutor-tutee pre-test reading attainment differential was above or below the median of the sample.

Significantly more reading tutees than mathematics tutees said that they would like to be a tutee again (χ^2 = 5.53; d.f. = 1; p <0.05) and that they would like to be tutored in the same subject area again rather than change (χ^2 = 5.38; d.f. = 1; p <0.05). The tutees' expressed wish to change

Table 3.2 Comparison of mean pre-test and post-test Reading accuracy (NARA) scores of mathematics and reading tutees

Suject area tutored	number of pupils	Pre-test mean	Post-test mean	F Test comparing change from pre-to post-test	Probability (1,41)
READING	24	26.08	35.69		
				9.00	p≤0.001
MATHS	21	32.24	34.57		

partner was not affected by whether the tutor was from the same school class or an older one or whether she/he was of their own or the opposite sex.

Informal observations by the experimenter who ran the sessions and by ten regular teachers, (observing through a small window in a closed door) suggested that pupils were unusually well behaved, never presented discipline problems and were fully occupied in their designated tasks.

Discussion

The results of the present study can be summarised as follows:

1 'Learning-by-teaching' occurred in some, but not all, groups of peer tutors: it occurred for tutors of reading to the opposite sex, but for none of the other groups formed by the interaction of the primary and secondary independent variables listed earlier. Theories regarding the mechanism of 'learning-by-teaching' that rest on the premise that tutors learn *simply* because they teach are, therefore, not substantiated by these findings.

2 'Learning-by-teaching' did not result simply from increased exposure to the subject-matter in which attainment gains are made: the non-tutors and *all* groups of tutors had exactly the same exposure to reading material during the programme, yet the reading attainment of only one group of reading tutors exceeded that of non-tutors. This finding suggests that greater exposure to subject-matter is not necessarily the cause of the 'learning-by-teaching' reported in some tutoring pro-grammes (eg Cloward, 1967; Morgan and Toy, 1970; King, 1982) and not others (eg Page, 1975; Ramig and Ramig, 1976).

3 'Learning-by-teaching' was not a simple result of teaching the subject-matter in which attainment gains are made: reading attainment resulted in only one of the groups of reading tutors tested. However, since none of the groups of mathematics tutors made reading attainment gains it might be deduced that tutoring reading was a necessary but insufficient condition for reading attainment gains in this programme.

4 'Learning-by-teaching' was apparent for those tutoring reading to opposite-sex tutees, but not for those tutoring reading to tutees of the tutor's own sex or tutoring mathematics to tutees of the opposite sex. It was the interaction of the effects of tutoring the opposite sex and tutoring reading that appeared to produce the result. A mechanism for these attainment gains is suggested by the finding that significantly more tutors of the opposite sex than tutors of their own sex wanted to change partners; similarly, informal observations revealed that most of the pupils opted to spend their free time in single-sex groups. It could

be hypothesised that somehow (perhaps because of the novelty of the social interaction or because the opposite-sex tutor and tutee have nothing 'in common' but the tutoring task) tutors of opposite sex tutees had more 'engaged time' studying the tutoring material than other groups. Bloom (1980) draws a distinction between 'engaged time' and 'exposure time'; he claims that the former, rather that the latter, is highly related to attainment. The relationship between 'engaged time' and attainment gains in peer tutoring programmes deserves further investigation.

5   The Student's Perception of Ability Scale (Boersma and Chapman, 1979) did not differentiate groups. However, since 'self-concept' is variously defined and this scale measures factors that are qualitatively different from other measures (Boersma and Chapman, 1978; 1979) the evaluation is not definitive. Using different measures in separate programmes, Gardner (1978) found that the self-concept of tutors improved relative to controls, whereas Morgan and Toy (1970) found that it did not. It is recommended that, in future studies, observable behaviours associated with improved self-confidence are measured; such as frequency of contributions to class discussions and/or the number of social contacts initiated. It is also suggested that, when interpreting these studies, evoking 'self-concept' as an intervening variable is likely to complicate rather than clarify the findings.

6   Reading tutees improved their reading attainment significantly more than mathematics tutees who read by themselves for the duration of the reading tutoring sessions: this demonstrates that peer-tutoring in reading was effective. It also shows that the attainment gains did not result either from the increased attention and social interaction they experienced as tutees or from increased exposure to text. The finding that tutees preferred being tutored in reading to being tutored in mathematics warrants further investigation.

Follow-up studies in other schools were attempted. For a variety of reasons, outside the schools' control, it proved impossible to hold sessions more than once a week. The attainment differences found in the study reported in this chapter, in which sessions were held twice a week, were not replicated. The failure to replicate the findings, when sessions were held less frequently, suggests that attainment gains may not occur if the frequency of sessions is too low; this factor should be investigated further. Failure to replicate the findings does not diminish their value but it does suggest that one should avoid premature generalisation. As a test of the premise that the benefits to the tutor are caused by acting as a tutor, the results are important: acting as a tutor does not always produce attainment gains but has been proven to produce significant gains in certain circumstances.

Conclusions

In conclusion, at least one closely-defined group of tutors attained more than non-tutors, no group of tutors attained less than non-tutors, pupils tutored in reading attained more than those who read alone (ie the mathematics-tutees) and all participants behaved well with minimal supervision. It was also found that a sizable controlled study capable of yielding cause and effect relationships was readily conducted within the ongoing school situation. It is, therefore, recommended that research into this low-cost method of education be continued.

Acknowledgements
This research would not have been possible without the support of the SSRC. The author is also grateful for the cooperation and assistance of the schools involved and the advice of Dr G Wagstaff, Department of Psychology, University of Liverpool.

Correspondence
Dr M H Kennedy, Northern College of Education, Hilton Place, Aberdeen, AB9 1FA.

4 PERACH: A nationwide student tutorial programme

Barbara Fresko and Amos Carmeli

The PERACH Project, initiated in 1974, deploys university and college students as tutors to needy children all over Israel. Begun on a small scale, the project has gradually developed into a large scale scheme in which more than 12 000 tutors are active annually. Most tutoring is conducted on an individual basis: tutor and tutee meet twice weekly in two-hour sessions over the course of an academic school year. Tutors are not simply private instructors, but are expected to stimulate a desire to learn, reinforce self-confidence and broaden a tutee's base of general knowledge and experience. Some group tutoring exists as well, in which the emphasis is more academic than personal. PERACH has also begun to sponsor a number of enrichment programmes in the areas of health, sports, nature and the arts, through which university students can apply their particular interests and skills for the benefit of disadvantaged children. As compensation for their activity, all tutors are awarded a partial tuition-rebate.

PERACH reaches children in all sectors of Israeli society: in the cities, towns and rural areas, in both the religious and secular school systems, and in the Jewish, Arab and Druze communities alike. Children are recommended as candidates for tutoring by either their teachers or their school counsellors. While most tutees tend to be pupils in Grades 4–7, there are some children in the project as young as Grade 1 and others as old as Grade 12.

In principle, any university or college student can serve as a tutor, and indeed tutors come from all academic and social backgrounds. Since tutoring is conducted outside school, pairing of tutor and tutee takes into account the proximity of their homes. Also, insofar as the tutor is expected to serve as a positive role-model for the child, an effort is made to match them on certain traits which would facilitate identification, such as gender, ethnicity and religiosity.

Evaluation which accompanied the project during its initial five years indicated very high satisfaction among tutors, tutees, parents and teachers, although measurable impact on the achievement and attitudes of tutees was often marginal. Continuous informal feedback from various sources over the years has led to greater operational efficiency, increased numbers of tutors, and a branching out beyond individualised tutoring.

Introduction

Tutoring programmes aimed at providing instructional support to under-achieving learners have multiplied greatly in many countries during the past few decades. Differences exist among programmes with respect to duration, focus, structure, tutor-training, and the traits of both tutors and tutees. This variety has led to varying results regarding impact on the cognitive growth of both tutor and tutee (see, for example, Andersen, Licht, Ullman, Buck and Redd, 1979; Allen & Feldman, 1973; Cloward, 1967; Davis, Snapiri and Golan, 1984; Bloom, 1984; Cohen, Kulik & Kulik, 1982; Eisenberg, Fresko and Carmeli; 1980, 1981; Fresko and Eisenberg, 1985) and on such affective variables as motivation, self-concept or attitudes towards school (see Cloward, 1967; Cohen et al, 1982; Eisenberg et al, 1980, 1982b).

Some attempts have been made by researchers in experimental and quasi-experimental settings to clarify the conditions under which tutoring is most likely to succeed. The results of some of these studies have led to the following conclusions:

1 Tutoring-effectiveness tends to improve when tutors have been trained and/or tutoring is structured (Cohen et al, 1982; Davis et al, 1984; Niedermeyer, 1970).

2 Tutoring is more effective when meetings are frequent but do not extend over relatively long periods of time (Cloward, 1967; Fresko and Eisenberg, 1985).

3 Ethnic similarity of tutor and tutee has a positive effect on tutoring results (Cloward, 1967, Fresko and Chen, in 1989), gender similarity has little effect (Cloward, 1967; Devin-Sheehan, Feldman and Allen, 1976) and cross-age tutoring is more productive than peer tutoring (Bloom, 1975, Cohen et al, 1982; Devin-Sheehan et al, 1976).

4 Tutors who are motivated by intrinsic rather than extrinsic rewards tend to be more satisfied by, and less critical of, their tutoring experience (Fresko, 1988; Garbarino, 1975), and are more likely to exhibit positive attitudinal-change as a result of tutoring (Hobfall, 1980).

While research findings may serve as a guide to those involved in establishing a new tutoring scheme or revamping an existing one, they cannot, of course, be the only considerations taken into account. Who will tutor? How will tutors be recruited? Who is to be tutored? Where will tutoring take place and when? How much training will be provided to tutors? These are only some of the questions which must be resolved. Obviously, the demands and realities of the educational system must be considered in a search for solutions, taking into account the human, material and financial resources which are available.

The purpose of the present paper is to present a description of a particular tutorial project which was conceived more than 15 years ago in Israel and which has grown, developed and matured over the years. The name of this project is PERACH which in Hebrew means 'flower' and at the same time is an abbreviation for the words 'tutoring project'.

PERACH: A description

PERACH, the largest tutorial undertaking in Israel, deploys approximately 12,000 university and college students, annually, as tutors to needy school children. In return, tutors receive a rebate which amounts to approximately 40% of their tuition fees. This project was originally conceived as an answer to two social problems. On the one hand, tutoring was intended to help put a halt to the widening achievement gap between the 'advantaged' and 'disadvantaged' sectors of the population (Lewy and Chen, 1977). On the other hand, the award of a tuition-rebate was intended to enable students to meet the ever-rising costs of higher education.

The possibilities of the programme were realised after a two-year piloting (1972–1974) at the Weizmann Institute of Science in Rehovot, during which about 50 university students and staff voluntarily worked with children in the area. The following year about 70 students tutored children in other communities. Subjective impressions of the gains made by the tutored children were very encouraging. In 1976–77 PERACH began operation out of all seven universities in the country. During that year 900 students participated. Each year since has witnessed a continuous growth in the number of tutors; in 1989, figures exceeded 12 000.

Undoubtedly, the fact that PERACH gradually became an established institution on university campuses contributed considerably to its ability to attract more and more students. However, from the start, growth was one of PERACH's aims. A strong commitment to enlisting as many young people as possible to its task has led project directors to branch out in two distinct directions. On the one hand, tutor recruitment has been extended beyond the university student population to include other post-secondary school students, most particularly those in teacher colleges. On the other hand, project activities have been expanded beyond individualised tutoring to include group tutoring and special-enrichment programmes in the areas of health, sports, science, nature and the arts.

Despite these changes, the basic philosophy and operating procedures characterising the project have remained essentially unaltered throughout the years. The main features of the individualised tutoring programme, which still occupies more than 85% of PERACH tutors are described below.

Tutorial sessions

Tutor-tutee pairs are required to meet twice weekly in two-hour sessions over an eight-month period. Location and content of sessions are determined by the pairs themselves. Meetings generally take place alternately in the tutors' and tutees' homes.

Since the guiding ideology of PERACH is to provide each tutee with the type of help he or she requires, the focus of tutoring may vary greatly from pair to pair. Hence sessions may concentrate on general study, on homework, on enrichment activities of educational, cultural or practical value, or on doing things which enhance the tutor-tutee relationship on a personal level. Sometimes group activities are organised, in which many tutor-tutee pairs participate together. It should be pointed out that despite the variety, many tutors nevertheless devote a substantial amount of time to remedial study or doing homework.

Tutor guidance

Tutors are required to confer individually once a month with the PERACH coordinator who is responsible for them, in order to discuss and plan specific tutoring activities. They must meet with the tutee's teacher at least three times a year on an individual basis and twice a year in collective gatherings of teachers and tutors. In addition, ideas are exchanged and guidance is provided to tutors in the form of thematic monthly meetings in which they meet in groups of 30–50 with their coordinator. Written materials are also provided periodically to the tutors; these include educational games, puzzles and other activities which could be applied in tutorial sessions.

Tutors are also encouraged to consult the child's teacher, school counsellor, school psychologist or any number of professionals affiliated with the project, whenever they need additonal assistance. A recent survey of 1125 tutors indicated that 70% indeed seek out guidance, usually turning either to the PERACH coordinator who is responsible for them or to the child's teacher. (Although the coordinators are themselves paraprofessionals, they receive regular guidance throughout the school year from the PERACH professional staff.) According to the surveyed tutors, guidance is needed in order to help them deal with the emotional problems of the tutee (31%); the tutee's learning problems (23%); the tutor-tutee relationship (25%); or the tutee's social problems (21%).

Selection of tutees
Although tutoring takes place outside school, PERACH operates through the public school system. Schools selected have high proportions of disadvantaged pupils, are interested in participation, and are located in areas easily accessible to the student-tutors. In the project's early years, schools tended to be those which were situated near the universities. Since many students commute in order to study, participating schools have come to include also those schools located in areas in which a sizeable number of tutors reside. In this manner, PERACH has been able to reach children in regions all over the country.

Children are recommended as candidates for tutoring either by their teachers or by school counsellors. About 65% of the tutees are pupils in Grades 4–7, although tutored children are found in Grade 1 as well as in Grade 12. Approximately 75% are of North African or Asian-Jewish origin, 15% are Arab and 10% are of European or American-Jewish background. More than two-thirds of the children have three or more siblings, signifying that they come from relatively large families.

Selection of tutors
Participation is open to virtually any university and teacher college student, although potential tutors are interviewed at the start of the year and unsuitable types are rejected or discouraged from joining. Tutors tend to be evenly split by gender and by year-of-study, and to distribute themselves among the various major areas of study. Compared to the ethnic distribution of Israeli university students in general, PERACH has a large over-representation of Jewish tutors from North African or Asian origins and tutors from the Arab sector.

Tutor-tutee matching
Since tutoring takes place outside school, proximity of residence is one of the main considerations in the pairing of tutor and tutee. Insofar as the tutor is expected to serve as a positive role-model for the child, an effort is made to match on traits which would facilitate identification. Accordingly, children from religious homes are matched with religious tutors, Arab school children are matched with Arab tutors, and pairs tend to be formed by gender. Ethnic background is not taken into account in the matching of Jewish pairs since, as stated above, most children are from the North African and Asian group.

Administrative structure
Administration of the PERACH project is hierarchical. A public board composed of government, university and student representatives directs

project activities, and a Central Office supervises the work of local project managers at each of the universities. Each local manager, who may be aided by up to three assistant managers, is responsible for anywhere from 15 to 50 coordinators. These coordinators who are past PERACH tutors, each supervise the activities of 30–50 tutors active in one or two schools.

The Central Office is responsible for the main financial and administrative functioning of the project, which includes coordination and supervision of activities on the national level, regular contact with government bodies and other public offices, solicitation and distribution of funds, training of workers, preparation of guidance materials for tutors and coordinators, book-keeping and record-keeping.

Day-to-day operation is carried out at the universities by the local staff. Local managers are concerned with the overall functioning at their centres, including the selection of schools, publicity on campus, recruitment and supervision of coordinators and contact with university, municipal and school officials. They meet semi-monthly with the other managers and the Central Office directors to plan and coordinate activity on the national level.

Coordinators are responsible for operation within the specific schools. Their duties include maintaining contact with the schools throughout the year, matching tutors with children, supervising 30 to 50 tutor-tutee pairs, and meeting monthly with their tutors in private and as a group. The smooth functioning of the project essentially rests on their shoulders since they are the individuals who have contact with the teachers, tutors, tutees, and the children's parents, as well as with the local management.

PERACH is essentially a student-run project. Almost all the assistant managers and coordinators as well as the tutors are students. Moreover, at each university, the project is affiliated with the Dean of Students and the local student union which provides office space and facilities.

The basic administrative structure has remained virtually unchanged over the years, despite extensive growth and expansion of the project. The gradual increase in the number of tutors, tutees and schools involved annually has required a proportional increase in PERACH workers for continued efficient operation. Accordingly, more coordinators are employed, and assistant local managers have been added.

Perhaps the most significant change which has occurred concerns the role of local manager. Originally, managers were also students, which meant that there was a high yearly turnover of all PERACH workers. With the growth of the project, it became more and more imperative to maintain at least one stable figure at each university who was experienced in the operation of the project. Therefore, managers today are not students seeking temporary employment but individuals with management experience who are hired on a more permanent basis.

Budget and Funds

About 83% of the PERACH budget goes towards the tuition rebates, and about 8% towards salaries of coordinators. The remainder covers tutors' travel expenses, the salaries of managers and secretarial staff, and other daily operating costs.

During the early years of PERACH, the Ministry of Education and the Bernard van Leer Foundation of The Hague contributed considerably both to the day-to-day operating expenses and to the funding of tuition rebates. Other public and private agencies also donated student scholarships. Today, financial support is provided largely by the universities, the Council of Higher Education and the Ministry of Education. In essence these bodies have channeled many existing scholarship funds into PERACH and have thus made the granting of much scholarship money contingent upon social service.

Evaluation

From 1978 to 1983, formal project evaluation was supported by the Bernard van Leer Foundation. During this period, studies tended to concentrate on the effect of tutoring on the tutees.

In the first study, the academic progress of a sample of tutored children was compared to that of a sample of non-tutored children in mathematics, reading (Hebrew), and English (Eisenberg, Fresko and Carmeli, 1980, 1981). The tutored children were not found to be at an advantage on standardised tests, although parents, teachers and tutors all rated the project very highly, reporting that most of the tutored children were demonstrating progress in school, participating more in class, doing homework more regularly, and exhibiting more positive attitudes towards school.

In the same study, questionnaires for measuring affective changes were also administered to both samples using a pre-test post-test design (Eisenberg et al, 1980, 1982b). Results showed PERACH children to possess more positive attitutes toward school, to report more often on participation in class, and to be doing more leisure-time reading. Tutored children did not differ from non-tutored children on measures of self-concept and aspirations.

A follow-up study of these same samples was conducted two years later (Eisenberg et al, 1982a; 1983b). This study revealed that children from the tutored-group had dropped out of conventional school settings less often than those from the non-tutored group. They also possessed higher aspirations and reported doing homework more regularly. The two groups did not differ, however, with respect to self-concept, satisfaction in school, type and level of curriculum, and eligibility to take matriculation examinations.

In a later study, mathematics and reading skills were measured over a two-year period for children tutored two years, one year, and not at all (Eisenberg et al, 1983a; Fresko and Eisenberg, 1985). Findings indicated that one year of tutoring yielded cognitive gains, particularly in mathematics; however, a second year of tutoring did nothing to augment them. Less emphasis on achievement-goals during the second year appeared to account for these results.

In general, evaluation of project outcomes for tutees has proven quite difficult. While testimonial evidence abounds acclaiming the worth of the project (for example, in the survey mentioned earlier, only 4% of the tutors expressed dissatisfaction), studies have shown it to have only a small impact in both cognitive and affective domains. The main impediment to clear-cut evaluation lies in the fact that project goals are neither specific nor sharply defined. Hence, as mentioned before, tutoring activity varies considerably from one tutor-tutee pair to another. Such a situation implies that the impact of tutoring is likely to differ in content and intensity from pair to pair. Evaluation efforts cannot possibly take into account all these tutoring variations.

Since 1983, no formal evaluation has been conducted due to lack of funds. However, two sources of data have supplied some evaluative information:

1   The Central Office has occasionally distributed questionnaires in order to obtain feedback from tutors and coordinators (for example, the survey mentioned earlier);

2   Graduate students at the various universities have been encouraged to do theses or other papers on tutoring using PERACH as their focus.

Information derived from these sources has tended to be mainly descriptive, emphasising tutor-responses to the tutoring experience. In one correlational study, results of a questionnaire administered to a large sample of tutors revealed that those who acknowledged joining only for the tuition rebate reported less change in their tutees and were more critical of the project than those whose motivation included an intrinsic interest in tutoring (Fresko, 1988). In another study, tutor satisfaction was examined and found to be higher among tutors who felt that their tutee had changed, who had established a cooperative working-relationship with the tutee, who were from the same ethnic group as the tutee, and who were preparing to enter a helping profession (Fresko and Chen, 1989).

To conclude, it should be noted that evaluation has proved particularly illuminating with respect to formative issues. Research results have been influential in decisions regarding operation and tutor guidance.

Concluding remarks

We have tried to present the essence of the PERACH tutorial project and its development from a small-scale educational initiative to a large and established intervention programme. It should be clear by now that PERACH is more than simply a tutoring project. It attempts to attack the problem of the underachieving child in a comprehensive manner by trying to provide the type of specific help need by each tutee. In this sense, a PERACH tutor is actually a mentor.

Despite its 'age' and experience, PERACH does not claim to have all the answers. Changes have been made and will be made in the future. In any case, it seems as if this project will continue to be a dynamic presence on university campuses and in disadvantaged schools all over Israel for some time to come.

Correspondence
Barbara Fresko, Department of Science Teaching, The Weizmann Institute of Science, Rehovot, Israel 76100

5 Cambridge STIMULUS

L A Beardon

This chapter describes the setting up of a voluntary service scheme for Cambridge University students to assist school teachers in their classrooms helping children learn. In the first two years of the scheme, 91 volunteers from 23 Cambridge colleges have worked in 16 local schools, both primary and secondary, in Mathematics, Science, CDT and Computing and other lessons. The paper reports and analyses the responses to questionnaires completed by teachers, children and volunteers and considers ways of maximising the benefits for all concerned. The scheme operates in one university city but the same sort of pattern of operation could apply elsewhere.

The chapter analyses some of the ways in which volunteers work as classroom assistants: not just helping children when they find difficulties with their work but encouraging them to discuss their ideas and so develop oral skills and also assisting with practical work in and out of the classroom. Having extra adults around enables teachers to plan activities which would otherwise be difficult to manage. Increasingly, pupils are becoming aware of assessment criteria; they appreciate individual help in gaining the necessary skills and understanding. This applies across the ability-range from those with recognised learning difficulties to the high fliers. Where volunteers have particular expertise to offer, this can be used to enrich the children's experience. The paper also discusses the educational experience for the volunteers themselves; the volunteers as role-models; the effects on recruitment to the teaching profession; the organisation of orientation sessions for the volunteers; the importance of planning and of aims agreed between teacher and volunteer; and the sensitivity needed in the implementation of a scheme of classroom assistance.

Introduction

STIMULUS is an acronym for Science, Technology, Informatics and Mathematics Undergraduate Links between University and School. It is a community study service programme organised by the University of Cambridge Department of Education, in which university students volunteer to assist teachers in local schools. It is similar to 'The Pimlico Connection' which has been running at Imperial College, London for 14 years (Goodlad, 1985, Goodlad and Hirst, 1989, Chapter 5). The students help children with their school work in Mathematics, Science, Computing, Information Technology or Craft, Design and Technology. The students are themselves studying Mathematics, Natural Sciences, Engineering, Computer Science or Economics; they are not on Education courses or Initial Teacher Training courses, nor is there any academic credit associated with this experience. This work constitutes study service, which is defined by UNESCO to be 'work in which students combine study leading to the award of an academic qualification with some form of direct practical service to the community, not competing with paid professionals but doing work which would not otherwsie have been done' (Goodlad, 1982).

In order to evaluate the scheme, and to enable it to be tailored as far as possible to the perceived needs of all the participants, questionnaries are completed termly by the volunteers, school children and teachers involved. This article outlines the aims and operation of STIMULUS, and analyses the results of the questionnaires; in addition, it discusses the effects on the community and the implications for the learning and personal development of the volunteers and of the children.

When classroom volunteers are an available resource, the issue arises of how to make the best use of them. Indeed, realising the benefits, it is a resource that might be tapped in more localities if teachers sought it. Optimising the potential advantages of such help in the classrooms generates ideas which can transfer to other types of voluntary help (eg from a sixth-former, a parent, or a recently-retired engineer). Reflection on the STIMULUS experience and analysis of the questionnaires has raised some important issues about classroom management and making the best use of classroom volunteers. Some of the ideas about ways in which teachers can organise their classroom to the best advantage when they have helpers apply to other sorts of help in the classroom, from support teachers and welfare assistants as well as from voluntary untrained helpers.

As a response to the University Grants Committee (UGC) invitation in December 1986 for proposals for initiatives to improve the supply of teachers in shortage subjects, and with funding from the Manpower Services Commission, Kenneth Ruthven of the Cambridge University Department of Education carried out a feasibility study (Ruthven 1987) and set up the pilot scheme. A coordinator was appointed and the programme was piloted in the 1987/88 academic year as one of the new initiatives funded by the UGC.

The aims and benefits of the scheme are however, much more far-reaching than simply improving the supply of teachers. One of the STIMULUS aims is 'to give students first-hand experience of the classroom which may encourage them to consider a teaching career'. To date, there have been 91 volunteers (34 in the pilot year), from 23 Cambridge colleges, working in 16 local schools. According to the University Careers Service, a total of 90 out of the 3331 graduates in the shortages subjects entered teaching in the five years 1983–1987, that is 2.7%, as compared to 8% for the graduate population of the university as a whole. Of the 34 volunteers in the STIMULUS pilot study, 27 had previously considered teaching as a career: afterwards, 8 said they were keener to teach, and 17 felt just as keen to teach as before. One student who had not previously considered a teaching career said she was 'greatly encouraged towards teaching' and two said that they were 'somewhat' encouraged. Many students said that they now realised that teaching was a much more challenging job than they had ever thought it to be and they felt more attracted to it on that account. One student wrote 'it made me realise that teaching isn't so much about what you know but how you communicate it'.

What is a volunteer?

Certainly teachers, children and welfare assistants are not volunteers; for one reason or another they *have* to be in the classroom. The mere fact that people are prepared to give their time freely is often a boost to the morale of teachers and pupils. Many primary schools use parents and other helpers to listen to children read, help with music, crafts and with physical education, and in a variety of other ways, and local experts are sometimes invited in to talk to children about their special interest. In secondary schools (apart from assemblies), there is much less experience of using voluntary help and the one-adult-one-class situation is the norm.

It is important that volunteers are introduced to pupils and that there is no ambiguity about their role in the classroom. Where this is not done, both pupils and volunteers may feel uneasy and the children are inhibited from asking for help. As studies in Room Management (RM) with handicapped pupils and in integrating children with special needs into mainstream classes have shown (Thomas 1985, 1986), the benefits of voluntary help in the classroom are increased when the roles of the adults are made explicit. In a RM scheme, the 'Individual Helper' concentrates on working with individuals for 5 to 15 minutes each. Having organised tasks for all the children, the 'Activity Manager' concentrates on the rest of the children in the class, paying particular attention to praising and encouraging those who are 'busy' and giving minimum attention to those who are not 'on task'. The 'Mover' facilitates activites by organising materials and dealing with any interruptions to routine.

The volunteer works under the direction of the teacher to carry out a programme prescribed by the teacher and, as such, should be a valuable resource for the teacher. It is crucial that the teacher has a clear plan based on knowledge of the school pupils and their requirements and on a realistic assessment of the volunteer's capabilities. The plan needs to be discussed and negotiated so that there are agreed aims and a clear understanding about it, but the teacher may wish to do this in stages so that there can be flexibility and so that later stages can be planned according to the outcome of earlier ones. The teacher needs to be able to count on attendance and to be able to terminate the arrangement if necessary. Defining roles and informing the helpers about the aims, tasks and procedures for the lesson is the teacher's responsibility, but with good management (s)he does not have to be three people at once, giving the required attention to an individual, managing the engagement of the whole class and ensuring that flow is maintained.

The operation of the STIMULUS scheme

Students and Directors of Studies receive information about STIMULUS at the end of term; applications are made for the following term so that volunteers can visit schools from the first week of the university term. Students can choose the time of the week for visits; they can select upper-secondary, lower-secondary, junior or infant classes, and offer one or more school subjects. The coordinator contacts all the local schools (ie those within 5 miles from the centre of Cambridge) and matches the requests from the schools with the subjects offered and preferences expressed by the volunteers. Half-day orientation sessions are held in the Department of Education before lectures start at the beginning of term, and during the school half-term. Students make at least seven visits to their schools, and some continue for a second term. They usually work, in pairs, with the same class(es) at the same time each week.

Training of volunteers

The orientation sessions are intended to prepare the volunteers for the range of classroom scenes they will take part in. Most volunteers are aware that, even in the few years since they left school, there have been considerable changes in teaching, and their own experience will have been far from typical. These sessions are informal and responsive to the ideas, experience and perceptions of the volunteers and to the questions they raise. They have the opportunity to examine some of the resources (texts, worksheets and equipment) being used in the schools.

Students who have been STIMULUS volunteers in previous terms recount and discuss their involvement. Some of the pupils' questionnaires from previous terms are used to show the range of their attitudes and opinions of the scheme, and also, incidentally, their abilities to write and to express themselves.

A video has been made showing STIMULUS volunteers working in a variety of classroom situations. This is used to give volunteers some idea of what to expect and to promote discussion about the ways of being most effective in helping children learn. Videos of classrooms showing experienced teachers working with small groups of slow learners, and with children doing investigations, are shown and discussed.

The volunteers are given a list of typical situations which they might encounter in the classroom: working in small groups, they talk about the best ways of coping with the given situations. Then the whole group, with the coordinator, share their ideas. The coordinator is able to give them encouragement and boost their confidence by leading the discussion in such a way that the volunteers' own ideas are used to bring out the important points of which they should all be aware. Above all, volunteers are encouraged to draw out the *children's* ideas and find out how much the children understand by asking them questions. If a child does not know how to proceed, the volunteer encourages the child by asking simple questions they *can* succeed in answering, until they can see for themselves what to do next. Discussion covers the difference between open and closed questions and the ineffectiveness of simply showing children how to get answers without understanding the method.

Another important issue raised, using examples of children's work, is the variety of methods appropriate for particular tasks, together with the importance of recognising children's own methods and discriminating between those that are valid and those that need to be modified. Sensitivity as to when and when not to intervene in children's work is an important issue for discussion in orientation sessions and between volunteer and class teacher.

One of the school teachers and the coordinator usually run the mid-term training session together. At half-term there is opportunity for feedback; students share their experiences, discuss how far their expectations of the scheme are being met, and plan to solve any problems that may have arisen.

Visual aids and practical equipment are discussed in connection with particular topics that the volunteers have seen being taught in their schools. The students do some communication exercises, for example one in which they sit back to back, one student describing a diagram and the other drawing it from the description.

Support and assistance with the preparation of appropriate classroom activities is available from the coordinator at any time during the term and some volunteers themselves plan and carry out short teaching projects with small groups of pupils. For these volunteers a list of 'tutoring techniques' similar to the one supplied to tutors in the 'Pimlico Connection' is useful (Goodlad and Hirst 1989: Appendix A).

The volunteers' views

So far, 63 volunteers (27 pilot year) have worked in secondary schools, 28 volunteers in primary (seven pilot year), 51 in Mathematics, 28 in Science, five in Technology, three in Computing and four in general primary subjects.

One of the aims of STIMULUS is 'to give students the opportunity to develop their social, organisational, problem-solving and communication skills in a practical context'. According to many of their comments they enjoyed 'seeing the working of a school from inside'; 'gaining insight into teaching maths at school'; 'meeting teachers, discussing education and helping kids'; 'being able to communicate your knowledge to someone who finds it difficult to grasp and eventually gets there'; and 'having the chance one afternoon each week of doing something completely different'. 33 questionnaires were returned; the volunteers' opinions of the benefits they derived were as shown in Table 5.1.

Volunteers certainly did not want to be observers; rather, they valued 'the opportunity to get to know the children' and appreciated 'feeling needed'. It came as a surprise to some. The enjoyment and satisfaction obtained from working with slower learners and young children came as a surprise to some of the volunteers. Typical comments were:

'What I like best was getting to know a remedial set of 4th year, a nice experience'.

'It was very satisfying seeing people understand something for the first time especially the low-ability pupils who tended to think they were no good'.

'I found teaching the younger childern much more pleasurable than expected, nice to catch them while they're still enthusiastic'.

Students do not undertake this commitment without consulting their Director of Studies. It is most usual for the volunteers to be in their second year when the effects on their own studies should be minimal. Where STIMULUS did interfere with students' studies, the problems usually arose in meeting deadlines for handing in work; the students said themselves that this would not have occured had they been better organised.

Typical reflections on the experience included: 'learning communication skills is probably the hardest and most profitable thing to do and this would

Table 5.1   Opinions of STIMULUS students about the benefits of
being a helper

Volunteers considered that	(percentages n = 33)			
STIMULUS had benefited them:	greatly	somewhat	not at all	not sure
• by reinforcing knowledge of some aspect of their subject;	0	19	69	12
• by giving practice in communicating;	58	42	0	0
• by giving insight into how others perceive their subject;	38	41	16	6
• by increasing their self-confidence;	13	66	13	9
• by meeting people from a different social background;	13	32	48	6
• by giving feeling that they were doing something useful;	44	41	9	6
• by aiding decision about a career.	42	35	8	15
• Other effects: interference with studies.	6	34	54	3

have been easier to develop in small groups over a slightly extended period',
and 'more time would be better'. Indeed, some volunteers did make extra
visits to their schools and some continued for a second term.

The teachers' views

In the pilot study there were 12 teacher-responses to the questionnaires (see
Table 5.2) and many discussions with teachers about the scheme. Although
full written details had been sent to schools, and there had been discussion
with all the Heads of Department (or Headteachers in the case of the
primary schools) it was clear that some of the classroom teachers knew little

Table 5.2 Opinions of teachers about the STIMULUS scheme

Teacher responses to questionnaires. With STIMULUS volunteers lessons were: n = 12			
easier to handle	17%	harder 17%	the same 66%
more enjoyable	33%	less 0%	the same 67%
pupils learned more than usual	42%	less 8%	the same 50%

about STIMULUS and in future would be able to plan to make more effective use of the voluntary help. 'The rules of the new game' were not very clear to them, especially at the start – but with time, and with more information supplied directly to assistant teachers, this problem should be overcome.

From discussion, it was clear that not all teachers interpreted the questions in the same way. One teacher answered the question about the lessons being easier to handle by saying that more advance-planning was involved 'in terms of needing to organise the work on an individual basis in order to make as much use as possible of the volunteers' but she also said that 'they were of great help to me with a set of lower-ability pupils who need as much help and attention as possible'. The advantage of the children getting more individual attention, and hence relieving some of the pressure on the teacher, was recognised by all the teachers involved. A teacher from another school wrote 'it enabled the least, and most-able, students to have more time spent with them and, I think, particularly helped the brighter ones'.

In relation to enjoyment, teachers mentioned liking 'contact with university-level students', 'having an extra pair of hands in the classroom', and 'the chance to talk to someone involved with recent maths developments'. It was quite clear that these teachers appreciated the contact and help from the volunteers, and that this can only have a beneficial effect on morale, particularly as the volunteers obviously had an increased respect for teachers and a better understanding of the job teachers have to do.

The 42% of the the teachers who thought that the children learnt more interpreted the question to be about the total effect for all the children in the class. One primary teacher expressed concern that the volunteers were too eager to prompt the children to give correct answers and that these children would have learned more had she been teaching them herself, but naturally inexperienced and untrained volunteers will rarely be as effective as the professional, although the novelty-value of their presence, the extra individual interest taken in pupils and increased time spent with them should be of benefit to their learning.

Another teacher disliked the use of the term tutor, with its implications of directing and controlling learning and having charge of a person's education. In Cambridge, where the term is used for college tutors, it seems inappropriate and it is being dropped altogether from use in connection with STIMULUS.

The pupils' views

Table 5.3 gives pupil responses to the questionnaires. Typically the children liked 'having someone else to help so that there was someone else to turn to if the teacher was busy', and that 'the teacher was able to come around and help us individually as there were other adults in the room', having 'more one-to-one tuition', and 'if you needed help you didn't have to wait for 15 minutes in a queue'. Children also wrote that 'more work got taught', 'it gave me insight into different ways of approaching problems', and 'he explained everything very clearly and made us feel comfy'.

It is crucial that the volunteers are introduced to the children by their usual class teacher and that their presence in the classroom is explained so that their role is well defined. Some children thought that the volunteers seemed nervous or anxious: certainly it came across strongly when talking to volunteers that the experience had increased their self-confidence, but that ambiguity over their role in the classroom is likely to contribute to their unease and may also prevent children from seeking their assistance. In some cases, the children were puzzled as to what they were doing there, but in future this can be avoided. The children liked the volunteers to wear their name badges so that they could remember who they were and many children mentioned that they liked the volunteers 'to be friendly like asking us our names'.

Some volunteers had actually taught the whole class from the front and the responses from the pupils were very positive: 'it gave us the opportunity to experience different teaching methods with someone nearer our own

Table 5.3   Opinions of the pupils about the STIMULUS scheme

Pupil responses to questionnaires (n = 367). With STIMULUS volunteers lessons were:			
more interesting	30%	less 16%	the same 54%
easier to follow	38%	harder 12%	the same 50%
more enjoyable	29%	less 19%	the same 52%
I learned more than usual	24%	less 16%	the same 60%

age'; 'it made a change, I concentrated more because of an unfamiliar face'; 'they explained things quite simply, it was easy to understand and they made a gallant effort'.

Some of the comments from top sets reflected an attitude of reluctance to make use of the help offered: 'if I had needed them I am sure they would have made a lot of difference', and 'they would really have been better helping a lower set who needed their help as most people in our set could already do the work without help'. It was a common experience of volunteers in different schools that children working on individualised work schemes (usually SMP 11–16) were mainly interested in getting through the booklet and getting answers and did not often show much interest in really understanding or talking about what they were doing. This highlights the necessity for good judgement about how and when to intervene. One pupil wrote 'their help would have been better if they weren't so eager to explain things', and 'they told you things you did not really want to know'; but opinions differed: 'it would have been better if they told me a bit more and not what the answers were'.

One of the most valuable features of STIMULUS could be that children have more opportunities to discuss their work because the tutors have more time than the teacher to give them all their attention and to listen to them individually. For the children to get the maximum benefit, teachers need to help children to see the value of this to themselves, because children do not always realise the importance of oral work. Sensitivity is needed on the part of the volunteers because children may dislike interruption: 'they asked me questions about the work and I already knew the answers' and 'sometimes they would come and interrupt you and talk to you while you were getting on fine'.

Some children made very useful comments about the sort of help they liked: 'their help would have been better if they had explained everything not only verbally but also on paper', and 'if they came to the point straight away, and if they had objects to help you learn like abacuses boxes and cubes'.

Maximising the mutual benefits

It has been clear from the responses to questionnaires, and from de-briefing sessions, that although the volunteers were involved in many different classroom situations, all parties have seen benefits to themselves from the scheme. In some cases, volunteers simply circulated around the classroom helping pupils as they saw opportunities to do so. In other cases, the teacher structured the situation so that the volunteers were used according to some pre-arranged plan, for example to work with a small group of children for a whole session on an experiment or assignment.

One teacher reported that she had used volunteers to work with pupils following the SMP graduated-assessment scheme (criterion-referenced assessment). The volunteers were able to give the children extra practice, on an individual basis, in the particular areas which they found difficult, together with help interpreting longer questions in written tests, and developing oral, practical and mental skills. Another suggestion was 'that volunteers are put in classes where project-work, investigations and group-work are taking place' seeing these as situations in which the helpers can give more than where pupils are working on individual written tasks.

Discussion and oral skills

Children need practice in expressing their ideas clearly. A volunteer can give undivided attention to individual children, listening carefully to what they say and helping them to put into words what they want to say. It can be daunting for some children to speak out in front of a whole class but their confidence can be built up, their vocabulary extended, and their powers of communication developed, with this sort of individual help. A student volunteer with a secondary class working on an individualised workscheme described the part she had played 'mainly wandering around the class asking each child what they were doing and getting them to 'talk through' the questions they were on at the time and showing them new methods where appropriate'.

Discussion in groups gives more children a role and more opportunity to contribute their own ideas than a whole-class discussion but a teacher's time has to be divided between different groups. A perceptive volunteer can sit with a group mainly listening to their talk but occasionally supplying a word or explanation and helping the children develop oral skills as they work on a problem together. Another student-volunteer wrote about his experience with an infant class 'the children became much more autonomous when given more practical and attractive tasks and it is important to let them talk and establish 'rules' amongst themselves'.

'Catching up'

In the light of Warnock and the 1981 Education Act, recognising that 20% of children experience difficulty at some stage of their learning, and with research indications that *the amount of individual help* and *the time that the child is able to remain 'on task'* are most significant in overcoming these difficulties, it follows that, as Thomas (1986) suggests, 'it is improvements in organisational strategies rather than refinements in instructional method which will have the greatest payoff for children with special needs'.

It is interesting to note that in Japan differentiation is deliberately avoided. Students have the same curriculum, and hard work is the recommended way of overcoming all difficulties (Monk, 1988). In our culture we may wish to concentrate on individual needs, entitlement, flexibility and support for pupils with learning difficulties and to move away from selection and consequent 'labelling' of children, while at the same time taking care not to impose excessive pressures on them. Mixed-ability teaching makes great demands on the teacher if the pupils are to be given appropriate help and not to be left to struggle alone. The contribution that volunteers make gives that extra flexibility to the teacher, and the opportunity of more individual support for pupils; it is particularly valuable in mixed-ability classes.

All teachers will have met the 'I never could do .....' syndrome. Whether they use the volunteer to help other pupils while they themselves do the remedial teaching, or vice versa, having the presence of volunteers makes it possible to give the one-to-one attention, and the patient, and very often time-consuming, help necessary to rebuild the pupil's confidence and help them overcome their difficulty.

Graded assessment schemes and testing for the National Curriculum will present well-defined hurdles for pupils to clear. Volunteers can assist pupils in developing specific skills in order to succeed in clearing these hurdles. One of the reasons for failure at all levels is difficulty in reading and interpreting written instructions; volunteers can encourage pupils to read the instructions phrase-by-phrase, prompting them to ask themselves questions like 'What do these few words tell us?', 'What do we have to find out?', 'Have I seen a problem like this before?', 'Have I met this word anywhere else before'? These heuristics and others such as those described by Polya in *How to solve it* (1945) can be brought into play and pupils helped to overcome reading-comprehension difficulties by tackling the reading phrase-by-phrase instead of expecting to understand the piece of text all at once.

Developing understanding

One pitfall for inexperienced teachers is described by a primary teacher involved in this scheme:

'the volunteers showed a marked lack of insight into the teaching process and were too interested in getting right answers, which they supplied if the children weren't very forthcoming. The students seemed to believe that if the children could repeat what they had been told then they understood it.'

This comment formed the basis of a very useful discussion at the half-term orientation session and some extra insights were developed. However, the other side of this coin is that children, particularly those engaged in individualised work-schemes, very often set their own goals in terms of finishing as many cards, pages or booklets as they can and are more interested in answers than in understanding. Provided that the teacher helps the pupils to adjust this perspective they can make good use of volunteers to discuss their work with them. It is very often the most able child who sees success in terms of quantity of work but who could most benefit from the opportunity to discuss the work with the volunteer and to take on a more challenging aspect of it.

Practical work

Practical work and assessment can be easier for teachers to organise with volunteers in the classroom, particularly when the pupils are low-attainers. Having extra adults around enables teachers to plan practical activities both in and out of the classroom which would be difficult to manage otherwise.

Organising practical assessment in Mathematics with limited equipment and without any laboratory assistants has been a problem in many schools; in some cases it has been tackled by using a circus of activities. Good use can be made of volunteers to check equipment and to check pupils' results in their progress around such a circus.

Environmental mathematics and science

The rich possibilities for work outside the classroom are often not fully exploited. Having other adults to help, particularly when the adults have special expertise to offer, can greatly facilitate this.

Role models

One of the STIMULUS aims is to provide pupils (particularly girls) with positive role-models of young mathematicians, scientists and technologists; to date there have been 33 women volunteers and 58 men, and 8% of them have been from ethnic-minority groups. From the pupils' comments there were indications of the 'role-model effect': 'she is very approachable and clarifies most maths problems quickly, it was an ideal time for extra teachers because our exams are coming up' and 'I liked having a chance to talk about what he was doing and just talking to him about future maths I might be doing'. This is perhaps an intangible benefit, but talk about university studies or 'off-syllabus work' is likely to help motivate and broaden the education of pupils. Just as visiting local industry and talking to female engineering apprentices can influence 14-year-old girls to opt for 'male' subjects (Royal Society 1986), getting to know the STIMULUS volunteers can help to counteract negative stereotyping. It may influence pupils to decide to go on studying beyond 16 and to choose Mathematics or Science. Other pupils commented that their volunteers had a good sense of humour, and very good rapport existed between pupils and volunteers – yet these same volunteers were also described, to their surprise and amusement, as 'yuppies' by some of the pupils.

Surprisingly in this small city where university buildings dominate the city centre, our volunteers found that some pupils knew nothing about the university. They did not know what those buildings were, nor did they realise that so many young people choose to go on studying until they are in their twenties.

Education for the volunteer

Most of this article has concentrated on maximising benefit to pupils and teachers. To do so one also needs to take account of the reasons people have for volunteering to help children learn and whether the expectations of the volunteers are met. It is equally important to maximise the benefits to the volunteers.

The majority of volunteers had at some time considered teaching as a career, and certainly the STIMULUS experience raised their awareness of what the job involves. For the minority for whom the experience revealed that teaching was not the career for them it was helpful to have found that out; they were no less positive than the other volunteers about extended pieces of coursework, problem-solving, investigations and group-work and other teaching methods they had seen but had not themselves benefited from in their own schooling. Many students remarked that thinking more about ways of facilitating learning had in some way helped them in their own studies. A group of volunteers told their University Mathematics lecturer that now they understood his problem in helping them to understand things they were finding difficult. Referring to the experience of assisting a child with decimals who was struggling because of lack of understanding of place value, one student said that it had helped her to get her own difficulties with her studies into perspective and to fight feelings that barriers are inpenetrable with the knowledge that usually such barriers can be overcome.

The scheme is intended to give students the opportunity to develop their social, organisational, problem-solving and communication skills in a practical context. They all thought that it had given them practice in communicating ideas of their subject, 79% said it had given them insight into how other people perceive their subject, 79% thought it had helped to increase their self-confidence, 85% said that they had enjoyed the feeling that they were doing something useful outside the university and 77% said that it helped them in making a decision about their career.

With so few hours in the classroom, one cannot be very ambitious about student-led projects but when volunteers want to introduce an appropriate experiment or investigation it can be very worthwhile. Student volunteers have reported that through working with children, particularly on a project they have introduced themselves, they have learnt a lot about the scientific method and about learning processes. They have realised that they had been taking a lot for granted and underestimating the amount of learning experience and training required. It is essential to avoid volunteers feeling that they are merely passive observers but there are many alternative ways of involving them fully which do not depend on the volunteers suggesting their own projects.

Conclusion

As teachers become more used to having this new resource they should be able to make even better use of it: enabling pupils to have more individual help; maintaining activity flow in the classroom; keeping pupils 'on task' for a higher proportion of time; and giving themselves more time to be aware of how children are performing. Even teachers with 'eyes in the back of their heads' who have 'Withitness' and who manage 'Overlapping' brilliantly (Kounin 1970) can share responding to pupils with their helpers hence they can be even more effective than if they had to simultaneously confront and deal with several issues all the time. This requires the combination of a clear understanding of the role of the helper, spelt out before the lesson, and the willingness of the volunteer to respond to cues from the teacher during the lesson.

As with other resources, teachers need to plan how to manage the learning experiences in their classes to make good use of the resource for the benefit of all the participants; it does not 'just happen'. As one teacher in our scheme wrote: 'I found the experience all very worthwhile but it would be better if we could have more time together before a lesson'. According to a volunteer: 'I could have gone over selected topics with a group of pupils who found that section difficult'. This sort of help would be likely to be more effective if the volunteers were given some advance warning and a chance familiarise themselves with the appproach used and to prepare for it. With the goodwill that exists on the part of volunteers, such planning can be well worth the effort.

The effects of the scheme on the participants and on the community need to be monitored, but there is no doubt that the majority of the participants have derived benefits from it. For the university students it has provided an opportunity to develop interpersonal skills in a different environment from that of the university. For teachers and pupils it has provided valuable support, giving many youngsters more individual help and attention than the teacher is able to give alone. There is need for further research on the interactions between all the participants, and for evaluation and development of the support systems and other aspects of the project in order to maximise these benefits.

Correspondence:

Mrs L A Beardon Mathematics Initiatives Coordinator,Cambridge University Department of Education,17 Trumpington St., Cambridge CB2 1QA

6 Tutoring as field-based learning: some New Zealand developments

John Jones

Since 1986, undergraduate students from the University of Auckland have been acting as tutors in school classrooms. About 80 science students and 25 law students have been involved for periods of up to 15 weeks. Evaluations suggest that significant benefits have resulted for tutors, tutored students, and their institutions as a result of tutoring activity. These benefits can be categorised as cognitive gains within specific subjects, more general shifts in attitudes and aspirations, and general 'empowerment' of a broader constituency. It is argued that a credible framework for the tutoring process is that of field-based education, and that an ecological stance – 'helping oneself while helping others' – is applicable. During 1989, an academic credit course, 'Tutoring in Science', is being offered for the first time as a second-year paper in the Faculty of Science. After a five-week induction programme, university students spend 15 weeks tutoring in secondary schools; in a final reflection phase they write reports based on their experiences.

Introduction

In its most general form, peer tutoring is any system of instruction which capitalises upon the potential which students have to teach each other. Both the tutored and those who do the tutoring learn from the experience. Goodlad and Hirst (1989) have described a wide variety of settings in which peer-tutoring has been organised. Such settings, within formal educational institutions, have ranged from early primary to university and polytechnic classrooms. The focus of this paper is a university setting in New Zealand.

The predominant ethos within university teaching is that of the handing over of knowledge from 'expert' lecturer to 'novice' student. Lectures are still the major teaching strategy, and most staff subscribe (in large part, at least) to what Fox (1983) has called a 'transfer theory' of teaching. Within this mode, students are largely passive and are rarely required to actively construct meaning during classroom teaching. In *tutoring* activities too, it is usually the university staff member who dominates and is most intellectually active. ('Tutoring' here means small-group teaching which involves some degree of interaction between students and a staff member.) However, there are other possibilities, based around the notion of peer-tutoring, which involve students in much more active teaching/learning roles. Goldschmid and Goldschmid (1976) have described two arrangements in a review of such activities in higher education.

1 Peer-tutoring refers to any arrangement where 'competent' students act as a teaching resource for less 'competent' classmates.

2 'Parrainage' consists of senior students in an institution acting as academic and social mentors for their more junior colleagues.

Both of these arrangements capitalise upon the potential which students have to act as a provider of, as well as a drain upon, teaching resources. It is possible to view any course as a series of demands made on students (writing assignments, passing tests, etc). Students involved in a course are arguably the most under-utilised potential resource associated with that course.

Students can also act as tutors outside the confines of their own institution. One example is the Pimlico Connection (Goodlad *et. al*, 1979; Goodlad, 1985; Goodlad and Hirst, 1989, chapter 5) which, for more than a decade, has seen university science students working in neighbouring school classrooms. A similar scheme has been running at the University of Auckland since 1986. From its action-research origins, it has developed to the stage where university science students may now obtain academic credit within a BSc degree for a paper which is based upon tutoring in schools. The aim of this paper is to describe that development, introduce a related move in the Law Faculty and place these within an appropriate conceptual framework.

Tutoring and community service: a 'Field' activity

When students work outside the confines of the institution for any extended period of time, it is often in a 'field' setting: the geography 'field-trip' is possibly the most familiar example. Traditionally, field-based subjects have been associated with the natural sciences in particular – but there is no *a priori* reason why that should be the case. Longeran and Andresen (1988), in a useful consideration of field-based education, write as follows:

The notion of 'field' is used here to cover any area or zone within a subject where supervised learning can take place via first-hand experience, outside the constraints of the four-walls classroom setting ... It is unnecessarily limiting to apply the 'field' denotation *only* when it is literally a 'green field'. The broader perspective proposed here may demonstrate how both the potential and practice of field-based learning may be considerably more widespread than generally imagined.

(p64)

In the kind of field-work which is carried out in 'green field' settings, there is a keen consciousness of possible environmental impact by the learners. Ecological maintenance principles are firmly adhered to, and the country-code directive, 'leave it as you found it', is an axiom. When we move out of the non-sentient green field setting into human social field settings, then some important differences emerge. In particular, some obvious ethical considerations – analogous to those between researcher and researched in the area of social science – come into play. An arrangement in which students learn by immersing themselves in a human field setting, and give nothing to that social context, is morally dubious. In sentient fields, the ecological principle is modified to become 'leave it *better* than you found it'. Another motto might be 'helping oneself through helping others', and in this respect the philosophy has much in common with that of Community Service (Goodlad,1982). A service activity implies a direct benefit to a client community; but there is no reason why, at the same time, the providers of that service (and their home institutions) should not derive direct positive outcomes from the experience.

In the next section, schemes which involve the use of university students as tutors in school classrooms are analysed in terms of the benefits which might accrue to participants, institutions and the wider community.

Students as school tutors: who benefits?

Over the period 1986–1989, science students from the University of Auckland have been acting as tutors in local school classrooms. For the first three years, the work was funded as a research project by the government Department of Education; during 1989 the tutoring is proceeding as part of a paper for which students earn academic credit. Arrangements have been similar to those described by Goodlad *et al* (1979) in relation to the 'Pimlico Connection'. In outline, the main features of the scheme in each of the years have been as follows.

1986
22 science students tutored in four secondary schools, for a period of ten weeks, under the direction of the regular class teacher. A group of five or

six students visited the same school, once a week, for a period of about two hours. Over this period they typically acted as tutors in two classes – one Form 3, one Form 4. Each week they returned to the same classes, and generally each university tutor worked with the same small group of school students. University tutors were paid for the time they spent tutoring in school classrooms.

1987

During this year the arrangement was basically the same as in the previous year, with the difference that 15 students worked in *three* secondary schools over a period of 15 weeks.

1988

A major difference in 1988 was the extension of the tutoring scheme to incorporate Form 1 and Form 2 classes in primary/intermediate schools. 23 tutors operated in five schools (two secondary, three primary/intermediate) for a period of ten weeks.

1989

In 1989 a new subject, 'Tutoring in Science', is being offered for the first time as a cross-disciplinary paper in the Faculty of Science. After a five-week introductory programme, those enrolled spend the remainder of Terms 2 and 3 tutoring in local secondary schools. Tutoring arrangements are essentially the same as in the three previous years. During Term 3, a series of tutorials and seminars within the university will enable the tutors to reflect upon their experiences, and produce a 'research report'. Students are assessed for credit in terms of their practical performance in the classrooms, plus their end-of-project report.

In 1987 and 1988, a scheme operating out of the University of Auckland Law School also involved university students tutoring in school classrooms. The aim of the sessions was to provide school students with information about the Law, and to facilitate a degree of empowerment in an area which many perceived to be 'threatening'. University students visited the school classrooms in a group of six, together with a qualified 'community lawyer'. They were totally responsible for the hour-long sessions, which used small-group work as the process. The university students involved in the project developed a series of problem-based units which were used with the Form 4 students. These units centred around stories set in contexts which were relevant for school students, and which aimed to project them into situations with which they could empathise. Typical concerns embodied in the units were under-age drinking, hire-purchase agreements, behaviour when approached by police-officers, etc.

In 1987, 16 sessions were run in two schools over a four-week period. During 1988, 14 sessions took place in the same two schools over a similar period of time.

Most of the Law students who participated in the scheme were able to count the experience as part of their Year 3 Legal practice, through a notional 'ten-hour attachment' at the Community Law Office which was included. (The actual time involved was very much more than this.)

The initial motive for both the science and law tutoring programmes was *service*; however recent developments have seen an acceptance that the tutoring, together with other associated activities, deserves academic credit. In this respect it is valid to view the tutoring activity as 'field-based' education in the sense described in the last section. However, in what is evidently a human-field context, the stronger ecological principle of improvement of the 'field' must be embraced. 'Helping others while helping oneself' is the basic philosophy. There are a number of potential benefits which might accrue to participants in the field-based classroom programmes, and it is possible for much of that potential to be realised in practice. In the discussion which follows, evaluation data which has been described in detail elsewhere (Jones and Bates, 1987) is drawn upon.

Advantages associated with the scheme may be categorised in terms of *personal* and *institutional* advantages for *tutors* and *tutored* respectively. In the wider sense, there are also benefits which might flow on to the community at large: some of these are indicated in the analysis which follows.

The conclusions presented in the following paragraphs are drawn from data which emerged out of open-ended interviews with participants in the tutoring schemes. All university tutors were interviewed at several points during the project, including at the start of their tutoring and shortly after it was completed. Each classroom teacher was also interviewed at the completion of the project, and at least one earlier point. School students completed a short, open-ended questionnaire after the tutoring was finished, and some were interviewed during the course of the series of classroom-visits by university tutors.

Advantages for the tutors

1   It is educational folk-wisdom that the optimum strategy for learning something is teaching it – and to a very great extent that intuition is borne out by experience. Moreover, the prescription is in line with recent research which suggests that deep, *quality* learning results from the active construction of personal meaning out of a body of information. Successful tutoring demands precisely that depth of knowledge. Thus, the activity of tutoring is a means through which university students are 'forced' to take a deep approach to subject matter, construct meaning, and come to a greater understanding of it.

A majority of the tutors who have been involved in the projects report that their understanding of subject-matter improved. The reported improvement occurred in one of two ways.

a) As a result of an introduction (or sometimes a re-introduction) to a particular subject, such as biology, which had not previously been studied in anything other than a cursory fashion.

b) Through the construction of a more integrated conceptual framework, incorporating elements from what had previously been conceptualised as separate disciplines: physics, chemistry, biology, etc.

2 A significant number of the science student tutors were contemplating teaching as a career; for example, nine out of the 15 tutors who were originally involved in 1987 were in this category. The experience helped practically everyone to come to a firm decision about entering teaching. By the end of their tutoring periods, about half of those who had been considering teaching were still very enthusiastic; the other half, though they generally enjoyed the experience, were adamant that a teaching career was *not* for them! All agreed that the experience had been worthwhile in helping them to come to a decision.

3 There is a common feeling among Auckland University staff that new graduates are not sufficiently articulate within their chosen disciplines. This feeling is not confined to the Science Faculty – nor indeed to staff. A survey of Commerce graduates (Jones,1985) indicated that the graduates themselves considered that their 'communication skills', including oral proficiency related to their subjects of study, were relatively undeveloped – and yet were crucial for success in their work. Over the past few years these concerns have manifested themselves in requests to the author for 'seminar skills' workshops, for science students about to embark upon postgraduate study. Workshop sessions on seminar presentations for beginning MSc students are now a regular feature of some departments in the university. Tutoring offers another context in which students may develop their skills at communicating, through using the language of science in an appropriate manner.

The Law students saw the tutoring as an opportunity to communicate with a group who are potential clients, but with whom they rarely come into contact, ie young people from ethnic minority and lower socio-economic backgrounds. From that perspective it is a valuable part of professional preparation.

The benefits to *tutors* outlined above have led to acceptance by academic staff that 'Tutoring in Science' constitutes a valid university paper. Students experience intellectual (and probably social) development through engaging in what is essentially a field-based learning experience. In summary, the main benefits for university students are:

1 Enhanced understanding of science concepts, through teaching.

2 An opportunity to try out teaching as a career – and to learn something about the ways in which children learn science.

3 The opportunity to become more articulate within the discipline, and

to develop communication skills which are appropriate for a range of audiences.

There is another important benefit which almost all of the university students involved in the scheme reported. That is the feeling that they are doing something useful and worthwhile with their university learning. The opportunity to offer a positive contribution to the community was something which many students found very significant. It is an aspect which should not be under-estimated, in terms of students' positive attitudes to intellectual material.

At the same time that university students benefits on an 'individual' basis, there are potential (and actual) positive aspects for the university as an institution.

Advantages for the institution

1   Universities do not project a particularly positive image of themselves to the population at large. This fact is implicit in recent political moves in the UK and Australasia (at least) which have sought to exert greater control over universities, and diminish real *per capita* resources available. A recent goverment report on *Post-Compulsory Education and Training in New Zealand* (Hawke, 1988) has suggested sweeping changes in the New Zealand tertiary education sector. Underpinning many of the recommendations is an implied criticism of the universities – their management structures, their accountability and the extent to which they 'serve' their communities. From the viewpoint of a university academic much of this appears unjustified and based upon misconceptions of university practices. However, taking a rather wider perspective, it must be acknowledged that universities are not in touch with their potential constituency as well as they might be. Academic freedom has often been taken to mean complete autonomy in the determination of the curriculum, and the freedom to organise teaching and learning environments without any serious consultation with actual and potential client communities.

Tutoring schemes are one means by which universities can interact productively with the surrounding community, in ways which are consistent with an essential university ethos. At the same time it is a partnership: all participants help themselves while helping others. Perhaps universities should be looking more to the 'marketing of their images', without engaging in the intellectual and moral bankruptcy which the activity sometimes implies.

2   Over the past decade in New Zealand there have been mounting expressions of concern about the extent to which school students are 'turning off science'. This manifests itself in diminishing student

enrolments in science subjects (especially at university), and in a poorer conceptual grasp by those students who do continue with a study of the discipline (Putt *et al*, 1985).

Much of the problem may be due to a poorly-prepared, and hence over-stressed, teaching workforce (Clark and Vere-Jones,1986). The development of a comprehensive system of tutoring in schools by university science students might help to ameliorate the situation, in the following ways:

a) More well-prepared science graduates might enter teaching.

b) University students might act as positive and credible role-models for school students, and provide encouragement for them to continue in science subjects.

c) School students might become more confident about their ability to cope with science, and attain better achievement in the subject as a result of more individualised tutoring from university students.

Evaluation interviews with school students and with teachers have suggested strongly that c) and – to a rather lesser extent – b) are occurring as a result of tutoring schemes. As an example, Jones and Bates (1987) report the following perspective of a particular teacher.

> The third-form students became much more *confident* as a result of the tutors' input. They realised that they could do things for themselves and work through difficulties without necessarily going to the teacher. This increased confidence has carried through after the tutors have left.
>
> (p 103)

3   In common with an international *status quo*, universities in New Zealand are socially-elitist institutions. (Jones, 1982). Students originate predominantly from high socio-economic, professional, highly-educated backgrounds. A recent review of New Zealand universities (Watts,1987) has drawn attention to these facts, and suggested that the universities take steps to change the situation. Two particular aspects need to be addressed.

a) Participation in university education in New Zealand is low in comparison with countries which have a similar socio-cultural and industrial make-up: the participation-rate needs to be increased.

b) In particular, enrolment-rates from ethnic minority and low socio-economic groups need to increase markedly.

One of the very explicit objectives of the original tutoring schemes at Auckland was associated with the positive *general* role-models which university tutors might offer to school students. In this way, university education might become more psychologically accessible for school students from socio-cultural groups who are not traditionally university entrants. It was this focus which led to the extension of the science tutoring scheme to Forms 1 and 2 (in addition to Forms 3 and 4) during 1988. Research into school students' educational and vocational aspirations (Crothers and Jones, 1987) suggested that early adolescence is a crucial time for the formation of such attitudes. By the Form 3/Form 4 level, school students' aspirations have firmed up to a large extent, and have passed from 'fantasy' to a 'realism' which is often based on role-models within a close social ambience. It is significant too that by this stage there are distinct differences in aspirations based on social and ethnic backgrounds.

To date, the results of the scheme at the Form 1/Form 2 level in 1988 are inconclusive, so far as changing attitudes are concerned. *Some* school students certainly developed new aspirations as a result of the university student presence in their classrooms. Whether this will eventually convert into the hard currency of university enrolment is less certain.

As far as the universities are concerned then, tutoring schemes offer strategies for a potential increase in enrolments. At Auckland, further developments are under way, including reciprocal visits to the university by school students, in the company of their university tutor 'buddies'; funding has also been obtained for the production of a compendium of video and print material for teachers to use in schools as part of an overall programme which might include tutoring activities.

Advantages for the tutored students

1   *Within the specific subject* ie science, the advantages to the students are the flip-side of those which have already been described for the universities. Having more individual attention from the university student tutors in their classrooms leads to many school students becoming more confident about their ability to handle the subject. The following comments are typical of very many which school students have made.

> 'They made our work easier...they explained and gave me an example.'
> 'They are different from the teachers. They sort of relate things more clearly to us than in the scientific way our teacher does.'
> 'We could understand them better. I found out more than I did in weeks [before].'

In turn, the increased confidence leads to better academic achievement. In several cases, teachers who have been involved in the tutoring scheme have reported that, following the university students tutoring:

a)   the overall class achievement on tests improved markedly over what was 'usual';

b)   some class members began to show a potential and a competence which had not previously been evident.

2   University students are able to act as credible role-models for school students who previously had little or no contact with tertiary-educated people. There were many cases, too, of university students being able to offer careers and educational programme planning advice to school students. This aspect of the potential benefit transcends the boundaries of specific school subjects.

3   The tutoring project in which the Law students are involved has its focus beyond the specific school curriculum. It is designed to empower school students, and enhance their confidence in an important and potentially intimidating aspect of their lives: ie dealing with the Law. Feedback from the school students suggests that the tutoring *has* been useful in this respect. It is worth noting too that in the case of at least two young Pacific Islands women-students, the tutoring has had a direct effect on their careers. These students were in a sixth-form class which was visited by a university student tutor group in 1987. This university student group contained Pacific Islands women Law students, and the experience was significant enough to persuade the school students that *they* should aim for university – with the result that they are both currently enrolled.

4   It has become evident, too, that for many school students the simple experience of being *listened to*, and having an opinion considered seriously by an adult, is a confidence-booster. This is especially the case for some ethnic-minority students, for whom second-language English status and cultural norms often constitute serious constraints to their ability to make contributions in normal class discussions. The process is especially significant when the university student and the school student involved are from the same cultural background. In an evaluation of the project (Jones and Bates, 1987), examples of this are documented; for example:

> A Samoan tutor found that his ability to speak Samoan to Samoan students had helped them to understand science. Explaining a concept in Samoan intially led to a basic understanding which was subsequently able to be continued into a discussion in English. There also appeared to be a positive role-modelling effect associated with Pacific Islands tutors helping students who are from that region.
>
> (p.47)

Advantages for the school

1   University student-tutors have the potential to be a considerable additional resource for the particular school. Out of the Auckland projects three distinct, though related, aspects have been noted.

a)   University students can bring to a subject area an expertise which the regular teacher does not possess. This is particularly true of some primary/intermediate schools, where the teacher taking science classes is largely untrained in the discipline. In some cases too, the university students were able to provide equipment and materials (on a loan-out basis) for use in junior classes. (A flask of liquid nitrogen provided a 'magic' afternoon for one particular Form 1 class!)

b) In the case of the Law students' tutoring scheme, they were able to provide expertise and 'empowerment' through knowledge and experience which school teachers did not possess at all. It was especially significant that Community Law Service solicitors were also involved in the project. While this injected a credible professionalism, it also provided a link between potential client and community resource. The university tutors performed an important role as catalyst, in bringing about communication and interaction between community solicitors and their constituents. In this way the particular scheme offers the potential for *direct* social transformation within a community. This is in contrast to the science tutoring scheme which can only affect the client community indirectly, through the mediating agency of the school and the actions of its student clients within that formal educational setting (see Jones and Jones, (1987), for a more extensive discussion of this point).

c) When student tutors are present, there is the opportunity for teachers to organise learning processes which are difficult to facilitate in a single-teacher classroom. Successful 'practical' work in classrooms (whether hard science, discussion-based assignments, or whatever) demands low-key supervision and a rapid 'consultative service' for school students who require it. Having an extra four or five adults present makes it possible to achieve. (There were several cases of teachers organising real *experimental* work, as distinct from closed-end exercises, when science students were present in their classrooms.)

Conclusions

Having university students acting as tutors in school classrooms can benefit both *tutors, the tutored* and their *institutions* in a variety of ways. Some of the benefits are of a cognitive kind, concerned directly with academic competence in a particular subject area; others relate more to affective factors – attitudes toward a subject, self-confidence, educational and vocational aspirations. There is also the possibility that tutoring schemes are catalytic in bringing about closer co-operation between institutions, and between institutions and their constituent communities.

While tutoring schemes may usefully be viewed as community service, it may be equally productive to conceptualise and organise schemes as 'field-based' education. Student tutors, through reflection on their experiences, can learn in a field-based context. Proper arrangements will insure that the 'human ecology' of the sentient field context in which tutors operate also benefits from the experience.

Correspondence:
John Jones, Higher Education Research Office, University of Auckland, Private Bag, Auckland, New Zealand.

7 Experience of proctoring over three years at Nottingham Polytechnic

B L Button, R Sims and L White

Over the past three years on the sandwich BEng honours degree course in Mechanical Engineering, 92 final-year students have helped 234 first-year students and 176 second-year students to learn. This we have called proctoring. Each proctor, a final-year student, led a group of either about four second-year students or about eight first-year students who were either designing or detailing a product. The proctors were responsible to the lecturer for organising their own particular group and for the general progress of the group project.

For all students, proctoring was a part of a group-project for Engineering Design. The proctors were assessed mainly on the quality of their written report on their particular group, and not on their performance as proctors. The assessment of first-year and second-year students continued to be based on either a log book and/or a group report and an oral presentation.

Proctoring has given all the students the opportunity to use and develop their communication skills in a friendly and supportive environment. The majority of proctors appeared to enjoy the opportunity to use and develop their accumulated knowledge and skills, and to develop their organising, planning, cooperation and leadership skills. The proctored students gained from the experiential knowledge of the proctors. Feedback was obtained from questionnaires completed by students and from the written reports submitted by the proctors. This feedback has been analysed and acted upon.

The introduction of proctoring need not increase the workload of students or lecturers and it can provide more opportunites for subject integration between different years of a course and the integration between subjects.

This academic year, proctoring has been extended to first-year HND students who are proctored by final-year degree students, and to the subject of Computing. Proctoring has also been included as a part of the Polytechnic's Enterprise in Higher Education Programme which will involve all its lecturers and students over the next five years.

Proctoring could be extended to include the personal tutoring of students by students instead of, or as well as, by lecturers.

The authors believe that proctoring in some form should be a part of all primary, secondary and tertiary education.

Introduction

What is proctoring? Proctoring occurs when students help less advanced students to learn (Button, 1985). It:

- creates a situation where students have to communicate with one another;
- provides an opportunity for students to develop their organising, planning, cooperation and leadership skills and to pass on some of their experiential knowledge;
- need not increase the workload of students or lecturers;
- can provide more opportunites for subject integration between different years of a course and the integration between subjects.

Over the three academic years 1985–8 proctoring has involved over 500 students on our sandwich BEng honours degree course in Mechanical Engineering. An account of the first-year's experience is given by Button et al (1987). This account is for the whole period and covers: how proctoring is organised; how proctoring relates to assessment; the student's attitudes to proctoring; and how proctoring has been extended and could be developed.

Organisation

All the students involved in proctoring were briefed about the aims of proctoring and the outcomes that can be expected.

Final-year students were the proctors. They were each responsible to a lecturer for organising a small group of students doing either the design, or the detailing, of a product for a part of the coursework for Engineering Design. The groups consisted of either about eight first-year students or about four second-year students.

The introduction of proctoring has not changed what, or how much, work the first-year students and the second-year students do in Engineering Design. To keep the same work for final-year students it was necessary to replace about one-quarter of the content of Engineering Design by proctoring. Proctoring takes up about four per cent per annum of the timetabled workload of students involved in proctoring.

For the last three academic years 234 first-year students were proctored by 46 final-year students. During the last two academic years 46 final-year students proctored 176 second-year students. A detailed breakdown of the students is given in Table 7.1.

Table 7.1 Summary of proctoring 1985-8
(Figures in parentheses give the number of questionnaires returned.)

Session	Proctors		Proctors	
	Year	Student numbers	Year	Student numbers
1985–6	4	14 (12)	1	98 (77)
1986–7	4	18 (9)	1	78 (62)
	4	26 (10)	2	98 (42)
1987–8	4	14 (11)	1	58 (33)
	4	20 (10)	2	78 (40)

Example

The design and manufacture project for the first-year Mechanical Engineering degree students during the academic year 1987-8 is typical of the proctoring activity.

60 first-year students were given the task of producing assembly drawings from a set of detail drawings for a textile machine mechanism. The mechanism consisted of eight identical sub-assemblies, so eight groups of seven or eight students were formed; each group being made responsible for the manufacture of a sub-assembly.

All groups were proctored by a final-year Mechanical Engineering degree student for the first 12 of the 18 weeks devoted to the project. The timetabled contact was one hour per week during the design period.

After an initial briefing the proctors were left to determine how to achieve their objectives. It was soon noticed that a significant delegation of responsibilities was not taking place in any of the groups. The lecturer then suggested that a group leader be appointed and that other members of the group be given the following jobs:

- manufacturing officer
- progress chaser
- buyer
- quality controller
- drawing officer
- fitting officer.

This structure is an attempt to mirror the responsibilities in the industrial situation with the proctor taking the role of section leader, and the group leader his assistant.

Such organisation was especially necessary during the period when the proctor was not present, for example after the 12-week period when the group was given the opportunity to manage itself but under the overall supervision of the lecturer.

Assessment

As the work of the first-year students and second-year students remained unchanged with the introduction of proctoring, their assessment continued to be based on either a log book and/or a group project report and an oral presentation.

The assessment of the proctors was based mainly on their written reports. This meant that the final-year students were not assessed on their performance as proctors, but rather on the quality of their report. The guidelines for the content of the report were as follows.

1   Project title
2   Group membership
3   General discussion about the project
4   A detailed description of the more important technical problems
5   The individual roles of the members of the group, their reactions and contributions
6   Personal problems that were encountered and how they were dealt with
7   Any comments the proctor may wish to make, regarding your personal experience and what could be done in future to give students a better experience.

Survey

Similar questionnaires were prepared for proctored students and proctors. To each of the nine items in their questionnaire the students were asked to respond on a six-option scale: *true for me* (+ 3 + 2 + 1) or *not true for me* (– 1 – 2 – 3). The questionnaire finished by asking the students to respond freely about what impressed them most, and least, favourably about proctoring.

254 proctored students and 52 proctors completed their questionnaires, representing a 62 and a 57 per cent return respectively. The detailed breakdown of the student's responses is included in Table 7.1.

Tables 7.2 and 7.3 give the percentage of the responses made by the students during 1985-8 to each item considered *true for me*. Since the responses made by the first-year students and the second-year students were not significantly different, the average percentage is that reported in Table 7.2. The only exception is the response to item 4a.

More than 70 per cent of proctored students thought that proctoring was helpful and preferred to work with a proctor. More than 90 per cent of the proctors thought that proctoring was a useful experience and preferred to proctor. The difference of over 20 per cent suggests that some proctors only communicate with part of their group. A greater percentage of proctors (76 per cent) than proctored students (63 per cent) would have preferred more time proctoring.

About 90 per cent of the proctors discussed the project outside timetabled periods, but only 46 per cent of first-year students did; for second-year students this increased to 71 per cent. It is encouraging to note that discussions took place on other topics. Virtually all the students felt friendly to one another. 96 per cent of proctors cared about their groups but only 74 per cent of proctored students thought they did. Again this suggests that proctors only communicate with part of their group. This lack of communication with the whole group is also borne out by the fact that only 21 per cent of proctored students thought the proctors authoritarian, whereas almost 89 per cent of the proctors thought they were. 90 per cent of the proctors thought they would have benefited had there been proctoring when they were first-year or second-year students. A lower percentage of proctored students (71 per cent) expected to benefit from being a proctor in their final year.

Almost half of all the students thought that other subjects should be proctored as well. Computing was singled out by about 70 per cent of all students. This demonstrates that students realise the benefits of passing on experiential knowledge.

Also included in Tables 7.2 and 7.3 are responses made by students for 1985–6. When the responses to items 1 to 3 are compared to those for 1985–8 they illustrate that a greater percentage of the students think that proctoring is worthwhile. Surveying all the responses, it is clear that overall the final-year students have a more positive attitude to proctoring than do the first-year and second-year students.

Free responses

A selection of the free responses is included because they show in more detail what the students think about the most, and the least, favourable impressions of proctoring. The free responses are categorised under different headings to show the different aspects of proctoring, namely: communication, cooperation and leadership, organisation and planning, experiential knowledge and attitudes and values.

Table 7.2 Summary of proctored student's responses 1985–8

Item	True for me/ per cent
1 Proctoring was helpful	71
2 I prefer to work with a proctor	74
3 I would prefer more time with a proctor	63
4 I talked to the proctor outside the timetabled period about:	
a) the project	54*
b) other topics	43
5 The proctor was friendly	93
6 The proctor was authoritarian	21
7 The proctor was uncaring	26
8 I expect to benefit from being a proctor in my final year	71
9 Subjects other than computing should be proctored	47
10 Computing should be proctored	72

* 46 and 71 per cent for first-year students and second-year students respectively.

Table 7.3 Summary of proctor's responses 1985–8

Item	True for me/ per cent
1 I found proctoring a useful experience	94
2 I would have preferred not to have been proctored	8
3 I would have preferred more time to proctor	76
4 I talked with the group outside the timetabled periods about:	
a) the project	89
b) other topics	76
5 The group was friendly towards me	100
6 The group followed my lead	89
7 I cared about my group	96
8 I expect I would have benefited from being proctored when I was a first-year student	90
9 Subjects other than computing should be proctored	43
10 Computing should be proctored	70

Least favourable impressions by first-year and second-year students

Communication
There is a possibility of breakdown of communication between lecturers, proctors and students.

Cooperation and leadership
He was bossy.
He was not very dominant.
The fact that proctoring did not work was due to the proctor being an ineffective leader.

Organisation and planning
Bad organisation severely reduced the usefulness of proctoring.
Lack of time designated to proctoring.
The proctor did not know what he was doing.
Still being forced to have proctoring meetings when they were no longer needed.

Experiential knowledge
They were not very experienced.
Had not got a real manufacturing background.
Not always correct with his advice.
His knowledge of basic engineering was non-existent.
The proctor had little (or no) more technical knowledge than ourselves.

Attitudes and values
Lack of interest and commitment.

Most favourable impressions by first-year and second-year students

Communication
Easy to talk to a proctor at my level.
Getting discussions going.
Help in finding information.
Ability to explain technical detail.
Talking about the subject of Engineering Design.
He was helpful with advice on other areas.

Cooperation and leadership
The proctor was always approachable.
The proctor was very helpful.
Teamwork was at a premium.
The proctor was friendly.
Carried it out as a leader of a cohesive group.
The proctor adopted a total professional attitude throughout the design periods.

Organisation and planning
The idea of being organised.
The proctor organised well.
He was helpful with the initial organisation.
Attendance of the proctor every week.
He turned up on time.
The proctor was able to timetable the development of the project invoking a degree of self-discipline within us.
Our proctor was able to marshal our ideas into relevant areas.
Familiarity with Polytechnic procedures.

Experiential knowledge
The experience he had gained through the course which he could relay to myself.
Could talk on an informed basis about any problem which occurred.
Knowledge of the proctor.
Helpful advice on the rest of the course.
Gave useful advice on technical matters.
Introduction to background material that could only be known or utilised by a student.
Knew where to make start and gave hints and direction in which to go.
His alternative ideas.
Attitudes and values.
The idea was excellent.
Gave interest to the project.
The enthusiasm of the proctor.
Regarded us as capable of thinking for ourselves.

Least favourable impressions by final-year students

Communication
We should be taught more communication skills.

Organisation and planning
The organisation was very poor.
Insufficient time allocated to proctoring.

Attitudes and values
General lethargy by students towards proctor.

Most favourable impressions by final-year students

Communication
The opportunity to develop communication skills.
Working closely with students who were prepared to listen to my advice.

Cooperation and leadership
The chance of some responsibility and the chance to show or having a go at showing leadership qualities.
The chance to practice man management without the various industrial drawbacks.
Good preparation for dealing with people.
The cooperation of the members of the group.
Working closely with lecturers.
Development of ideas.
The group responded well.
Being involved with a large team of people.

Organisation and planning
The opportunity to develop organisation skills.

Attitudes and values
The commitment from the group was keen and enthusiastic.
Attitude of lecturers towards proctors was good.
Enjoyed being a group leader.
The chance to help other students.

The reports

Generally the reports contained what has already been described but there are the following notable exceptions.
'Initially I was against the idea of final-year students proctoring first-year and second-year students. I believed that this was too much to ask in time and effort. I now retract this statement and would completely encourage proctoring.'
'I found proctoring to be the most valuable aspect of the four-year course.'
'I think the degree course in general may benefit from final-year students

acting as personal tutors to first-year and second-year students alongside the normal system of lecturer personal tutors.'

Conclusions, actions taken and suggestions

1 The majority of the 500 students who have been involved in proctoring have enjoyed it and have benefited from the experience; with a more positive attitude being taken by final-year students.

2 Proctoring is now well established in the Department for degree students doing Engineering Design. This is continuing, but this year proctoring has been extended to HND students and to the subject of Computing.

3 To make proctoring successful it is absolutely essential that all the students and the lecturers involved are briefed beforehand about its organisation, aims and expected outcomes.

4 A repeated criticism of professional engineers is their lack of ability to communicate (Beuret, 1983). Proctoring provides an opportunity for students to overcome this criticism.

5 It is currently estimated that only 65 per cent of graduates enter professions for which they have specific training (Association of Graduate Careers Advisory Services, 1988). This highlights the importance of the hidden curriculum, which proctoring so admirably brings into the open. Communication has already transferred from the hidden curriculum to the formal curriculum. It is time for other professional skills to make this transfer and at the same time higher education teachers should use better methods of assessing these skills.

6 To maintain and improve the quality of the proctoring experience feedback is essential.

7 Proctoring could be extended to include personal tutoring of students by students instead of, or as well as, by lecturers.

8 Proctoring has been included as one of the 12 identifiable activities in the Polytechnic's Enterprise in Higher Education Programme which will progressively involve all lecturers and students over the next five years (Button, 1989).

9 Proctoring in some form should be a part of all primary, secondary and tertiary education.

10 There is a need to state the behavioural objectives for proctoring and to demonstrate scientifically that these have been achieved.

Correspondence
Dr R Sims or Professor B L Button, Department of Mechanical Engineering, Nottingham Polytechnic, Burton Street, Nottingham, NG1 4BU.

8   An experiment in same-age peer tutoring in higher education: Some observations concerning the repeated experience of tutoring or being tutored

Nancy Falchikov

In this chapter, a replication and extension same-age peer tutoring study, carried out at Napier Polytechnic, Edinburgh, is described and comparisons made between the outcomes of this study and those of the original one. In the earlier study, students were randomly assigned to the roles of tutor or tutee, or to a study-alone condition (the 'control' group). One-to-one tutorials were arranged and carried out in tutor-tutee pairs. The effects of the scheme on achievement and attitudes were assessed, and compared with those from the more extensive body of literature on peer tutoring among school-age students. The findings for tutors were in line with the positive effects generally noted in younger populations for cross-age as opposed to same-age tutoring — that is to say, they perceived the scheme to confer benefits and performed at a level which was consistent with their ability. Tutees also perceived the scheme to be beneficial, though to a lesser extent than did tutors, and also performed at an appropriate level in terms of their ability. Tutees appeared to enjoy, and benefit from, the one-to-one aspects of the scheme, and its flexibility. However, the findings also reinforced the warning-signals in the literature with regard to being assigned a tutee-role. For example, tutees expressed some lack of confidence in their tutors. Both tutor and tutee groups listed the time and organisation required as the least-liked features of the scheme (Falchikov and Fitz-Gibbon, 1989).

The follow-up study aimed to investigate the effects of repetition of role on both tutor and tutee. In this study, some students simply repeated the roles they had occupied in the first study, while others attempted peer tutoring for the first time. In one tutor-condition, material for the tutorial was obtained by book-research on the part of tutors rather than by attendance at a filmed lecture. Procedures followed those of the earlier study. One-to-one tutorials were arranged and conducted by student pairs. Feedback on the scheme and attitudes of participants was again obtained on completion of the exercise. A short test was conducted after three weeks and an unannounced retention test after a period of three months. While, overall, the questionnaire and semantic-differential responses suggested that the exercise was less well-liked than on the original occasion, some positive changes were observed. For example, tutees no longer expressed lack of confidence in their partners. There was also some indication that experience at the task may have improved test performance. Once again, tutors perceived themselves to have benefited from the scheme in terms of increased independence, thought and structure, and in the amount of learning that had taken place. 'Experienced' tutors also felt themselves to be more confident and critical as a result of the experience. Similarly, some tutees felt themselves to be more thoughtful as a result of the exercise, and, as on the first occasion, listed 'one-to-one relation benefits' and 'flexibility' as best-liked features. Possible sources of increased dissatisfaction were investigated and the video presentation of material was identified as one likely source.

Finally, ways of increasing perceived benefits to tutees are discussed and suggestions for future research include the recommendation of a scheme of co-tutoring or peer-assisted learning for use with same-age groups in higher education.

Introduction

One-to-one tutoring is recognised as an exceptionally effective teaching method. Bloom (1984) reported that, given a trained personal tutor, 98% of students academically out-perform those taught in conventional class-rooms. It is clearly not possible to implement such a strategy for the benefit of the majority of students; such personalised instruction is reserved for a privileged few. However, in order to provide more universal one-to-one tuition, there are benefits to be gained if use is made of the great resource of the students themselves. Not only do students involved in peer tutoring programmes achieve considerable gains in terms of learning (eg Cohen et al, 1982; Cook et al, 1985–86), they also appear to benefit in other ways. For example, Smith (1977) found that, in an undergraduate maths class, students showed both content gain and improved attitude towards the subject after working with a partner. Allen (1976) notes that the helping relationship which characterises one-to-one peer tutoring seems to be beneficial to both partners. He observes that, in a wide variety of situations the individual who helps others experiences 'positive dividends of a psychological nature'. Kammer (1982), reporting the use of peer tutoring in nursing education, concludes that a teaching-method which encourages students to use each other as a resource seems more effective and economical than traditional methods. Levin (1988), explicitly comparing four different educational interventions for cost-effectiveness, found that cross-age tutoring yielded 'four times the increase in achievement for each dollar of cost as the least cost-effective program (lengthening the school day)' (p 52). Peer tutoring was found to be the most cost-effective of the four interventions.

In spite of demonstrated benefits, peer tutoring, particularly outside the schools, tends to be viewed more as a 'therapeutic enterprise' (Hedin, 1987) than as a basic instructional method available for use by any teacher. In higher education, there appears to be little use made of peer tutoring other than in cases of postgraduate students acting as paid teacher surrogates. There is also little systematic research being carried out in this area. Recent studies of peer tutoring tend to be examples of Hedin's therapeutic enterprises. For example, peer tutoring has been used successfully with under-achieving students (Pigott et al, 1986), with behaviourally-disordered students (Scruggs et al, 1985) and with handicapped students (Cook et al, 1985-86).

A recent study by Falchikov and Fitz-Gibbon (1989) addressed questions associated with peer tutoring in the context of higher education. Their study involved same-age pairs (being administratively preferable to cross-age pairs) and bore some resemblance to Cornwall's (1979) conception of Peer Assisted Learning. That is to say, the scheme was based on the assumption that 'the ability to help other students to learn is not dependent on academic superiority and that there are intrinsic qualities of the relationship between peers which are unique and can be exploited in a teaching-learning interaction' (p 33). The study here reported built on this earlier one.

The original study

A same-age tutoring project was carried out at Napier Polytechnic, Edinburgh; it involved first-year students studying psychology as part of a four-year degree in catering and accommodation studies. Students were randomly assigned the roles of tutor, tutee or independent study student. The results of the first study (Falchikov and Fitz-Gibbon, 1989) corresponded to others found in the literature for cross-age populations (eg Cohen, Kulik and Kulik, 1982). The peer tutoring experience was perceived by the undergraduate participants as being worthwhile and as conferring benefits irrespective of group membership. Post-performance measures found no statistically-significant differences between groups, but hinted at superior performance on the part of tutors in the post-test and at improved tutee performance on the retention-test. Neither tutors nor tutees appeared to be disadvantaged academically as a result of their experiences.

Qualitative measures, however, pointed to lack of confidence in the tutor partner on the part of some tutees.

Rationale for the follow-up study

It can be argued that, as with any skill, practice at tutoring, even if it does not actually achieve perfection, will lead to considerable improvement. Similarly, tutees, reassured to some extent by the performance-measures following the first experience of being tutored, will settle into their role, increase their trust in their tutor, and do even better a second time. If, however, there is something intrinsic to the role of tutee in a same-age peer tutoring situation that makes the scheme undesirable under these circumstances, we might predict a clearer indication of tutee-discontent on repeating the peer tutoring exercise. The present follow-up study was designed to address these questions. Furthermore, as the ability to research a new topic is a valuable skill for undergraduates to acquire, the study also introduced a research variation in the tutor task, in order to investigate effects of devolving more responsibility to tutors over the preparation of their tutorials.

Method

The follow-up study was carried out between February and May 1987. In this study, students acting as tutor or tutee repeated their roles in the same pairs as in the first study, though one group of tutors fulfilled a modified research role in this variant. Students who had acted as 'controls' and had studied independently in the earlier experiment were also assigned the roles of tutor and tutee. In this way, the present study could make a direct comparison between 'experienced' and novice tutors and tutees. A video-lecture on the topic of 'Attitudes' was prepared in conjunction with a social psychologist, and delivered by the same experienced lecturer as in the earlier study. This was viewed by two of the three tutor groups during the normal class hour. All tutors are subsequently identified by the prefix 'TO', tutees by 'TE'. Information in parentheses indicates the method of acquisition of material for the tutorial. 'V' tutors viewed the video lecture and 'R' tutors researched their topic. The 'experienced' tutors TO(V2), had carried out a similar task in the earlier study, while the other group, TO(V1), were performing the task for the first time. The third tutor group, TO(R), were given detailed references from a readily available textbook on social psychology, and written hints on structuring their tutorial. The lecturer offered her services as a consultant should any tutor wish to discuss her or his tutorial plan. (No tutor availed her- or himself of this offer).

The three corresponding tutee groups are referred to as TE(V2) ('experienced' tutees), TE(V1) (first-time tutees) and TE(R) (tutees of research tutors). Tutors and tutees were again expected to arrange a one-to-one tutorial at a mutually convenient time during the week following the video presentation or book research. All participants were encouraged to spend time over and above the minimum required to carry out the exercise. After the tutorial had taken place, a feedback questionnaire was completed. This contained open-ended questions and some semantic differential ratings of the scheme itself and of student responses to it. Questions relating to the attitudes of tutors and tutees towards their partners and to the quality of the working relationship were included. A short test, comprising 10 multiple choice questions and two short essay questions, was conducted after an interval of three weeks. An unannounced retention test, also comprising both multiple choice and short questions, was completed the following May.

Results: questionnaire responses

Best-liked features of the scheme
The pattern of responses to this section immediately suggested a less favourable response to the exercise than on the previous occasion. This time, of the 39 responses, 24 were positive in nature, nine negative and six participants made no comment at all. Of the positive responses, in the three tutor groups the most frequently cited best-liked feature fell into the category labelled 'personal and study skills benefits'. Next most frequently occurring were responses appreciating the flexibility of the system. Response rate of research tutors was particularly low, the only two responses received falling into the 'content' category. Tutee groups rated 'flexibility' and 'one-to-one relation benefits' as the best-liked features. Negative responses were variations on the theme of 'nothing'.

Least-liked features of the scheme
Features least-liked overall by tutor groups were the time-consuming nature of the task and a lack of motivation for it. New tutors differed from the other two groups by making only one reference to time. Tutees overall rated 'organisation' as the least desirable feature of the exercise, with 'time' the next most frequently cited. Groups TE(R) (tutees of research tutors) and TE(V1) (tutees of novice tutors) made a single reference each to lack of confidence in their partner, whereas the 'experienced' tutees, TE(V2), did not.

Changes in participant perceptions on repeating the experience
Best-liked feature most frequently listed by tutors on both occasions of
tutoring was 'personal and study skills benefits'; those of tutees were
'flexibility' and 'one-to-one relation benefits'. Thus, the peer-tutoring experience appears to elicit similar responses on both occasions. The most
frequently-listed feature liked least by tutors, namely 'time', similarly remains constant on repeating the experience. Tutees, however, appear to
perceive things differently on the two occasions. The lack of confidence in
partner expressed by about a third of the tutee group on the first occasion has
been replaced by problems with organisation and time in the present study.

Semantic differential measures

Responses of the tutor-groups to the statement 'The scheme of tutoring/
being tutored makes you...' are shown in Figure 8.1. Although the number
of participants making up each group was small, group percentages were
calculated in order to facilitate comparisons between groups and with
results of the earlier study. All tutor groups appear to perceive the
experience as conferring benefits: they claim to be independent, to think
more, learn more and to be confident and critical as a result of the
experience. In addition, 'experienced' tutor groups TO(V2) (those who had
viewed the video) and TO(R) (the tutors who had researched their
material) rate the scheme as aiding structure. Tutee responses are shown in
Figure 8.2. While some benefits are perceived as resulting from the
experience, particularly by group TE(R) (tutees of research tutors) whose
members feel they think more, learn more and are more critical. Once
again, however, in this repeat study, tutees generally feel that they do not
derive as much benefit from the scheme as do tutors.

Responses to another set of bipolar adjectives following the statement
'The scheme of tutoring/being tutored is...' are shown in Figure 8.3 and
Figure 8.4. There appear to be differences in responses among tutors,
depending on the sub-group membership. Tutor group TO(V2) (the
experienced tutors repeating the roles already practised in the previous
study) seem to rate the scheme most highly of the three tutor groups. At
least half of the group perceive the scheme as challenging, helpful and
beneficial, easy and enjoyable. However, overall, tutee groups perceive the
scheme *more* positively than do tutors. Patterns of responses for experienced
tutees (groups TE(V2) and TE(R)) are similar. Tutee group TE(V1), for
whom this was the first experience of being tutored, rated the scheme as
more enjoyable, easier, less challenging yet more beneficial than did the
other tutee groups.

Fig 8.1 Tutor Groups   The scheme makes you.....

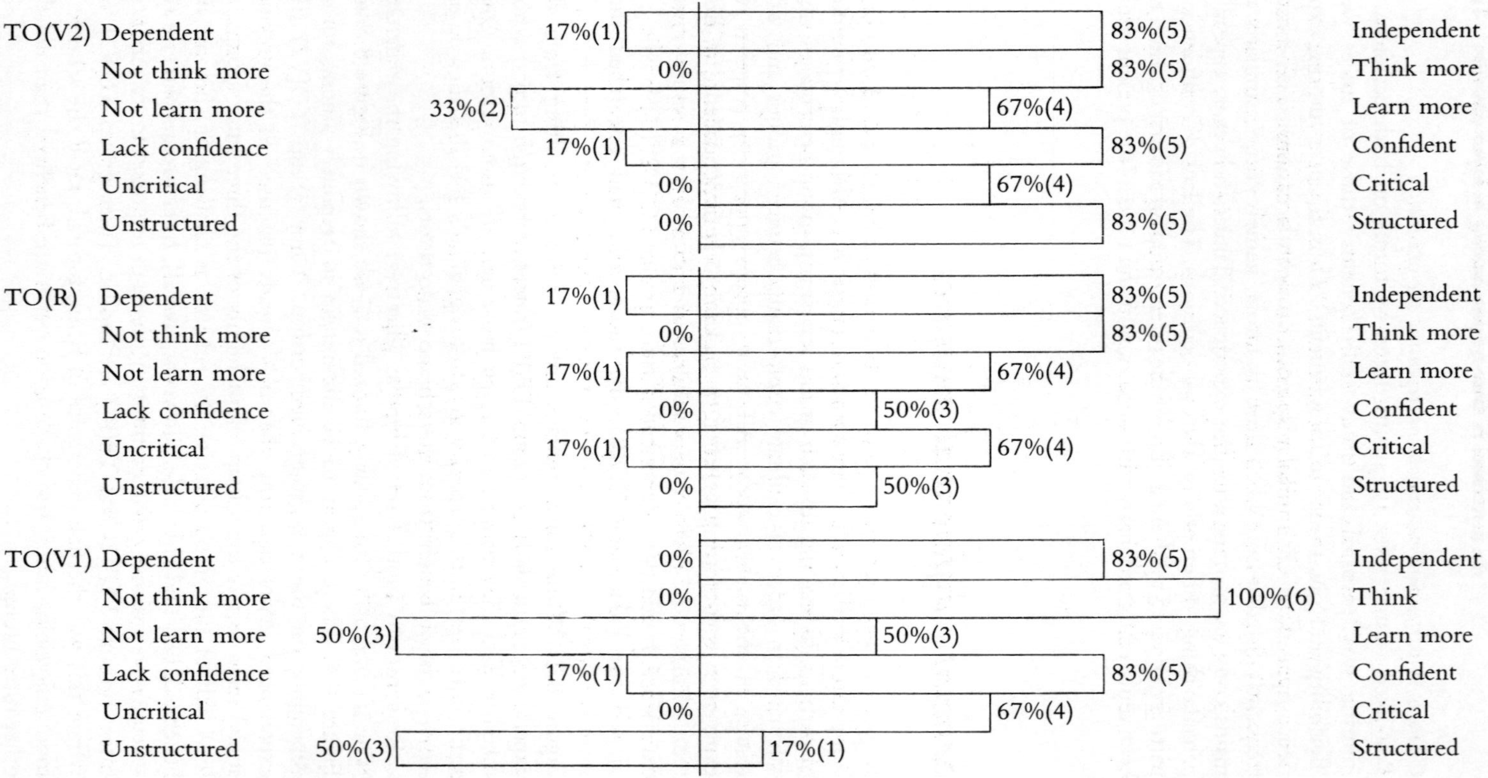

TO(V2)

Category	Value	Opposite	Value
Dependent	17%(1)	Independent	83%(5)
Not think more	0%	Think more	83%(5)
Not learn more	33%(2)	Learn more	67%(4)
Lack confidence	17%(1)	Confident	83%(5)
Uncritical	0%	Critical	67%(4)
Unstructured	0%	Structured	83%(5)

TO(R)

Category	Value	Opposite	Value
Dependent	17%(1)	Independent	83%(5)
Not think more	0%	Think more	83%(5)
Not learn more	17%(1)	Learn more	67%(4)
Lack confidence	0%	Confidence	50%(3)
Uncritical	17%(1)	Critical	67%(4)
Unstructured	0%	Structured	50%(3)

TO(V1)

Category	Value	Opposite	Value
Dependent	0%	Independent	83%(5)
Not think more	0%	Think	100%(6)
Not learn more	50%(3)	Learn more	50%(3)
Lack confidence	17%(1)	Confident	83%(5)
Uncritical	0%	Critical	67%(4)
Unstructured	50%(3)	Structured	17%(1)

Figure 8.2 Tutee Groups   The scheme makes you.....

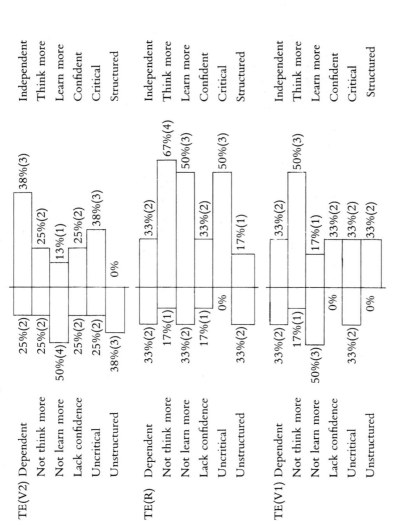

Figure 8.3 Tutor Groups

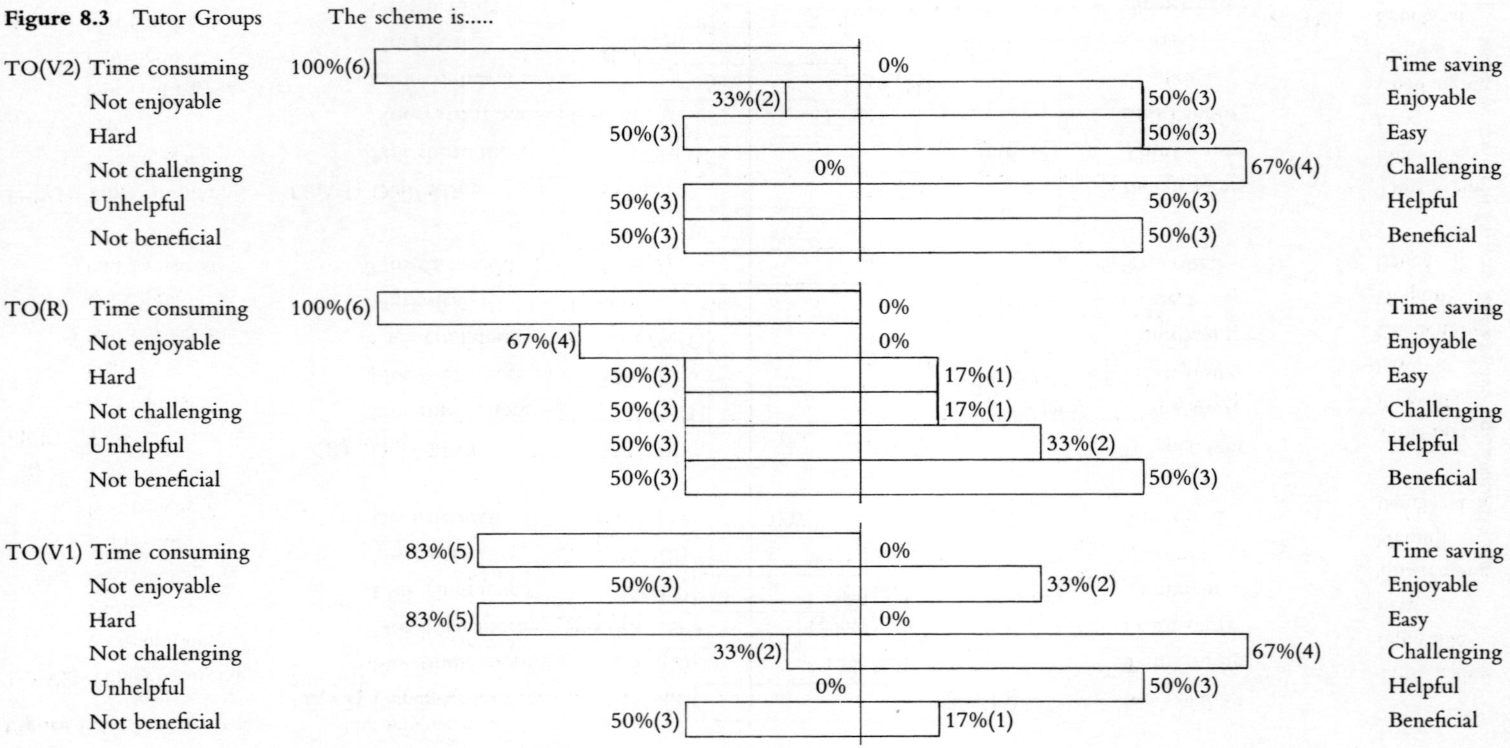

The scheme is.....

TO(V2)

Time consuming	100%(6)	0%	Time saving
Not enjoyable	33%(2)	50%(3)	Enjoyable
Hard	50%(3)	50%(3)	Easy
Not challenging	0%	67%(4)	Challenging
Unhelpful	50%(3)	50%(3)	Helpful
Not beneficial	50%(3)	50%(3)	Beneficial

TO(R)

Time consuming	100%(6)	0%	Time saving
Not enjoyable	67%(4)	0%	Enjoyable
Hard	50%(3)	17%(1)	Easy
Not challenging	50%(3)	17%(1)	Challenging
Unhelpful	50%(3)	33%(2)	Helpful
Not beneficial	50%(3)	50%(3)	Beneficial

TO(V1)

Time consuming	83%(5)	0%	Time saving
Not enjoyable	83%(5)	33%(2)	Enjoyable
Hard	50%(3)	0%	Easy
Not challenging	33%(2)	67%(4)	Challenging
Unhelpful	0%	50%(3)	Helpful
Not beneficial	50%(3)	17%(1)	Beneficial

Figure 8.4 Tutuee Groups

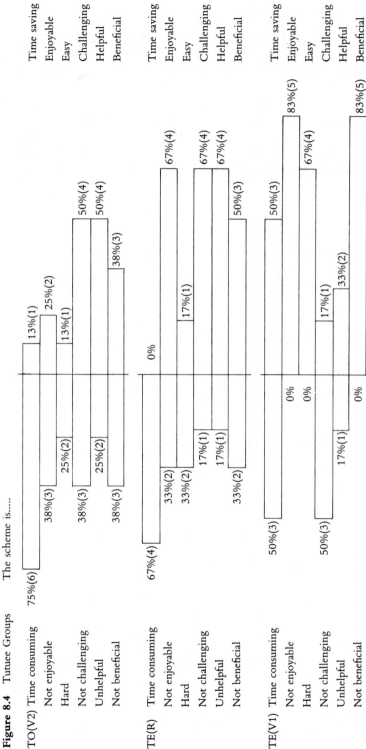

The scheme is.....

TO(V2)

	Time consuming		Time saving
Not enjoyable		13%(1)	Enjoyable
Hard	25%(2)	25%(2)	Easy
Not challenging	38%(3)	13%(1) 50%(4)	Challenging
Unhelpful	25%(2)	50%(4)	Helpful
Not beneficial	38%(3)	38%(3)	Beneficial

75%(6) — Time consuming
38%(3)

TE(R)

	Time consuming		Time saving
Not enjoyable	33%(2)	0% 67%(4)	Enjoyable
Hard	33%(2)	17%(1)	Easy
Not challenging	17%(1)	67%(4)	Challenging
Unhelpful	17%(1)	67%(4)	Helpful
Not beneficial	33%(2)	50%(3)	Beneficial

67%(4) — Time consuming

TE(V1)

	Time consuming		Time saving
Not enjoyable		0% 83%(5)	Enjoyable
Hard		0% 67%(4)	Easy
Not challenging		17%(1)	Challenging
Unhelpful	17%(1)	33%(2)	Helpful
Not beneficial		0% 83%(5)	Beneficial

50%(3) — Time consuming
50%(3) — Not challenging
50%(3) — Time saving

Comparing Figure 8.1 with Figure 8.3 points to an interesting contradiction. Figure 8.3 suggests that tutors, on the whole, have a somewhat negative opinion of the peer-tutoring *scheme*. Figure 8.1, on the other hand, indicates that, in spite of their poor opinion of and attitudes towards the *scheme,* they perceive the personal *benefits* derived from it to be great. Tutees register less-extreme ratings for both statements (Figure 8.2 and Figure 8.4), but present a more consistent picture. In the case of tutees, the scheme itself receives a higher rating than that registered by tutors, but the personal benefits derived are perceived to be fewer than those noted by tutors.

Changes in participant-perceptions on repeating the exercise

Extreme caution must be exercised in making quantitative comparisons, due to the small numbers of participants involved (particularly in the more recent study where tutor and tutee groups were subdivided). None-the-less, some differences are qualitative and others appear to be quite large.

For tutor group TO(V2) (the 'experienced' video-watching tutors) the greatest benefit of having done the task before appears to be in terms of independence ratings (which show an increase of 27% in the follow-up study) and structure (+ 20%). While there is an increase in the overall proportion of group members who experience an increase in confidence (+ 20%), there is also an increase in those who do not (+ 17%). For tutor-group TO(R), the research tutors, there is also a perceived increase in independence. Other changes, though mostly very small, tend to be for the worse. The response profile of tutor group TO(V1) (the first-time tutors, originally part of the 'control' group) has aspects in common with both tutor and independent study group profiles from the earlier study. For example, independence ratings for tutor group TO(V1) in the present study resemble those of the earlier independent study group. The high confidence rating in the present study (83%) more closely resembles that of the phase 1 tutors (63%) than that of the independent study participants (46%).

Comparing the present study ratings of tutee groups with those from the earlier investigation, many differences are apparent. All changes indicated by tutee-group TE(V2) (tutees of 'experienced' video-tutors) for example, appear to be for the worse. The repeated experience of being tutored by the same same-age peer appears to be a negative one for some participants. This, however, does not seem to be the case for tutee group TE(R) (tutees of research-tutors). Ratings for this group present a similar pattern to those recorded at the end of the earlier study. That is to say, they perceive themselves to be thinking more, to have learned more and to be more critical as a result of the experience. They, too, were tutored by the same same-age peers as in the earlier study, though in the repeat study their tutors were given more responsibility for the preparation of the tutorial than in the first case. In spite of their negatively-perceived experiences, the research-tutor group TO(R) seem to have provided a good tutorial service to their tutees. On comparing responses of first-time tutees (group TE(V1)) with their responses as independent study students in the previous investigation, a very gloomy picture emerges. Their new status as tutees appears to have reduced their independence rating by 59% to 33%. This more closely resembles the 38% recorded by the tutee-group in the first experiment. Comparing this first time tutee, TE(V1), independence rating of 33% with the 83% rating of the TO(V1) group (who had shared the status of independent student with the TE(V1) group in the earlier study) and with the 56% of the original tutor group, suggests that the experience of independent study makes the subsequent experience as tutee particularly unsatisfactory, while tending to produce very independent, confident and thoughtful tutors.

Summarising the changes signalled by questionnaire and semantic differential responses, we see that increases in confidence characterise two of the three tutor groups. For tutee groups, the repeated experience of being tutored has led to a reduction in the lack of confidence in partner which characterised the earlier study, but, for two of the three groups, in other respects the scheme is perceived more negatively than on the previous occasion. In cases of both tutor and tutee, the 'odd one out' is the research condition. Research-tutors experience an increase in independence rather than in confidence, but otherwise recorded changes seem to be for the worse. Research tutees, however, appear to maintain the benefits perceived on completion of the first study.

The relationship between tutors and tutees

Tutees were invited to assess their tutors on 14 items using a five point scale (see Appendix Qu. 6). Tutors, similarly, assessed their tutees on ten items, again using a five-point scale (Qu.7). All participants were then given the opportunity to assess the working relationship globally (Qu.9) using a five-point scale. For tutor and tutee ratings of each other, average ratings were calculated (0–5), with high scores indicating a favourable rating. Data relating to tutor and tutee attitudes and to the quality of the working relationship are summarised in Table 8.1. It should be noted that most scores are at or above the average rating of 3. Comparing tutor and tutee responses to the quality of the working relationship, we see that six pairs are in complete agreement, three from the experienced pairs group, two

Table 8.1 Quality of working relationship

Tutor-tutee pair	Tutor's rating of tutee	Tutor's rating of working reln	Tutee's rating of working reln	Tutee's rating of tutor	Tutor's rating of tutee-tutee's rating of tutor
TO-TE(V1) GROUP					
1	4.25	4	4	4.07	+ 0.18
2	3.00	5	4	3.43	− 0.43
3	4.2	4	5	3.86	+ 0.34
4	4.1	4	3	3.93	+ 0.17
5	3.56	5	4	3.64	− 0.08
TO-TE(R) GROUP					
1	3.1	5	5	4.57	− 1.47
2	3.78	5	3	3.36	+ 0.42
3	2.44	3	4	3.5	− 1.06
4	3.78	4	5	4.57	− 0.79
5	4.00	4	4	4.00	0
6	3.22	4	3	3.71	− 0.49
TO-TE(V2) GROUP					
1	4.3	4	4	3.93	+ 0.37
2	3.1	4	2	2.13	+ 0.97
3	4.1	4	3	2.93	+ 1.17
4	3.56	4	4	3.43	+ 0.13
5	5.00	5	4	4.93	+ 0.07
6	3.00	4	4	3.71	− 0.17

(Left margin labels: First time tutor-tutee pairs; Research tutor-tutee pairs; Experienced tutor-tutee pairs)

from the research pairs group and the remaining one from the first time tutor-tutee pairs. Only one individual rating fell below the average score. Where discrepancies occur, tutee ratings of the working relationship tend to be lower than those of tutors.

A comparison of tutor ratings of tutees with tutee ratings of tutors is shown in the extreme right-hand column of Table 8.1. A positive score indicates higher ratings on the part of the tutor than of the tutee, a negative score the reverse. There appear to be differences according to experimental condition. In five of the six experienced pairs, tutee ratings are below those of their tutors. In the group of first-time tutor-tutee pairs, the positive and negative scores balance, while in the research group, in only one pair is the tutee rating below that of the tutor. Again it is difficult to interpret these data and unwise to generalise from such small samples.

Tutor and tutee responses to presentation of material

We must consider whether the dissatisfaction expressed concerning the investigation was related more to the mode of transmission of information than to other causes. Was the video well presented and the topic of equal interest to participants? Was the topic presented in a motivating way by tutors? If tutor dissatisfaction is related to presentation, then we might look for differences in ratings of subject matter and presentation between groups encountering the topic by video rather than by book research. As all tutees were introduced to the topic in a one-to-one tutorial, then we must look to factors other than the quality of the video when considering any dissatisfaction in this group. Figure 8.5 presents subject matter ratings for four types of participant: tutors seeing the video, their tutees, book-research tutors and their tutees. Most favourable ratings overall are made by tutees, particularly by those whose tutors did not see the video (group TE(R)). They rate the subject-matter and presentation as clear, stimulating, easy to understand, important and very relevant to the course (100% response in the latter case). They are equally divided as to whether it was interesting or lacking in interest. Their tutors, however, tended to rate the subject matter less positively. A comparison of responses of tutor groups TO(V1 and V2), who were introduced to the subject matter by means of the video, and group TO(R), who researched the topic themselves, shows that, on four of the six scales, the researchers rate the subject matter more highly than the video watchers. Ratings of tutees (none of whom saw the video) are highest of all. So, although the subject-matter was rated highly overall, the least-favourable ratings were made by those participants who viewed the video lecture. Thus, we may be able to attribute some tutor dissatisfaction to presentation of subject matter.

Test results

The immediate post-test
The immediate post-test took place during lecture time and was completed by only 28 out of the class of 44. The timing of the post-test was somewhat unpropitious, being very near the end of term, when attendance at lectures is generally poor. However, there did not appear to be any systematic bias in the pattern of absences. The results of both the immediate post-test and the retention test are shown in Table 8.2. The group means and standard deviations for Highers entrance qualifications are also shown. ('Highers' are Scottish post-GCSE examinations). These provide some general indication of ability. Once again, it is clearly unwise to generalise from these data, given the very small sample sizes. However, patterns within the results may

Figure 8.5 Subject matter ratings for the four conditions (Numbers refer to percentages of participants)

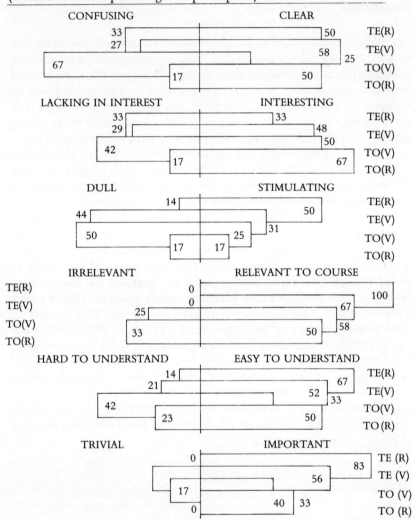

Table 8.2   Tutor and tutee scores on cognitive measures

TUTOR GROUP TO(V2)	n	Mean	(Experienced tutors) Std.Dev
HIGHERS	5	63.00	9.75
MC. POST	5	6.40	1.52
SQ. POST	5	22.40	2.19
TOT. POST	5	28.80	3.63
MC. RET	3	2.33	0.58
SQ. RET	3	2.00	1.00
TOT. RET	3	4.33	1.53

TUTOR GROUP TO(R)	n	Mean	(Research tutors) Std.Dev.
HIGHERS	7	61.67	17.51
MC. POST	7	5.71	0.95
SQ. POST	7	18.86	3.39
TOT. POST	7	24.57	3.78
MC. RET	7	2.14	1.21
SQ. RET	7	1.71	0.95
TOT. RET	7	3.86	1.77

TUTOR GROUP TO(V1)	n	Mean	(First-time tutors) Std.Dev.
HIGHERS	4	53.75	7.50
MC. POST	4	6.50	1.00
SQ. POST	4	15.75	2.75
TOT. POST	4	22.25	3.50
MC. RET	3	2.33	0.58
SQ. RET	3	1.67	1.53
TOT. RET	3	4.00	1.73

TUTEE GROUP TE(V2)	n	Mean	(Experienced tutees) Std.Dev.
HIGHERS	3	48.33	10.41
MC. POST	3	5.00	1.00
SQ. POST	3	19.33	3.06
TOT. POST	3	24.33	3.79
MC. RET	5	2.00	1.22
SQ. RET	5	1.80	1.64
TOT. RET	5	3.80	1.30

TUTEE GROUP TE(R)	n	Mean	(Tutees with research tutors) Std.Dev.
HIGHERS	3	55.00	13.23
MC. POST	3	6.33	1.15
SQ. POST	3	19.00	1.00
TOT. POST	3	25.33	2.08
MC. RET	8	2.63	1.19
SQ. RET	8	1.50	0.93
TOT. RET	8	4.13	1.81

Table 8.2 (cont'd)

TUTEE GROUP TE(V1)			(First time tutees)
	n	Mean	Std.Dev.
HIGHERS	6	56.00	14.32
MC. POST	6	3.83	2.14
SQ. POST	6	14.83	4.26
TOT. POST	6	18.67	2.58
MC. RET	6	1.67	0.82
SQ. RET	6	2.17	1.33
TOT. POST	6	3.83	1.47

Key
HIGHERS   Scottish post grade examinations
MC   Multiple choice questions
SQ   Short essay questions
POST   Immediate post-test
RET   Long term retention test
TOT   Total scores

provide useful clues for further research. Entrance qualification scores ('Highers') suggest that there is variation in ability-level across the six groups. For example, the two highest-average entrance scores are both achieved by tutor groups, the 'experienced' video-tutors, TO(V2), and the research-tutors, TO(R). Overall, tutors appear to have slightly higher scores than their tutee peers. Total post-test scores for tutor groups seem entirely consistent with their differing ability levels. Performance of tutee groups, however, cannot be accounted for simply in terms of ability. For example, the lowest-ranked ability-group, the tutees of 'experienced' tutors, TE(V2), achieve test scores comparable with those of higher ability groups. Conversely, the third highest ability-group, tutees of novice tutors, TE(V1), seem to perform very poorly overall at post-test. First-time tutors as well as first-time tutees score least well within their respective groups.

The retention test
Patterns hinted at in post-test scores are not evident in retention scores. In terms of retention, neither experimental treatment nor ability appear to bear any clear relation to test scores.

Summary and discussion

In spite of some negative ratings, the present study has tended to confirm the view that peer-tutoring is an appropriate educational method for use in higher education. Although the participant-responses are more mixed than on the first occasion, substantial benefits remain. Interpretation of results has been hampered by very small sample sizes but the study has highlighted some of the possible pitfalls of one particular form of the scheme, and has provided a number of pointers to improving its use.

In contrast to their earlier experience of tutoring, in the present study tutors rated the *scheme* negatively, although this effect is least marked in the group of experienced tutors. In spite of this negative rating, the *benefits* of the scheme were perceived by tutors to be even greater than on the first occasion. The performance of the experienced group of tutors on the post-test (which exceeds that of any other group) is consonant with these perceptions. The *scheme* is rated more positively overall by tutees than by tutors, with new tutees rating it highly. Least-enthusiastic tutees were the experienced group, TE(V2). In spite of their more positive rating of the scheme, tutees perceive themselves as achieving fewer *benefits* from it than do tutors. It seems that, even with a minimum of perceived-benefit, tutees continue to have faith in the scheme. On average, approaching 60% of this group rate it as enjoyable and beneficial (compared with less than 40% of the tutor group). Responses of tutees to repeating their role appear to be dependent on the status of their tutors. For example, tutees of research-tutors respond more positively to the repeated peer tutoring experience than do those of the video-tutors. It is not entirely clear why this should be the case. However, changing the status of tutors may also have the effect of improving the response of tutees. We should do well to take note of the response of tutors to the video-lecture style presentation of new material. One interpretation of this is that the traditional lecture may not be the best way to introduce new information to students.

Some aspects of this peer tutoring study, then, present us with a dilemma. It seems that tutors, particularly those repeating the task of tutoring, benefit from the scheme, and yet rate it negatively and experience little enjoyment in carrying out their task. It is as though they see the scheme as a dose of nasty medicine — unpleasant, yet doing one good in the end. Similarly, research-tutors, who perceive the scheme particularly negatively, at the end of the day rate the subject-matter more highly than other tutor groups.

Why do tutors rate the scheme so much more negatively than on the first occasion? Trimbur (1987) suggests that tutors may have unrealistic expectations. For example, they may expect the performance of their tutees to improve dramatically as a result of their tutoring. If this does not occur, as in the case of the present studies, these expectations may backfire. If this happens, tutors may blame either the students they work with, or themselves 'and their feelings of inadequacy can turn into a debilitating sense of guilt about not getting the job done' (p 22). While this may or may not be true in the present study, it seems unlikely, given the high ratings of the working relationship recorded, that tutor-dissatisfaction is attributable solely to difficulties with this relationship.

It is more likely that tutor-dissatisfaction may be attributable, in part at least, to the video-lecture presentation of the original material. This explanation, however, cannot apply to the research tutors who did not see the film. For them, the demands on their time posed by the research task may have been too great. (The group unanimously rated the scheme as time-consuming on the semantic differential measure and all included time as the least liked feature of the scheme). This pressure of work may have given rise to a negative halo effect which resulted in the group's particularly negative rating of the scheme. Contrary to predictions, dissatisfaction with the *scheme* does not seem to be the primary focus of the problem as far as tutees are concerned, though we should not ignore the tendency amongst tutees to rate the working relationship and the tutor partner slightly less positively than do the tutors. What seems to be important, then, is the question of how to improve *benefits* to tutees.

Until the peer tutoring experience, these undergraduates have experienced education as almost exclusively involving a knowledgeable, powerful expert (the teacher) and themselves as possessing none of these qualities. It would not, therefore, be surprising if tutors, suddenly endowed with more knowledge and expertise (and, thus, with more power) than their tutees, should experience this as beneficial. Tutees must also be aware of the change in status of their tutors and, by the end of this follow-up study, appear to be responding to it. Whereas, in the original study, tutees were expressing a lack of confidence in their partner, this seems to be substantially reduced by the end of the present study. In addition, they may also identify the knowledge tutors bring to the tutorial as the main benefit of the scheme.

Given the somewhat mixed results of this study, it is appropriate to ask whether same-age peer tutoring in higher education confers enough benefits to justify its continued use. I believe it does, and suggest that a more pertinent question concerns the action required in order to improve the experiences of all participants. The present study suggests

1   At an administrative level, the allocation of more time in which to carry out the peer tutoring task might serve to alleviate some of the pressures experienced by participants;

2   Many participants, particularly tutees, found the organisation demanded by the task troublesome; an appropriate response to this dissatisfaction, in our case for example, would be to provide details of individual timetables (which varied from person to person and from week to week) at the point when tutor-tutee pairs were arranging their one-to-one tutorial, and to make the time available for these negotiations;

3   For tutees who still express lack of confidence in themselves or their partners, some reassurance may follow feedback from the lecturer on tutee performance measures from previous studies;

4 Tutees may also benefit from being made aware of the fact that tutors have, in the past, spent longer on their task than have tutees. If tutors spend more time on the task and, subsequently, benefit more from it, then so can tutees.

5 As some lack of motivation was experienced in all participant groups, regular reversal of roles might not only provide a motivating challenge to combat reduced motivation, but also allow all participants to experience the advantages and disadvantages of both roles. Cornwall (1979) terms this arrangement 'co-tutoring' or 'reciprocal tutoring'. In it, he claims, 'concern about the special knowledge or skill of the tutor disappears' (p 49). Similarly, same-age tutoring benefits were reported by Jason et al 1979 (in Kammer 1982) when students switched tutor and tutee roles.

In more general terms, further increases in motivation may follow from allowing tutor-tutee pairs a greater degree of choice of tutorial topic. Motivation may also be increased by a change of tutorial partner. Although, in the present study, there did not appear to be any incompatible pairings, it is not inconceivable that this could occur. Some provision should be made for the resolution of such problems, if only a willingness on the part of the lecturer to either help tutor-tutee pairs resolve their differences or to aid in the structuring of new pairs. Few benefits can be associated with the total breakdown of a working relationship. Given that novelty is a feature liked by many participants, it is possible that regular changing of partners may be beneficial in this respect. However, it is not yet clear whether there are long-term benefits associated with remaining in stable dyads. Harris (1987) advocates peer tutoring in groups of three rather than the more usual dyads. This system, she claims, not only increases learning but also encourages cooperation (which itself encourages more or better learning). Certainly, further investigations of the dynamics of both this variant and of the more usual dyad tutorial relationship may prove a fruitful line of enquiry (cf Ehly 1987). It also seems clear that, given the desirability of novelty, and in order to avoid flattening of the interest curve, same-age peer tutoring should be implemented for brief periods only, and regarded as one of a variety of teaching strategies available to teachers.

Thus, in spite of some warning signs in the outcomes of the present study, same-age peer tutoring must still be seen to offer actual and potential benefits to students. It is to be hoped that further studies implementing some of the modifications suggested will be carried out here.

Correspondence
Dr N Falchikov, Napier Polytechnic of Edinburgh, Colinton Road, Edinburgh, EH10 5DT.

Appendix

Peer tutoring/independent study questionnaire

NAME ....   Please circle as appropriate
TUTOR/TUTEE/INDEPENDENT
STUDENT
Card No. ....

1 What did you like *best* about this scheme?

2 What did you like *least* about this scheme?

In the following questions please place a "✔" in the box which best represents your views.

3 The scheme of tutoring/being tutored by a peer/studying independently makes you:

Independent						Dependent
Not think						Think
Learn more						Not learn more
Lack confidence						Confident
Critical						Uncritical
Unstructured						Structured

4 The scheme of tutoring/being tutored by a peer/studying independently is:

Time saving						Time consuming
Not enjoyable						Enjoyable
Easy						Hard
Challenging						Not challenging
Unhelpful						Helpful
Beneficial						Not beneficial

5   The subject matter was:

Left						Right
Clear						Confusing
Lacking in interest						Interesting
Stimulating						Dull
Relevant to rest of course						Irrelevant
Hard to understand						Easy to understand
Important						Trivial

6   *TUTEES only*
My *tutor* was

Left						Right
Confident						Lacking in confidence
Unhelpful						Helpful
Friendly						Unfriendly
Unenthusiastic						Enthusiastic
Well prepared						Not well prepared
Lacking in knowledge						Knowledgeable
Reassuring						Not reassuring
Relaxed						Tense
Supportive						Unsupportive
Not good at explaining						Good at explaining
Clear						Confusing
Well motivated						Poorly motivated
Unapproachable						Approachable
Well organised						Not well organised

7   TUTORS only
My *tutee* was

Confident						Lacking in confidence
Unhelpful						Helpful
Friendly						Unfriendly
Unenthusiastic						Enthusiastic
Well motivated						Not well motivated
Unwilling to learn						Willing to learn
Prepared to ask questions						Not prepared to ask ask questions
Tense						Relaxed
Critical						Uncritical
Approachable						Unapproachable

8   *TUTORS & TUTEES only*
Our *working relationship* was, on the whole:

very good	good	average	poor	very poor

9   My grasp of this subject now is:

very good	good	average	poor	very poor

10   Time taken on this project, *excluding* attendance at videotaped lecture.

1 hr	Between 1 & 2 hrs	Between 2 & 3 hrs	More than 3 hrs

9 Parental tutoring and reciprocal same-age tutoring

G R Arblaster, C Butler, A L Taylor, M Pitchford

This chapter contains a description of a commercial programme (Companion Reading) which uses parental tutoring and reciprocal same-age tutoring with six to eight year-old children in reading instruction. It also reports on how a very similar model of instruction, involving demonstrations followed by reciprocal tutoring, can be used in other subject areas with adult students as well as with children as young as five.

Data on the performance of a sample of 12, six to seven year-old children in peer tutoring settings was collected by the teachers involved to determine whether the children fulfilled their role adequately. The results obtained indicated that the children were highly proficient in correcting each others' errors. A survey of the attitudes of 22 of the children involved suggested that, two children apart, peer tutoring was viewed more positively than other academic activities by participants.

A questionnaire was also used to collect data on the parents' attitudes to peer tutoring and parental involvement. The majority of parents were positive in their response to parental tutoring and many also reported positive attitudes on the part of their children to peer tutoring. An overwhelming majority of parents wished the programme to continue.

The paper reports on the sort of management, training and planning techniques which have been found helpful in setting up teaching programmes which rely on the model of demonstration followed by reciprocal tutoring. Future directions for research are discussed in terms of peer tutoring and time on task, providing feedback for cognitive skills and increasing the range of applications for reciprocal tutoring.

Introduction

Companion Reading (Harrison and Gottfredson, 1983) is a commercial programme of initial reading instruction developed in the USA which incorporates both parental tutoring and peer tutoring (Companion Study) as a means of maximising one-to-one practice. A preliminary evaluation of children's levels of reading achievement before and after involvement in *Companion Reading* has been undertaken in Walsall (Howes et al, 1989) suggesting that gains in reading attainment in the region of one standard deviation are possible even with disadvantaged children who have previously failed to make satisfactory progress.

The aim of this paper is fourfold: first, to provide a brief description of Companion Reading; second, to look at data on childrens' performance in peer tutoring settings together with their and their parents' attitudes to tutoring; third, to describe the techniques which we have found helpful in setting up peer tutoring; and finally to speculate on how similar methods of instruction might be used in other curriculum areas.

Description of Companion Reading

Companion Reading is designed for use with American 'first graders' (6 +) or with older children who have failed in reading. It is designed to supplement, not replace, existing reading schemes, so that children continue to read their own reading book or any reading material which it is within their competence to read. In the present study it has been used over two years with both top infant and first-year junior children. The way *Companion Reading* works can best be appreciated by examining the activity-cycle for a typical lesson.

1 Teacher-led demonstration of selected reading skills
2 Companion study (peer tutoring)
3 Independent study
4 Mastery tests
5 Independent reading
6 The use of 'Share sheets' to keep parents informed of progress and enable them to provide fluency building and review practice.

The function of peer tutoring in this context is to provide immediate practice of the skills the teacher has demonstrated and also review practice of skills which have been introduced earlier. To this end the children are split into pairs and provided with a book of companion study exercises, these exercises also constitute the mastery test for the day's lesson.

The organisation of the peer tutoring component of the lesson also requires some elaboration. At the beginning of the year the teacher assigns companionships on the basis of a rule-of-thumb estimate of the children's performance, pairing the lowest-performing child with highest-performing child, the next highest performer with the next lowest performer and so on, until all the children have been paired up. This is illustrated in Figure 9.1.

During companion study the low-performing child takes the role of 'teacher' first and tests the higher-performing child. This maximises the probability of the lower-performing child receiving a model of correct performance additional to the one provided by the class teacher. The children then swap roles and the higher-performing child takes on the teacher role and tests his or her companion; the upshot is that there is a high probability of the lower performing child receiving a good correction for any errors made. Later in this paper we will provide evidence of the children's level of functioning in this respect.

Finally, under the heading of three positively-phrased rules (guide, check, praise), the children are taught how to guide their companion through the companion study exercise, check and correct errors and also praise correct performance. Our experience has been that children as young as five can master these skills to a very high level of competence.

The criticism which springs to mind about this model is that it may be unfair to high-performing children. However, research conducted by Schenkat (1987) into outcomes following the use of *Companion Reading* suggests that high; medium; and low-performing children significantly outperform matched peers in control groups where this model of instruction is not used.

To assess the degree to which the programme insures that children do not produce an unacceptably high level of errors and also to assess the

Figure 9.1 Rank ordering and assignment of peer tutors

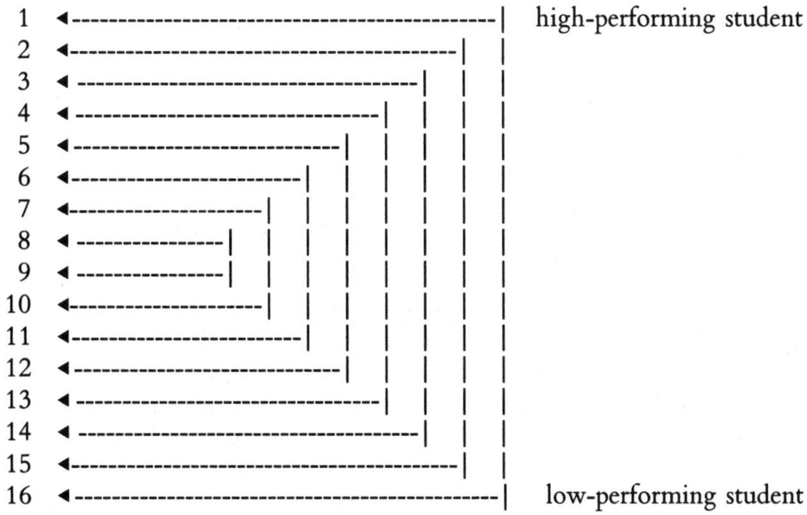

```
 1  ◄---------------------------------------------|   high-performing student
 2  ◄----------------------------------------|  |
 3  ◄ ----------------------------------|  |  |
 4  ◄ -----------------------------|  |  |  |
 5  ◄ ------------------------|  |  |  |  |
 6  ◄-------------------|  |  |  |  |  |
 7  ◄---------------|  |  |  |  |  |  |
 8  ◄ ------------|  |  |  |  |  |  |  |
 9  ◄ ------------|  |  |  |  |  |  |  |
10  ◄-------------|  |  |  |  |  |  |
11  ◄------------------|  |  |  |  |  |
12  ◄-----------------------|  |  |  |  |
13  ◄----------------------------|  |  |  |
14  ◄ ----------------------------------|  |  |
15  ◄-----------------------------------------|  |
16  ◄------------------------------------------------|   low-performing student
```

children's performance when errors are made, six pairs of children were tape-recorded during companion study. Table 9.1 shows the results:

In a similar study involving children at a different school, also using *Companion Study*, Howes et al, 1989, obtained very similar results. Specifically, 87% of all responses were correct during peer tutoring (compared with 89% in the current study) and of the 13% of errors which were made, 67% were corrected appropriately (compared with 11% and 87% respectively). However, it is probably more instructive to look at the tutor's performance when the tutee makes a comparatively large number of errors. In such circumstances it is clearly more critical that the tutor corrects errors than in the situation where the tutee makes perhaps one or two errors only. In Table 9.1 above, subjects 5, 7, 9 and 12 stand out as having made a relatively large number of errors (20% or more); nevertheless, the tutors have not been overwhelmed by this task and have provided 'good' corrections for 37 of the total of 42 errors made (88%).

Table 9.1   Accuracy rates during companion study and percentage of errors corrected by peer tutor

S	Correct	Errors	% Correct	+ Corrections	− Corrections	% + Corrections
1	49	1	98%	1	0	100%
2	48	2	96%	2	0	100%
3	46	4	92%	3	1	75%
4	48	2	96%	1	1	50%
5	38	12	76%	10	2	83%
6	47	3	94%	3	0	100%
7	40	10	80%	9	1	90%
8	49	1	98%	1	0	100%
9	40	10	80%	9	1	90%
10	41	9	82%	7	2	77%
11	48	2	96%	2	0	100%
12	40	10	80%	9	1	90%
$\bar{x}$	44.5	5.5	89%	4.75	0.75	87%

Key
S   — Subject
Correct   — Total number of correct responses
Errors   — Total number of errors
% Correct   — Percentage of all responses that were correct
+ Corrections   — Number of errors corrected appropriately by peer tutor
− Corrections   — Number of errors ignored or inappropriately corrected by
                       peer tutor
% + Corrections — Percentage of errors appropriately corrected

Children's attitudes to peer tutoring

In addition to the children's performance during companion study their attitude to peer tutoring is obviously of interest – in particular whether they like or dislike peer tutoring in contrast to other academic and social activities that they engage in within school.

To explore this area the children where asked to rate how much they did or didn't like the following activities:

- creative writing
- games
- companion study
- art
- playtime

In order to do this, 22 children were seen individually. After a short training session, they were asked to place their finger on the midpoint of the ladder shown in Figure 9.2 and then to move their finger to show whether they really like, like, don't like or really don't like the areas listed above. Table 9.2 shows the results obtained.

To summarise, in order of preference, children reported that their most and least favoured activities were as follows:

1 playtime and companion study (equal first)
2 games
3 art
4 creative writing
5 maths

Being rated equal in popularity to playtime is a creditable achievement for any academic activity. This finding also confirms our view that children seemed to particularly enjoy the peer tutoring component of the lessons and

Figure 9.2

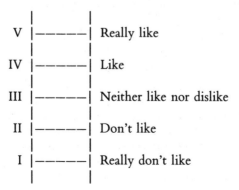

Table 9.2   Children's ratings of preferred activities

Rating				
//////////	Don't like	Neutral	Like	
Activity	I	II	III	IV	V
Writing	6	3	0	8	5
Games	0	3	0	4	15
Maths	4	6	2	6	4
C.Study	0	2	0	5	15
Art	2	4	3	4	9
Playtime	1	1	0	10	10

Key:
I   Really don't like
II   Don't like
III Neither like nor dislike
IV   Like
V   Really like

brought a great deal of commitment to this activity. In particular we are of the opinion that the children spend a very high proportion of their time 'on task' during peer tutoring in comparison to other academic activites. Additionally, children have frequently been observed to use the peer-tutoring skills they have learnt to help one another in other contexts. It is also worth pointing out that the companion study exercise is the mastery test for each lesson. It is understandable that people new to mastery learning may object to its emphasis on regular testing and wonder what effect this might have on childrens' attitudes to the subject being taught. Our view is that mastery testing is essential if children and teachers are to get feedback on increasing levels of competence; giving children the responsibility and status which goes with the tutor role can only add to their feelings of satisfaction at the progress they are making.

An integral part of the programme is the use of parental tutoring at home to provide fluency building and review practice and also to keep the parents informed as to the progress made by their children. A previous study (Howes et al, 1989) found that parents had a significant impact on the children's reading-fluency rates. In the present study, it was decided to look instead at the parents' attitudes to the programme. Therefore parents were asked their views on *Companion Reading* via a questionnaire. The question-naire used was the same as one used for the same purpose in the USA by Schenkat (1987). All of the parents of the 52 children involved in

Companion Reading in two classes (one top-infant class and one first-year junior class) completed and returned the questionnaires. What follows is a summary of the main results.

1 The majority of parents (90%) felt that the share sheets kept them informed of their child's progress in reading.
2 The majority of parents (90%) enjoyed listening to their child read the share sheet provided.
3 The majority of parents (71%) reported that their child was positive regarding the companion with whom they undertook the peer tutoring part of the lesson. In contrast, 17% of the parents reported that they viewed their companion negatively, 10% didn't respond and 2% said their child viewed their companion favourably sometimes.
4 The majority of parents (94%) were in favour of the programme being continued.

Discussion

So far we have dealt solely with results obtained using *Companion Reading* in one school. However, the model underlying this programme is essentially simple and we have found that the same model of demonstration followed by reciprocal tutoring can be used with different subject areas and different age ranges. Two examples from Walsall will suffice to give some idea of the potential range of application. Harris and Bland (1988) report the use of the same model with secondary aged pupils in chemistry lessons, to teach both practical and theoretical skills (using reagents to test substances, writing chemical equations, balancing equations, writing formulae and completing calculations). Typical of the comments made by the authors are that the lessons are of 'a far superior quality' to conventional lessons as a result of the use of reciprocal peer tutoring and that 'previously reluctant students blossomed'. Pitchford and Story (1988) also report the use of this model in providing in-service training for special needs coordinators in the use of structured-teaching formats (Carnine and Silbert, 1979).

From the experience accumulated in Walsall a few conclusions can be drawn regarding the steps which are required if this type of systems is to succeed when unsupported by commercially-produced materials. These are listed below.

1 There needs to be a careful task-analysis of the skills involved to guarantee that the students experience success and a level of correct performance in the region of 70–80% during the peer tutoring part of the lesson.

2   For the same reason, careful consideration needs to be given to how the skills are to be demonstrated to the students by the teacher.

3   High percentages of time-on-task can be expected during peer tutoring, consequently the students get through an awful lot of material. The problem is not getting the students to do enough; rather it is having enough for the students to do. For example Pitchford (1983), in an unpublished study where a class of children tutored each other using a paired reading approach, found that it took between a minute and two minutes for children to complete reading scheme books designed for first-year junior children. Consequently, major problems were experienced as those involved had continually to distribute fresh materials to the class.

4   Without training on correcting errors and the use of praise, children sometimes imitate the very worst they may see in the adults around them. In particular, they may ignore correct performance and deride or ridicule mistakes. Training in tutoring is simple and should on no account be neglected.

5   Activity-analysis (Medland and Vitale, 1984) is a very useful tool in deciding what tutoring behaviours may be required and identifying possible trouble spots. For example Pitchford (op cit) found that without the use of activity-analysis and the positively-phrased rules derived from this ('read together carefully' and 'read together quietly') children would read in unison, but not necessarily the same part of the page or at the same rate; levels of noise were unacceptably high. The introduction of the rules decribed above in conjunction with the contingent use of praise overcame these problems within one lesson.

The aim of activity-analysis is to list those things the student must do for the activity to proceed smoothly and successfully. Once this is done the next step is to identify those behaviours which are either new, complicated, potentially hazardous or have a history of problems. Next the teacher should frame a rule for any parts of the activity which meet the criteria listed above, introduce these rules to the children and use praise which gives feedback to the child when they follow a particular rule. For example, a praise statement designed to encourage children to follow the check rule used in companion study might be as follows: 'Well done Sanjit! You did a great job checking Amy and helping her to get it right.' A typical example of activity analysis is outlined in Figure 9.3.

Up to this point, we have discussed the use of reciprocal peer tutoring without saying precisely what its effects are. One reason for this omission is a simple one; all of the authors are involved essentially in fieldwork research. Under these sorts of conditions, it is simply not possible to conduct research on any large scale which can, for example, make a cost-benefit analysis of peer tutoring in comparison with other means of providing extra practice and the swift correction of errors. On the contrary,

Figure 9.3   Activity analysis: independent group work

Activity	Status
1 Class *select* appropriate reference materials.	/
2 Class *identify* relevant information.	x
3 Class *summarise* relevant information.	x
4 Class *collate* relevant information.	x
5 Class *communicate* relevant information to each other.	x

Key
/   Mastered
x   New, complex, has history of problems or potentially hazardous

In this example the students have already mastered item 1 but items 2, 3, 4 and 5, are all new and relatively complicated to the class. The teacher would therefore use the following rules:

Identify
Summarise
Collate
Communicate

Some rephrasing and amalgamation of categories might be required for younger children in which case the following rules may be preferable:

Choose
List
Tell

our imperative is not experimental rigour so much as that of actually teaching children and ascertaining whether or not the methods involved in peer tutoring are robust enough to be used in the classroom and appealing enough to motivate children. To the extent that we may have demonstrated that children proved competent at peer tutoring, actually appeared to enjoy it, and had communicated this enjoyment to their parents, we will have succeeded in our research.

Nevertheless, our experience in Walsall is such as to suggest some possible lines of future 'pure' research which fall under three main headings: engaged time, providing feedback, and expanding the range of applications.

There is little doubt that the higher the time students spend engaged on a task, the more quickly they will master it (see, for example Bloom, 1984). Even a casual observer cannot fail to be impressed with the high percentage 'time-on-task' that children demonstrate during peer tutoring. Comments to this effect feature frequently in teachers' comments regarding peer tutoring. It would be a relatively simple task to compare peer tutoring with other academic activities to determine which activities lead to the highest proportion of engaged time.

With regard to feedback, the learning of skills and concepts falls into two generic categories: those in which practice inevitably provides feedback and those where it does not (Engelmann and Carnine, 1984). For example, most motor skills provide feedback when they are practised; if the clutch is not depressed properly, the gears 'crunch'; if the toddler doesn't lift his feet correctly when walking, he falls over and gets a bump; if the footballer doesn't make contact with the ball, it won't go into the net. Although skilled tuition and feedback can accelerate the process of learning, nevertheless in all of these instances the environment (the gears, the ground, the ball) gives immediate feedback ('you didn't do it right, try again') and can shape the response so that the learner can discover for him or herself many of the skills and component skills required. The same is not the case when the learner is at the stage of basic acquisition in learning cognitive skills. For the beginning reader who makes a mistake, the environment remains mute and he or she can persist in the error until it becomes habitual. Unfortunately, until the learner has a large number of basic skills (that is, once they can read passages and rely on context to give them feedback and consequently are no longer at the stage of basic acquisition) the book simply doesn't say 'I'm sorry you got that wrong, the word is mat not man, now have another go.' A similar process can be seen to be at work in arithmetic in column addition 'without carrying' when the child adds the tens column first, not the units column first. The exercise book won't tell the child they've made a mistake, nor will the teacher unless alert to the dangers (the answer, if not the process it was arrived by, being very probably correct); but both teacher and child can expect some pretty strange feedback once column addition 'with carrying' is introduced and the child has to unlearn 'bad habits' before he can continue.

The point of this digression is as follows; as we have seen, peer tutors can provide immediate feedback for precisely those cognitive skills which tend not to give the child rapid knowledge of results. This is where its greatest value may lie and this is one area which would repay the application of pure research. In this respect, it is interesting that in one study conducted in Walsall (Edwards et al, 1988) using a time-series design with three subjects where fluency-data was collected, the addition of a peer-tutoring component seemed to lead to a faster reduction in errors than when peer tutoring was not present.

So far we have discussed peer tutoring in contexts where the primary task of the tutor is to test and check his or her colleagues' performance. However, valuable as its contribution in this context is, it is natural to wonder how its use can be extended into other situations. One form of peer tutoring which immediately springs to mind is what can best be described as 'disputation', whereby students debate particular topics or arguments with one another. Analogies are frequently drawn between the task facing the learner and the task facing a scientist (most notably in recent years by Siegfried Engelmann via John Stuart Mill) in deciding between a number of competing hypotheses on the basis of the evidence that can be collected. There is no question that constructive disagreement from colleagues helps scientists arrive at a clearer understanding of the factors which need controlling or manipulating; disputation could serve a similar service in schools for helping children identify important issues where no right or wrong answer may be available or identifying how to proceed to arrive at an answer. Again, this sort of topic would repay further research, particularly since 'disputation' as a means of instruction dates back at least as far as Socrates and has, like peer tutoring, been much neglected of late.

However, to return to where we began, the classroom, the beauty of the model we have described for the class teacher is that, unlike cross-age tutoring, same-age peer tutors are constantly to hand, no special timetabling arrangements are required, and this makes its organisation correspondingly simple. Furthermore, in reciprocal-tutoring, both children enjoy the status and high teacher-expectation which goes with taking the tutor role.

Another important consideration is the degree to which the use of peer tutoring frees the teacher from some of the 'legwork' of more conventional styles of teaching. As we have already seen, tutors can be relied on to correct immediately the majority of errors their peers may make. This in turn reduces the degree to which the teacher needs to be 'on the prowl' searching for children who are floundering and also decreases dramatically the delay between a child needing help and getting it. Consequently, the teacher can target his or her support far more carefully with a view to maximising its impact.

Moreover, contrary to many teachers' doubts when first introduced to the notion of peer tutoring, we have found that children as young as five, given the pre-condition of a minimum of training, become adept at tutoring. Some children of only seven go further and, without specific training, learn complex teaching skills to a level of proficiency which would do credit to professionals. The probability of incidental learning taking place must surely be greatly increased in classes and schools where the children see themselves as skilled contributors to the tasks of instruction and learning.

These children are tommorrow's parents. An important if long-term secondary gain may be an increase in the level of skill they will bring to helping their own children in the future.

Correspondence
Mr M Pitchford, Walsall Education Department Psychological Services, Lime House, Littleton Street West, Walsall, WS2 8EN.

10 Peer tutored Paired Reading: outcome data from ten projects

Keith Topping

In the context of a large-scale dissemination project, ten different peer tutor projects were conducted, and procedures and outcomes are reviewed in this paper. Pre-and post-test data are reported for all studies, while four studies also have baseline data and two studies have comparison group data. Two studies have follow-up data for the short and long-term respectively. The evidence reviewed suggests that peer tutored Paired Reading accelerates children's reading progress, with peer tutors gaining more than tutees.

The deployment of children as tutors for other children has a long history. Allen (1976) notes that it was not until the seventeenth century that the separation of pupils of different ages in educational establishments became common practice. Against this segregative trend, the Bell-Lancaster system was established in England and Wales towards the end of the eighteenth century. The basic feature of Bell's original system was some one-to-one tutoring by other pupils and, in addition, the teaching of entire classes by one older boy with the aid of younger boys as assistants. By 1816 about 100,000 children were said to be receiving education under this system. However, as the state began to provide money for education, the 'Monitorial' system fell into disuse. Related procedures were revived in the United States in the 1960s and interest is again being stimulated in the United Kingdom.

Peer tutoring

Reviews of early efforts in the field are provided by Allen (1976) and Sherman and Harris (1975). In a more recent review, Sharpley and Sharpley (1981) examine 82 peer tutor programmes, according to the characteristics of the participants, the characteristics of the tutoring process and the adequacy of research designs utilised. Sharpley and Sharpley (1981) conclude that recent work supports the claim that both tutors and tutees show attainment gains, and sometimes improve in social behaviour and attitudes to each other and the curriculum area of tutoring also.

The Sharpley review indicates that longer programmes do not yield better absolute gains than shorter programmes, that programmes involving training for the tutors produce better effects, that children who themselves have learning and behaviour problems can benefit from acting as tutors, that socio-economic status of the participants makes no significance difference, that one-to-one tuition can be more effective than small-group tuition, and that age-peer tutor projects are as effective as cross-age tutor projects. Cohen, Kulik and Kulik (1982) have also provided a review, meta-analysing 65 peer tutor programmes, many of them student theses.

Subsequently, Bloom (1984) reviewed the effectiveness of a variety of pedagogic strategies, and concluded that one-to-one tutoring was the only intervention which reliably produced the '2-Sigma' effect, ie the average student taught using this method produced attainment scores two standard deviations above the score of the average control group student taught under conventional group methods of instruction.

In the United Kingdom, interest in peer tutoring has grown in recent years. Goodlad (1979) has described a number of peer tutoring projects. More recently, the deployment of the 'Pause, Prompt, Praise' technique in a peer tutoring format has been described by Wheldall and Mettem (1985) and Wheldall, Merrett and Colmar (1986), and this technique may be expected to be more vigorously disseminated in the near future. A recent review of research from a European perspective, together with guidelines for operating peer tutor projects, can be found in Topping (1987).

Paired reading

This reading tutoring technique for non-professionals is now widely known in the United Kingdom and is becoming known internationally. Originally described by Morgan (1976) and Morgan and Lyon (1979), the use of the technique in action has been more fully outlined in Topping and Wolfendale (1985) and Topping (1986a).

As its simplest, the technique involves two phases. Children are allowed to choose their own books or other reading material at any level of readability within the competence of the tutor. Project coordinators may control readability to an overall ceiling reflecting the ability of the tutors, or teach the tutoring pair readability checking strategies, or both. On sections of text which are difficult for the tutee, both tutor and tutee read out loud together. The tutor adjusts to the tutee's natural reading speed and synchrony is established with practice. When the tutee makes an error the tutor repeats the word correctly and requires the tutee to do likewise before proceeding.

If the tutee refuses a word or struggles unsuccessfully with it for more than five seconds the tutor intervenes and supplies the word. Praise for correct reading at very regular intervals and for specified reading behaviours is emphasised throughout. When the tutee has selected an easier text which is more within the tutee's independent readability level, the tutee can choose to silence the tutor by a pre-arranged non-verbal signal. When the tutor becomes silent, the tutee continues to read aloud, until there is a failure to read a word correctly within five seconds, at which point the tutor corrects the error and the pair *resume reading together* (see Appendix).

The use of Paired Reading as a peer tutor technique was first reported by Winter and Low (1984) and further work is reported in Crombie and Low (1986). A small study is also reported from New Zealand by Limbrick, McNaughton and Glynn (1985), using a variant of the original technique. Encouraging results are reported in all three papers. Several further reports of peer tutored Paired Reading projects are available in the *Paired Reading Bulletins*.

The projects reported below were mounted in the context of a large scale Authority-wide Paired Reading dissemination exercise. Between 1984 and 1986 this had involved the running of 185 individual projects, most of which used trained parents as reading tutors, although a minority utilised adult volunteer, teacher volunteer or peer tutors. By the end of 1987, these projects had involved over 2750 children, and of these, norm-referenced data is available for 2370. At a time when many distractions in the teaching profession inhibited the involvement of parents as tutors, interest in peer tutoring has grown in the schools.

It should be emphasised that the purpose of the present paper is to review briefly ten projects in which peer tutoring employing the Paired Reading method was used. No claim is being made that these studies are truly experimental but they are demonstrations of effectiveness carried out in the real world of teaching and learning. Educational rather than statistical significance is what is being sought in these studies, which were carried out in a variety of situations with a minimum of central control and direction.

Method

All ten projects were operated by ordinary class teachers who were allocated no extra time for the purpose and received only minimal support from external sources. The projects themselves were thus very various in training methods, in monitoring of tutoring process and in evaluation design and method. However, in almost all cases training was carried out in groups by verbal instruction (and in some cases written instruction), demonstration of the tutoring behaviours, and supervised practice with feedback.

The age of the tutees ranged from eight years to 14 years and the age of the tutors from eight years to 18 years. A full range of socio-economic

Table 10.1 Outcome data from ten peer tutor projects

				Project details						Baseline data		Pre-post data					
												Mean pre-test reading age (years and months)		Mean gain (months)		Ratio gain*	
Project Number	n	Tutee age (yrs)	Tutor age (yrs)	Test used	Project period (wks)	Pre-post test period (wks)	Baseline test period (wks)	Follow-up test period (wks)	Data Subject	Mean gain (months)	Ratio gain*	Accuracy	Comprehension	Acc.	Comp.	Acc.	Comp.
1	5	8–9	10–12	Daniels Diack 1	5	22			Tutees			5:07.4			10.4		2.1
2	4	8	8	Neale	9	10			Tutees			7:03.3	7:00.3	3.2	4.2	1.4	1.8
	4			Neale		10			Tutors			10:05.8	10:08.0	3.7	8.0	1.6	3.5
3	23	11–13	16	Neale	6	8		12	Tutees			9:00.3	9:01.0	12.0	12.7	6.5	6.9
4	34	7–8	9–10	Primary Reading Test	10	10	43		Tutors	6.4	0.6		7:07.0		4.0		1.7
	35					10			Tutees				10:05.0		9.7		4.2
5	14	11–14	11–14	Schonell	5	7	13		Tutees	2.7	0.9		8:07.3		5.6		3.5
6	22	11–14	11–14	Schonell	5	7	13		Tutees	5.0	1.7		9:02.2		3.6		2.3
7	18	10	10	Burt	9	26	26		Tutees	1.5	0.3		9:00.7		8.5		1.4
	19			Burt		26	26		Tutors	4.4	0.7		12:06.0		4.8		0.8
	18			Daniels Diack 12		9			Tutees				8:05.3		12.0		5.7
	19			Daniels Diack 12		9			Tutors				10:05.1		8.8		4.2
8	12	11	11	Widespan	8	8			Tutees				10:10.0		7.7		3.9
	12			Widespan		8			Tutors				12:06.0		13.5		6.9
9	6	7–8	7–8	Neale	8	8			Tutees			8:04.8	8:00.0	10.5	9.5	5.7	5.1
	8			Neale		8			Tutors			10:00.9	9:11.8	14.0	12.5	7.6	6.8
10	13	11–12	16–17	Daniels Diack 12	15	20		52	Tutees				7:09.8		14.3		3.1

* Ratio gains = ratio of reading age gain to real time passed between testings.
Fuller details of the data are available on request from the author

Table 10.1 contd.

Project Number	Type of group	n	Comparison or control group data						Follow-up data			
			Mean pre-test reading age (years and months)		Mean gain (months)		Ratio gain*		Mean gain (months)		Ratio gain*	
			Acc.	Comp.	Acc.	Comp.	Acc.	Comp.	Acc.	Comp.	Acc.	Comp.
1												
2												
3										1.3	1.5	0.5	0.5
4												
5												
6												
7												
8												
9	Parent tutored	7	8:00.6	7:11.4	9.7	12.3	5.4	6.8				
	Teacher tutored	9	8:06.8	8:01.0	3.8	8.4	2.1	4.0				
10	Control group	29	10:03.7			8.8		1.9		6.4		0.5
	Control Group									8.2		0.7

status was represented in the projects. In seven of the ten projects, the tutees were retarded in reading by up to four years. The other projects were mixed ability projects in areas of above average socio-economic status.

It is important to note that these ten projects were the first of their kind operated consecutively in one local authority. Thus, they were carried out when the local experience of this kind of service delivery was by definition small, and this may be reflected in the results. In addition, the ten projects ran consecutively and the results presented in Table 10.1 are completely unselected, in contrast to many research reports (where the higher probability of publication of positive and statistically significant results encourages pre-selection by authors).

Process evaluation

The research into Paired Reading, whether peer tutored or not, has been unlike research into the pause, prompt, praise technique in that it has focused very little on process in terms of maintenance of tutoring behaviours and has been preoccupied almost wholly with product or outcome. In these projects, in many cases there was direct observation of the tutoring by a coordinating teacher, arrangements for self-referral of tutor pairs with problems and a form of self-recording which incorporated subsequent checking of records by the coordinator. In many cases there were also group and individual discussions with tutor pairs to review the operation of the project. However, very rarely was this information collected in a structured way which was amenable to subsequent analysis. Further details of some of these projects will be found in Bruce (1986), Cawood and Lee (1985), Free, Harris, Martin, Morris and Topping (1985), Gale and Kendall (1985), Lee (1986) and Townsend and Topping (1986).

Outcome measures

All the projects incorporated a reading test in their evaluation, but the sophistication of the research design varied considerably. However, baseline, comparison group and follow-up data are available in some cases. Seven different reading tests were used, all of which have been criticised on one count or another, not least with reference to the question of to what extent a formal reading test can hope to measure 'real' reading in a more natural environment.

The Neale Test (Neale, 1966) has been criticised for being very dated, for low inter-form reliability and for the biasing structure of its scoring system, particularly on the Comprehension scale. The Daniels and Diack Tests (Daniels and Diack, 1985) have been criticised for the lack of available information about their standardisation, whilst Test number 12 demonstrates a marked ceiling affect. Word recognition tests would appear to have particularly low validity for the assessment of the effects of a programme which emphasises reading fluently from continuous meaningful prose and their susceptibility to practice effects is well known.

The 'experimental' period for many of these projects was between five and ten weeks, and the validity and reliability of using reading tests to measure meaningful gains in reading ability over such short periods of time is questionable. Thus, the results from these ten projects are considered as a whole, since their combined significance is likely to be greater than their individual import.

In the wider dissemination project employing parent tutors, the subjective views of the child, parent and class teacher participants have been gathered by structured questionnaire (see Topping, 1986b, for details), data of this kind from the peer tutor projects are accumulating (Topping and Whiteley, 1990). There is a great deal of anecdotal evidence of interest and enjoyment on the part of tutors and tutees alike.

Results

The first two projects were small scale and used simple pre-post research designs. Outcomes were modest but encouraging, indicating that tutors as young as eight years of age could be effective using the Paired Reading technique.

Project 1

This project involved cross-age tutoring of five eight to nine year olds by 10 to 12 year olds. Three of the tutees were Asian, and two were non-readers at pre-test. Project length was five weeks, but the inter-test period was 22 weeks. Daniels and Diack Test 1 was carried out on the tutees, who gained in reading skill during the project at approximately twice 'normal' rates (see Table 10.1 for further details).

Project 2

This project involved age-peer tutoring with eight year olds. The four tutees had reading difficulties. The project length was nine weeks and the inter-test period ten weeks. The Neale Test showed that tutees gained in reading skill at a little more than 'normal' rates in accuracy and comprehension. The tutors gained at a little more than 'normal' rates in reading accuracy but at 3.5 times 'normal' rates in comprehension.

Project 3

This project was a very brief cross-age tutor project in which fifth form pupils who were shortly to leave school (or had already officially left) served as tutors for children from the Remedial Department in a High School. An external evaluator was used for this project. The unfamiliarity of this person to the children combined with the fact that Form A of the Neale Test was used for both pre-and post-testing (owing to doubts about inter-reliability of forms) may imply that a degree of practice effect is involved in the very large gains evident. Because of this uncertainty, a three month follow-up assessment was conducted, again by the same tester, after the long Summer holiday during which little reading ability gain would usually be expected, using a different form.

During the project 23 11 to 13 year olds were tutored by a small number of 16 year olds. The project length was six weeks and the inter-test period eight weeks. Neale test results on the tutees showed that during the project they gained at 6.5 times 'normal' rates in reading accuracy and at almost seven times 'normal' rates in comprehension.

At 12 week follow-up however, during which time tutoring had ceased over the long Summer holiday, progress decelerated sharply to less than normal rates. This indicated that while the post-test results appeared to be reliable, continued acceleration did not occur after the peer tutoring had ended.

Project 4

This project involved cross-age tutoring in the junior department of a primary school, in which 35 nine- to ten-year-old third-year pupils tutored 34 seven- to eight-year old first-year pupils. All the pupils in one third-year and one first-year class were involved, half the tutor pairs operating in one classroom and half in the other. The catchment area was of above average socio-economic status and the classes were mixed ability for this area. The project length was ten weeks, pre-post inter-test period was ten weeks and the baseline period 43 weeks. The Primary Reading Test (a group administered measure) was used in parallel forms, baselined for the tutors only. During the project, tutees gained in reading skill at 1.7 times 'normal' rates while tutors gained at over four times 'normal' rates. The tutors gained in reading skill very much more during the project than they did during the baseline period.

Project 5

This project involved age-peer tutoring with 11 to 14 year olds, in which both the tutors and tutees were drawn from the remedial department of a high school. The project length was five weeks, the inter-test period was seven weeks and the baseline period 13 weeks. During the project, tutees gained in reading skill at 3.5 times 'normal' rates, gaining much more rapidly during the project than during the baseline period.

Project 6

This project was a repeat of project 5, separated from it by a second baseline period when only normal class teaching was occurring. A number of the tutees participated in both projects. During project 6 the tutees gained in reading skill at more than twice 'normal' rates, but this represented only a slight acceleration over the baseline period, during which progress rates were well above 'normal'. This may reflect the involvement of some tutees in both projects. Unfortunately, no data on the progress of the tutors is available. However, these projects demonstrate the organisational feasilibity of deploying the peer tutoring technique on a large scale within a high school remedial department.

Project 7

This project involved a whole class of third-year junior children (ten year olds) of mixed ability in an area of relatively high socio-economic status. The results illustrate the doubtful inter-reliability of different reading tests. The project period was nine weeks, the pre-post inter-test period six months on the Burt Word Recognition Test and two months on the Daniels and Diack Test. The baseline period on the Burt Test only was six months.

On the Burt test, during the project the tutees gained in reading skill at slightly more than 'normal' rates and the tutors at slightly less than 'normal' rates. For the tutees, this represented a substantial acceleration over baseline rates of gain. However, on the Daniels and Diack test, during the project the tutors gained in reading skill at over four times 'normal' rates and the tutees at well over five times 'normal' rates.

In view of the substantial gains made by the tutors on the group test, even though this test has a marked ceiling effect for more able readers at this age, it is difficult to explain this result in terms which do not cast doubt on the validity of word recognition tests for measuring gains in the reading ability of able ten-year-old readers. The subjective impressions of this project were that it was particularly successful.

Project 8

This project was similar in organisation to project 7, but operated in a smaller class of 11-year-old fourth-year junior children. The project period was eight weeks, and inter-test period 8.5 weeks. Results on the Widespan (group) test in parallel forms showed that during the project period the tutees gained in reading skill at approximately four times 'normal' rates.

Project 9

This project had interesting additonal features. In a class of eight year olds, the eight most able readers were designated as tutors, while a half of the class were designated either as peer tutees or as children to receive parent tutoring at home, according to parent preference. The other quarter of the class formed the comparison group which received daily reading practice from the classteacher and access to a special, highly-motivating collection of books.

The project length and inter-test period were eight weeks. During the project, the parent-tutored children gained in reading skill at over five times 'normal' rates in reading accuracy and almost seven times 'normal' rates in comprehension. The peer tutees performed similarly in reading accuracy, but less well in comprehension, nevertheless gaining at five times 'normal' rates. However, the peer tutors showed the highest gains, of almost eight times 'normal' rates in accuracy and as well as the parent-tutored children in comprehension. The children receiving only teacher tuition with extra reading stimulation gained at higher than 'normal' rates, but did not do as well as any of the other groups on either accuracy or comprehension.

Project 10

This project involved cross-age tutoring of 11 to 12-year-old first-year children with reading difficulties in a high school by 16–17-year-old sixth form pupils. The project length was 15 weeks, the inter-test period 20 weeks and long-term follow-up data were gathered one year later. Results on Daniels and Diack Test 12 for the tutees and a comparison group of children with lesser reading difficulty showed that during the project the tutees gained in reading skill at three times 'normal' rates, while the comparison group gained at almost twice 'normal' rates.

At follow up 12 months later, the rate of gain had slowed markedly for both groups, although this may reflect test artifacts attributable to the structure of the measure. From pre- to post-test, the tutees gained eight points in raw score compared to two points in the comparison group, while at follow-up the tutees had gained a further three points compared to the comparison group's one.

Of interest with respect to project 10 is the qualitative assessment carried out in parallel by the project coordinators. At pre-test, post-test and follow up tutees were audio recorded reading two one hundred word samples of text drawn from everyday curriculum materials. The tapes were analysed according to total errors produced, number of refusals, number of self corrections and number of errors contextually originated (see Table 10.2). Reading rate was also calculated. The proportion of errors made by the tutees declined from pre- to post-test and had declined further at follow up one year later, although the presentation of a new, harder text elicited a higher error rate on that. The tutees' proportion of refusals declined markedly over this period, while the proportion of self-corrections increased markedly, and the introduction of the new harder text elicited

Table 10.2 Project 10: Qualitative shifts in reading behaviour

	Mean performance of tutees on reading analysis factors on various texts			
	A1 + B1	A2 + B2	B3	B3 + C
Errors as % of whole text	8.40	5.17	4.00	8.00
Refusals as % of total errors	27.46	15.85	6.15	12.46
Errors self corrected as % of total errors	19.67	27.85	45.92	34.27
Errors of contextual origin as % of total errors	27.27	34.13	54.69	47.27
Reading rate (words per minute)	66.27	74.00	86.23	77.20

Text passage A and the harder passage B were administered at pre-test (1) and post-test (2). At follow-up (3), passage A was not re-administered, being considered too easy for the pupils, but a much harder new passage (C) was administered. *Inter alia,* the table shows changed reading style generalising to text C. Complete data on only 13 tutees owing to sample attrition, although there is no evidence that this biased the results.

only moderate regression in these parameters of competent reading. Likewise, the proportion of errors of contextual origin showed steady improvement, which was maintained at follow up. The tutees' speed of reading also increased. Thus the use of peer tutored Paired Reading appear to have fundamentally changed the reading style of many tutees and these changes were sustained at follow up one year later even though no tutoring had occurred in the meantime.

Discussion

There is considerable evidence here to suggest that peer-tutored Paired Reading has substantial promise, although detailed information about tutoring behaviour during projects is lacking and the outcome data from these projects is expressed in such different ways that it is difficult to combine or meta-analyse.

Doubts about the reliability, validity and comparability of the reading tests used in these projects are substantial. However, it is well accepted by evaluators that it is considerably more difficult to demonstrate positive results on norm-referenced tests than on criterion-referenced measures or more subjective indicators of consumer satisfaction. It can be argued that the apparent irrelevance of some reading tests to the real processes of naturalistic reading is in fact a strength, in that they represent a stringent test of generalisation. Furthermore, the approach adopted here of citing gain scores in relation to real time passed has been rightly criticised by

Pumfrey (1987), who points out that a gain of six months on a reading age of seven years is not the same as a similar gain on a reading age of 11 years.

However, to give an approximate indication of overall trends, the mean ratio gains for all pre-post observations on all tests may be worth noting (see Table 10.3). This indicates that during projects, both tutors and tutees gained in reading skill at approximately four times 'normal' rates. In those projects which involved testing the reading progress of both tutors and tutees (mostly age-peer rather than cross-age projects), tutors clearly gained more than tutees on average. Tutees in cross-age projects thus appear to tend to gain more in reading skills than tutees in age-peer projects, although the latter do of course afford a double benefit.

Many other educational initiatives have reported simple pre-post gains which have subsequently not been substantiated by studies utilising better research designs. However, in the case of peer-tutored Paired Reading, the four projects incorporating baseline periods have yielded very encouraging data on four out of five data sets. In the two projects incorporating control or comparison group data, the results are equally encouraging, although given the small numbers involved in some of the project groups, the outcomes are likely to prove of greater educational than statistical significance.

The follow-up data is much more mixed. This is usual in educational research, but in the context of peer tutored Paired Reading projects which are typically of short duration we have to ask to what extent it is realistic to expect gains to endure in the longer term. While the follow-up results cited here do not indicate continued acceleration beyond the end of the project period, nevertheless it is encouraging that there are relatively few signs of 'wash-out' of experimental effects. Furthermore, the long term follow-up data of a qualitative nature are much more encouraging.

The evidence cited here would appear to merit the dissemination of peer-tutored Paired Reading on a wider basis. Indeed, many more such

Table 10.3   Mean pre-post ratio gains, all projects

	Data sets	Participants	Weighted mean of mean ratio gains
Tutors	8	109	4.25
All Tutees	14	202	3.81
Tutees in projects where tutors also tested	8	102	3.05

Means of pre-post mean ratio gains are given for all projects combined, irrespective of test used and including both accuracy and comprehension ratio gains, weighted by the number of project participants.

projects have subsequently been operated in the local authority which supported the ten projects reported here, although not all these were evaluated.

Further research should utilise fewer norm-referenced reading tests, conforming to modern standards of content and stability, validity and reliability. Much more detailed analysis of the process of peer tutoring using the Paired Reading technique is required, particularly fine grain analysis of tutoring behaviours, but this kind of research is labour intensive and practising teachers may be unable to find the requisite time. Further work is needed on gathering the subjective perceptions of project participants in a structured manner which renders them susceptible to analysis, and this data then can be related to purportedly 'objective' outcomes. Perhaps most crucially, the gathering of further long-term follow-up data will be invaluable and in this context the qualitative analysis of pupil reponse to naturalistic texts offers a productive way forward.

NOTE
The Paired Reading Bulletins are available internationally on inter-library loan or microfiche, or may be purchased from the following address:
Paired Learning Project
Psychological Service
Kirklees Metropolitan Council
Oastler Centre
103 New Street
Huddersfield HD1 2VA
West Yorkshire, England

Correspondence
Keith Topping, Director: Paired Learning Project (address as above)

Appendix: Paired Reading Procedure

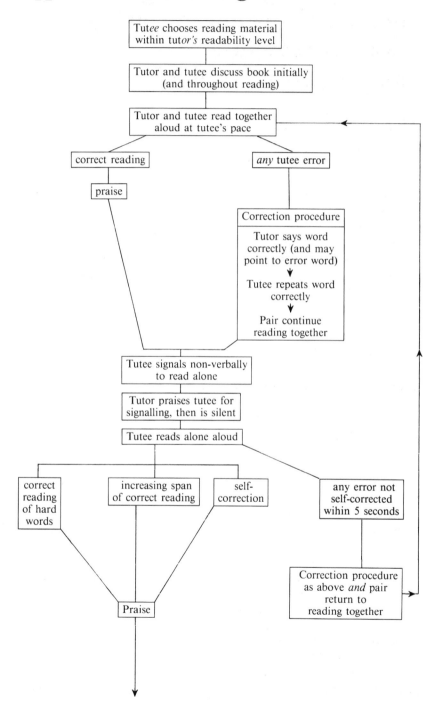

11 Cross-age tutoring – a controlled evaluation using poor readers in a comprehensive school

Mary Kennedy

This chapter reports a controlled evaluation of peer tutoring in a British secondary school using low achievers in the fourth and fifth form to tutor reading comprehension to low achievers in the first and second year. Tutoring produced significant reading attainment gains in tutors. There was no evidence that the reading attainment of tutees was affected by tutoring. Qualitative information about the programme is presented. The political implications of introducing a tutoring scheme are also discussed.

Introduction

There is evidence that educationalists have used students to tutor other students since the Spartan times of the eighth century BC (King 1982). In the eighteenth century AD, the Monitorial System of Bell (1797a) and Lancaster (1803) developed. In the twentieth century, particularly in the United States, a plethora of 'peer' and 'cross-age' tutoring programmes emerged. Anecdotal reports on these schemes cite improved attainment, self-esteem, behaviour, attitude to school, understanding of the difficulties facing school teachers and confidence to communicate amongst the benefits attributable to them (see, for example, review by the Center for the Study of Evaluation, Los Angeles 1978). Most of the published controlled studies of the effects of tutoring find that both tutors and tutees make attainment gains (Cohen, Kulik and Kulik, 1982). There are, however, methodological failings in many of these studies; these include comparing voluteer tutors with non-volunteer controls and/or trained tutors with untrained controls and subsequently deducing that improvements among tutors are produced by tutoring rather than the confounding effects of training or volunteer status (see reviews by Feldman, Devin-Sheehan and Allen 1976; and Kennedy 1985).

There have been a few controlled studies of cross-age tutoring programmes in British secondary schools. Fitz-Gibbon (1981), for example, conducted a controlled evaluation of the effects on randomly-selected 'low-achieving' and 'average' 14 year olds of a two-week period of tutoring 'fractions' to mixed-ability nine and ten year olds. She found that in one school class the attainment of tutors significantly exceeded that of pupils receiving 'normal classroom instruction', yet in another it did not. Several of the North American programmes that have produced attainment gains in the tutor used low-achieving teenagers from areas of social deprivation in this role (see, for example, Cloward, 1976).

In the comprehensive school used for the present study, there were a number of 14- to 16-year-old fourth- and fifth-form pupils who, despite years of extra tuition, fell a long way short of functional literacy. Their reading comprehension was particularly poor. Many of these pupils were frequent truants and behaved badly when they did attend. The school is located in an area of high unemployment, motivation being one of the hardest problems for the school staff. A controlled pilot-experiment in cross-age tutoring was, therefore, initiated. The major objective of the programme was to improve the reading comprehension of the fourth- and fifth- formers previously described. The scheme would also give first- and second-year pupils with low reading attainment some additional practice in reading and comprehension and provide them with experience of social interaction with older pupils. The programme minimised the input from the supervising teacher so that, if successful, it could readily be adopted as school practice.

Pupils

The school has five year levels: from 11-year-old first-formers to 16-year-old fifth-formers. Initially, the sample of 52 was made up of 13 pupils drawn from each of the first-, second-, fourth- and fifth-year groups. These pupils were selected because they had the lowest reading attainment within their year. Other factors, such as behaviour and temperament, were not taken into account. Fifteen pupils were absent for more than two experimental sessions and were excluded from the final analysis. The scores of 15 fourth- and fifth-formers (three female, 13 male) were used in the analysis of the effects of tutoring on the tutors. Twenty-two first- and second-year pupils (seven female, 15 male) were used in the analysis of the effects on the tutees. The fourth- and fifth-formers had a mean pre-test score of 17.6 on the NFER 'DE'/group reading test; the first- and second-formers had a mean pre-test score of 15.2 on the NFER 'BD' test.

Design and analysis

Experimental and control groups were formed through random allocation. Pupils had their attainment measured before and after the tutoring programme. The attainment gains of tutors were compared to those of their controls in a separate analysis from the one comparing tutees with their controls. Both analyses comprised two-factor mixed-ANOVAs with two independent levels (experimental tutor or tutee vs control) and two related levels (pre-test vs post-test). Repeated measures taken on independent groups of subjects were analysed because the more common practice of working directly with the incremental changes in scores can yield spurious findings (Nunally, 1975).

Measures (dependent variables)

Reading comprehension was measured at pre-test and post-test using NFER group reading tests: 'DE' for fourth- and fifth-formers and 'BD' for first- and second-formers. These measures were used because they could be administered within the time available and they have reasonable psychometric characteristics. Analysis and interpretation has been confined to the raw scores because many of the pupils fell below the range for which standardised scores are currently available. The possibility of developing a measure especially suited to this particular study was considered and, following Klaus 1975, rejected because it would be a highly resource-intensive process likely to produce an idiosyncratic test.

Method

Eleven 20-minute sessions were held for just under four weeks (ie three sessions a week) in an unused room during 'registration period'. Throughout the programme, intervention by the supervising teacher was minimal. At the first session, tutees chose their own books from a selection of reading books designed for readers in this age-group with low reading attainment. They were then introduced to the tutor to whom they had been randomly allocated. Each tutee was told that, during these sessions, the tutor would help her/him to read the book. Tutors were told that the tutees had particular difficulty understanding what they read and were asked to question them at the end of every couple of pages – or as they thought necessary. They were also asked to write a report on their tutee at the end of every session stating the page and book that they were on and how well they had perfomed. Tutors were to help tutees change their reading book if they felt the one chosen was too difficult. In subsequent sessions, tutors managed the tutees' progress without intervention or direction from the supervising teacher; she simply re-allocated pupils whose partner was absent, made sure reading books and report sheets were available and answered tutors' questions regarding how to pronounce 'difficult' words.

Questions regarding how to direct the tutees' progress were treated in a non-directive manner – the tutors made these decisions. At the end of each session the supervising teacher read each tutor's report and briefly discussed their tutee's progress with them.

The pupils in the control groups were told that there were not enough people available to partner them on this occasion but that 'next time they could have a go'. They spent the duration of the tutoring sessions in 'registration period' during which they were involved in a programme of discussion work and school-assembly preparation.

Group tests of reading-attainment were administered before and after the 11 tutoring sessions. Within each year group, experimental and control group subjects were tested together.

Results

The NFER DE score of tutors increased by an average of approximately 6.5 points (from a mean of 16.17 at pre-test to 22.67 at post-test); the control group did not increase at all (pre-test mean of 18.56 and a post-test mean of 17.56). The analysis of variance shows that the tutors increased their score significantly more than the control group by revealing a significant interaction between the effects of treatment and the test session (F = 5.70; df = 1,13; p≤0.05) – see Figure 11.1. There was no significant difference in the scores of tutors and controls at pre-test.

Figure 11.1 Reading comprehension mean scores

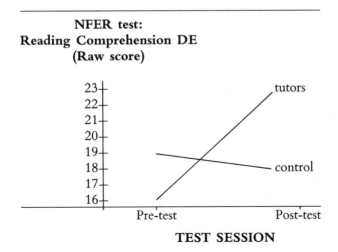

NFER test:
Reading Comprehension DE
(Raw score)

TEST SESSION

There was no evidence of any significant difference in the increase in score of tutees and their controls. There was, however, a highly significant increase when both groups were considered together: the mean score on the NFER BD increased from 13.96 at pre-test to 17.88 by the end of the programme ($F = 27.56$; $df = 1,20$; $p \leq 0.01$). There was no significant difference in the pre-test scores of tutees and their controls.

A less formal evaluation of other aspects of the scheme was also made. When asked individually at the end of the programme, all participants –except for one tutee – said that they would like to continue with the work. In an unstructured interview participants were encouraged to think of ways in which they might change the programme; the majority could think of no modifications but four pupils said that they would like to do it more often and a further three pupils said that they would like to do more 'different things': spelling, 'maths', 'English workcards' and reading games were among the suggestions. These observations supported the supervising teacher's impression that, if activities were not soon varied, enthusiasm would wane. The pupils' enthusiasm for the scheme was overwhelmingly demonstrated by the absence of discipline-problems and the tutor's total concentration on their teaching job.

Discussion

Support for the introduction of this type of tutoring scheme is provided by the discovery that, after only four weeks, the reading comprehension attained by low-achieving, non-examinee fourth- and fifth-formers who tutored exceeded that of a similar group who did not tutor. It was also found that the attainment of tutees was not slowed down by being tutored by older pupils with poor reading ability. Almost all the participants enjoyed the tutoring programme and expressed a wish to continue with it. It is worth noting, however, that some tutoring programmes do not produce attainment-gains in tutors (Kennedy, 1985; Ramig and Ramig, 1976; Page, 1975) and the causes of success and failure are unknown. In the present study, the 'learning-by-teaching' exhibited among tutors may have been influenced by any of the following factors:

1   The topic tutored (reading comprehension) was the one in which attainment gains were made – attainment gains may be confined to the topic tutored.

2   Tutoring sessions were held in a special room in which everyone was in a tutoring dyad – the results may not generalise to tutors used as classroom aides.

3   Tutors did not select their own tutees – pairing of tutor and tutee

according to pre-existing friendship may prevent attainment gains amongst tutors.

4   The tutor's role as teacher was emphasised by requiring them to keep records of their tutee's performance each session, giving them disciplinary responsibilty for their tutee and not appearing to closely monitor their activities; Allen and Feldman (1973) predict that these procedures will 'increase the likelihood of behavioural and attitudinal changes consistent with expectations for the role of teacher' (p 115); attainment-gains might not be produced if the tutor's role as teacher was not emphasised in these ways.

Any variation in the methods used in the present study requires thorough monitoring as it might prevent attainment-gains.

The first- and second-year pupils were distinguished from the fourth- and fifth-formers in that only the former group received intensive individual remediation of their reading skills on a daily basis. It is likely that this factor, compounded by the effects of repeated testing with the same measure, caused the highly significant increase in score of the younger subjects. This increase may have masked the effects of treatment. There is no question, however, that the tutoring programme provided the tutees with extra reading practice and encouraged them to communicate with older pupils. Furthermore, all but one tutee (the most able reader) said that they enjoyed being tutored and would like to carry on with it.

The present study was not designed to establish the mechanism through which attainment gains are achieved. However, since tutor and control groups were formed through random assignment, it can be deduced that the greater attainment of tutors is unlikely to have been produced by any qualitative difference between them and the controls. If allocation to tutor and control groups had been made on a differential basis (eg because pupils did/did not volunteer to tutor or because their teachers did/did not consider them suitable) this deduction could not be made. (Random allocation between tutor and control groups also maximises the possibility that the results of the present study will apply generally.) Since, in the present study, tutors were compared with a control group who attended 'form period' during tutoring sessions, it is possible that the tutors' attainment-gains resulted from an increase in the time for which they were engaged in reading. This contention is supported by the observation that the tutors were *fully and actively engaged* in reading text and reviewing its meaning throughout each tutoring session. Previous workers have drawn a distinction between 'engaged-time' and 'exposure-time' (eg Bloom, 1980) the former being more closely related to attainment gains than the latter. Reading attainment among low-achieving 14 to 16 year olds who tutor reading may be caused by an increased amount of 'engaged-time' spent studying text as compared to that produced by the more conventional remedial techniques to which they have been subjected previously. This possibility was not tested in the present study but deserves further investigation. In an earlier study (Kennedy, 1985), it was found that eight- to nine-year-old mixed-ability junior-school pupils who tutored peers to learn multiplication 'tables' were actively engaged in their task for significantly longer than a similar group instructed to learn the 'tables' by themselves.

The introduction of 'non-professional' school students as aides can be politically sensitive in the same way as schemes that involve parents. These issues are countered at a fundamental level by programmes, such as the present one, that aim to benefit both the tutor and the tutee. Furthermore, although it is not particularly time-consuming, the role of the supervising teacher is extremely important. In the present study, for example, one second-year girl wept for two sessions and would not speak because she had been assigned a male tutor and one fourth-year boy was mercilessly bullied by a gang of first-year boys in the playground because he had reprimanded his tutee for misreading a word in a tutoring session. Such extreme reactions will not be uncommon among pupils requiring learning support. The supervising teacher must deal with these situations without in any way diminishing the position of the tutor so that the likelihood of beneficial changes is not reduced. It is also the supervising teacher's responsibility to vary the tutoring activities to ensure that participants do not get bored: this should also be done without diminishing the tutor's role as 'teacher'.

Conclusions

Low-attaining 14- to 16-year olds who tutored the reading-comprehension of low-attaining 11- and 12-year-olds significantly improved their own reading comprehension and did not adversely affect that of their tutees. Participants worked hard and behaved well during tutoring sessions despite very little intervention by the supervising teacher. Social interaction outside the peer group was facilitated. Almost all participants expressed a wish to continue with the scheme. It is therefore recommended that cross-age tutoring be adopted into the repertoire of educational techniques used for children with special educational needs. Such schemes must, however, be monitored objectively because there is evidence that some schemes do not produce attainment gains amongst the participants. The present study demonstrates the feasibility of controlled evaluation within a single school – the generality of findings being maximised by random allocation between comparison groups.

Acknowledgements
The assistance of Mr Benard Tong is gratefully acknowledged.

Correspondence
Dr MH Kennedy, Northern College of Education, Hilton Place, Aberdeen, AB9 1FA.

12 Special education students as tutors: a review and analysis

Russell T Osguthorpe and Thomas E Scruggs

Qui docet Discet *(one who teaches learns)*
Learning is a social act *(Meiklejohn, 1882)*

Although accounts of cross-age and peer tutoring date back to the first century AD, only recently have special educators begun to investigate its effects with handicapped students. The purpose of the present article is to synthesise the results of these investigations, emphasising the effects of tutoring on the academic and personal/social skills of both tutors and tutees. In general, research has shown that handicapped and remedial students can be trained to tutor both peers and younger students in a variety of content areas. Results further show that academic and personal/social benefits come to special education students, as well as to those they tutor, although the data regarding academic achievement is more convincing than the data regarding changes in general self-esteem. Following the summary of results of tutoring, implications for instruction are discussed, and suggestions are given for improving the quality of future tutoring research.

Introduction

Tutoring is one of the oldest forms of instruction known to society. As early as the first century AD, Quintilian, in his *Institutio Oratoria,* described instructional settings where older children were tutoring younger children. Between the years of 1530 and 1550, additional accounts are given of tutoring programmes initiated in Germany and by the Spanish Jesuits in the College of Lisbon (Paolitto, 1976). These programmes emphasised the benefits that accrue to the tutors as well as to the tutees. Student monitors, teaching 10 students in a classroom, became a popular instructional approach in these early years.

In 1797, Andrew Bell, a Scotsman, developed one of the first exportable tutoring systems (Bell 1797). Bell had been asked by the British government to establish a school for orphans in Madras, India. Since Bell was not a professional educator, he broke from traditional patterns of British schools and created an elaborate educational system that was based on older students tutoring younger students. As the programme matured, Bell noted that classroom behaviour problems decreased, and that student academic progress accelerated. After Bell published his first account of the programme in 1797, Joseph Lancaster, a British educator, was intrigued by the system and began to disseminate it throughout the British Isles and France (Le Compte de Laborde, 1815). By 1816, there were about 100,000 children being taught in England and Wales using the Bell-Lancaster system (Bell, 1817).

The reasons for the decline in popularity of the Bell-Lancaster system are not completely clear. Some have suggested that educators began to be less satisfied with the quality of the instruction that untrained 8- or 9-year- old tutors were able to deliver (Dures, 1971). Others have asserted that as the supply of professional educators grew, and as they became better organised, it was to their professional and financial advantage to dismiss unpaid, untrained student tutors (Allen, 1976). Another societal force that mitigated against the Bell-Lancaster system was the increasing tendency of schools toward self-contained classrooms where students were segregated according to age. As children were placed in these graded classrooms, it became less convenient to have older students helping younger ones.

Purposes of tutoring

At first glance, tutoring may seem to have a simple and singular purpose: to transfer new knowledge to the tutee. But the purposes and measured effects of tutoring are neither simple not singular. Many investigators have been more interested in the benefits that accrue to tutors than to tutees. Bell, himself, was at least as impressed by the growth in his tutors as he was by the new knowledge transferred to other students. As early as the 1600s, Joachim Fortius said: 'If students wish to make progress, they should arrange to give lessons daily in the subjects they are studying, even if they have to hire their pupils' (Gartner, Kohler and Riessman, 1971, pp. 14–15).

This passage illustrates the philosophical basis for the many research studies that have focused on tutor growth as opposed to tutee growth. The assumption that tutoring programmes are established solely for the benefit of helping tutees learn academic skills is a common misconception. Equally incorrect is the view that tutoring is simply another teaching method, a technique for transmitting information. From their inception, tutoring programmes have been multifaceted experiments in socialisation. The first effect Bell noted in his programme was the improvement in classroom behaviour – not students' performance in a spelling bee, but their ability to attend and their willingness to help other students master the task at hand.

Since that time, teachers and other observers have noted that tutors often appear to gain as much or more than the students they tutor. Social benefits, such as improved self-confidence, self-esteem, attitude toward school, and responsibility, as well as academic benefits, have been reported (Allen, 1976; Jenkins and Jenkins, 1982). If such reports are true, it follows that special education students could stand to gain much from acting as tutors. In fact, tutoring, and other peer interventions, have recently been investigated within special education settings (Gerber and Kauffman, 1981; Krouse, Gerber, and Kauffman, 1981; Strain, 1981). Often, however, the focus has been upon the handicapped student as the recipient of the instruction. In addition, some previous reviews of tutoring have excluded many studies involving handicapped populations (Cohen, Kulik, and Kulik, 1982; Devin-Sheehan, Feldman, and Allen, 1976). The purpose of this paper, then, is to synthesise previous research literature in which special education students have served as tutors.

For the purposes of this review, 'tutoring' will be defined to include those investigations in which special education students delivered academic instruction to other students on a one-to-one basis. By this definition, studies in which students were employed as nonacademic behaviour change agents are not included here although by other standards the activities investigated may be referred to as 'tutoring'. Specifically, studies of cooperative play (eg, Morris and Dolker, 1974; Young and Kerr, 1979), self-feeding (eg, Gross, 1975), extinguishing tantrums (eg, Whalen and Henker, 1969), or imitation (eg, Whalen and Henker, 1969) are not included. In addition, the recent literature that has emerged on 'cooperative learning' (eg, Buckholdt and Wodarski, 1978; Madden and Slavin, 1983; Slavin, Madden and Leavey, 1984), although closely related to tutoring, has not been included as it is considered to be beyond the scope of the present review.

Using this more limited definition, research will be reviewed that measured the effects of tutoring on the academic performance and personal/social development of both tutors and tutees. First, findings will be analysed that focused on the benefits of tutoring for those receiving the instruction, the tutees. In most studies, the students serving as tutees came from special education settings, while in a few instances they came from the regular classroom. Second, research will be discussed that focused on the benefits that come to handicapped students who function as tutors. Unlike previous reviews of tutoring research, studies involving regular class students as tutors will not be included. Finally, conclusions and recommendations will be given for employing tutoring programmes in special education.

Tutee benefits

The hypothesis that handicapped students can serve effectively as tutors of other students has received convincing support in recent research literature.

The vast majority of experimental or quasi-experimental investigations conducted in this area have concluded that properly trained students are able to function effectively as tutors of appropriately selected tutees. These studies, conducted over a wide variety of content domains, are discussed according to the handicapping condition of the tutor.

Learning disabled or academically delayed tutors

Students who are themselves academically deficient have often been chosen as tutors of lower academically functioning tutees. Since the tutors in these investigations have most consistently exhibited reading disabilities, reading has generally been chosen as the tutoring content. From Table 12.1 it can be seen that eight of the 26 studies employed learning disabled (LD) students as tutors of reading or spelling (Epstein, 1978; Higgins, 1982; Lamport, 1982; Landrum and Martin, 1970; Mellberg, 1980; Osguthorpe, 1985; Scruggs, 1985; Top, 1984). As can also be seen in Table 12.1, the purposes and results of the eight studies were similar, but the methodologies differed substantially. For example, the length of treatment ranged from 6 to 14 weeks; the number of tutees ranged from 8 to 764; and the experimental designs varied greatly. In one of the more carefully conducted studies, LD and educable mentally retarded (EMR) students, as well as regular class students, were employed as tutors. Results of the investigation indicated that tutees gained equally from the intervention, regardless of the type or existence of handicap on the part of the tutor. Mellberg (1980) concluded that LD and EMR students could be as effective as non-handicapped students in the role of tutor.

In Scruggs' (1985) investigation, LD students were employed as either cross-age tutors of other LD students (Experiment 1), or same-age tutors alternating tutor and tutee roles (Experiment 2). Results of this investigation indicated that both tutoring configurations were effective in raising reading achievement of the tutees. In addition, cross-age tutees reported more positive attitudes toward school than did controls. In a similar study, Top (1984) trained fifth- and sixth-grade LD students to tutor academically delayed regular class first graders in reading. The results showed that even though first graders in a comparison group received an equivalent amount of reading instruction, the first graders who were tutored by the LD students performed significantly better on both criterion and standardized reading tests.

Higgins (1982) used an alternating tutor-tutee design, and found that students learned more spelling words when in tutoring and free study conditions than they did in a no-remediation control condition. Performance in the tutoring condition was not observed to be superior to that in a free study condition, however.

Finally, two investigations directly examined mathematics achievement. Singh (1982) found that in mathematics achievement subtests LD tutees

Table 12.1 Summary descriptions of empirical studies that included handicapped students as tutors

Study	Description	Design	Tutors	Tutees et al. (1971)	Findings
Brown et al. (1971)	Intra-class peer tutoring to improve sight word recognition	Pre-post, no control.	2 adolescent moderate MR	7 MR agemates	Tutors learned 20 sight words in 23 sessions of 25 minutes, taught 10 words in 15 sessions of 15 minutes, and taught 7 classmates 5 words in 10 sessions of 15 minutes.
Carlton et al. (1985)	Intra-class peer tutoring to improve sight word recognition	Pre-post, control. Classes randomly assigned.	30 adolescent mildly MR	30 adolescent mildly MR	Tutors and tutees learned significantly more sight words than did students in the control group who received normal class instruction.
Csapo (1976)	Cross-age tutoring to improve reading skills and reduce inappropriate behaviors in tutors.	Pre-post, no control.	6 adolescent juvenile delinquents	8 elementary age reading disabled	Tutors' and tutees' reading achievement improved after 6 weeks of daily 20 minute sessions. Tutors made more positive remarks and showed reductions in inappropriate behaviours.
Custer & Osguthorpe (1983)	Reverse-role tutoring to improve social acceptance of tutors (sign language taught).	Pre-post, no control	15 elementary age mildly MR	15 elementary age non-handicapped	After 8 weekly 30-minute tutoring sessions, tutors spent significantly more time with nonhandicapped peers during free-play time.
Eiserman & Osguthorpe (1985)	Reverse-role tutoring to improve social acceptance of tutors (sign language taught).	Pre-post, control. Classes randomly assigned.	17 elementary age mildly MR	17 elementary age non-handicapped	After 10 weeks of tutoring during 15-minute sessions three times per week, tutors interacted more frequently with nonhandicapped peers during free-play time than did students in the control group.
Epstein (1978)	Intra-class peer tutoring to improve reading skills.	Pre-post, four control groups. Students randomly assigned.	100 elementary age LD	100 LD classmates.	Tutors performed significantly better than students in control groups on criterion reading test. No significant differences between groups on time used to cover the words.
Franca (1983)	Peer tutoring to improve maths skills and personal/social skills.	Multiple-baseline across tutors and tutees.	BD adolescents	BD adolescents	Tutors and tutees showed improvement on maths skills, attitude toward maths, and social interaction. Slight or no improvement was shown on sociometric measures, self-concept, and teacher perceptions of behaviour.
Gable & Kerr (1979)	Cross-age tutoring to improve maths skills of tutees.	Single subject design	BD adolescents	Younger BD adolescents	Tutees showed significant improvement on criterion maths tests, while tutors' performance showed no change.
Higgins (1982)	Both peer tutoring and	Single subject	8 LD adolescents	8 LD adolescents	Both peer tutoring and independent

Author (year)	Purpose	Design	Tutors	Tutees	Results
	...tutor or tutee) to improve spelling skills.				Tutoring was not significantly better than independent study. Tutees improved more in spelling than did tutors.
Kreutzer (1973)	Cross-age tutoring to improve reading skills and social adjustment of tutors and tutees.	Pre-post, control. Students randomly assigned.	18 low achieving adolescents	18 BD elementary age	Following 5 months of tutoring (five 45-minute sessions per week) neither tutors nor tutees showed significant improvement over controls on reading.
Lamport (1982)	Cross-age tutoring to improve reading skills and personal/social skills	Pre-post, control. Classes randomly assigned.	24 LD elementary age	24 LD younger elementary age	Following 8 weeks of tutoring (three 30-minute sessions per week) tutors improved in their phonetic analysis skills and had a more positive attitude toward school. Tutees showed more improvement in vocabulary than controls. Other measures showed no differences.
Landrum & Martin (1970)	Cross-age tutoring to improve reading of tutors and tutees	Pre-post, no control.	412 disadvantaged, reading disabled adolescents	764 elementary age reading disabled	After 6 weeks of tutoring tutors gained 8.3 months as measured by a standardized reading test. Tutees gained 4.7 months.
Lane et al. (1972)	Cross-age tutoring to improve reading skills of tutors and tutees.	Pre-post, no control	8 BD adolescents	8 LD or BD elementary age.	Following 7 months of twice weekly sessions tutors gained 19 months on a standardized reading test, while tutees gained 14 months.
Lazerson et. al 1980	Cross-age tutoring to improve self-concept and behaviour. Tutors chose content to teach.	Pre-post, control. Students randomly assigned.	20 BD elementary age	20 BD younger elementary age	Following 5 weeks of tutoring (four 20-minute sessions per week) self-concept and behavioural measures showed trends in favour of tutors and tutees, but differences were nonsignificant.
Lombardo (1976)	Peer and adult tutoring to improve tutees' understanding of word meaning.	Pre-post, control Students randomly assigned.	11 adults; 11 MR; 11 non-handicapped elementary age	33 MR elementary age	Tutees performed equally well on the criterion vocabulary test, regardless of the type of tutor. Peer retarded tutors taught as well as graduate student tutors.
Maher (1982)	Cross-age tutoring and group counselling to improve academic performance and behaviour.	Pre-post, control, Students randomly assigned.	18 BD adolescents	6 mildly MR elementary age	Following 10 weeks of tutoring (two 30-minute sessions per week) tutors improved significantly on academic performance and had significantly reduced rates of absenteeism and disciplinary referrals than did students who received peer tutoring or group counselling.
Maher (1984)	Cross-age tutoring to improve language arts and mathematics of both tutors and tutees.	Multiple-baseline across tutors and tutees.	8 BD adolescents	8 mildly MR elementary age	Following 10 weeks of tutoring (two 30-minute sessions per week) both tutors and tutees showed improvement in maths and language skills.

Reference	Purpose	Design	Sample	Sample	Results
Mellberg (1980)	Cross-age tutoring to improve reading and arithmetic skills.	Pre-post, control. Students randomly assigned.	60 disadvantaged and LD, elementary age and adolescents	225 disadvantaged and LD elementary age	Following 7 weeks of tutoring tutors and tutees performed better than controls on both reading and arithmetic. Type of tutor was not a factor.
Osguthorpe et al. (1985)	Cross-age, peer and reverse-role tutoring to improve reading skills and social acceptance of tutors and tutees.	Pre-post, control. Classes randomly assigned.	85 LD, BD & MR elementary age	119 non-handicapped elementary age	After an average of 10 weeks of tutoring (three 20-minute sessions per week) tutors and tutees showed greater improvements in social acceptance and reading skills than did controls.
Scruggs (1985)	Cross-age and peer tutoring to improve reading skills of both tutors and tutees.	Pre-post, control. Students randomly assigned.	26 LD. BD elementary age	LD, BD elementary age	Following an average of 12 weeks of tutoring (two 30-minute sessions per week) tutors and tutees showed improvement in word attack skills.
Singh (1982)	Cross-age tutoring to improve maths skills of tutors and tutees.	Pre-post, comparison group.	100 LD adolescents	LD younger adolescents	After 9 weeks of tutoring (four 15-minute sessions per week) tutees improved in maths skills when compared to nontutored LD students. Tutors also showed more improvement in maths skills compared to nontutored LD students.
Snell (1979)	Cross-age tutoring to improve language skills of tutees.	Pre-post, control. Students randomly assigned.	12 MR	24 MR	Tutees showed greater gains on language ability than did controls, but mental age did not show improvement.
Stowitschek et al. (1982)	Peer tutoring to improve spelling skills.	Multiple baseline	12 BD adolescents	BD adolescents	After 10 weeks of 15-minute daily tutoring sessions, peer tutors completing the study all showed improvement in spelling performance as measured by criterion tests.
Swenson (1975)	Peer tutoring to improve social acceptance, self-esteem, arithmetic skills of tutors and tutees.	Pre, mid and post with control. Students randomly assigned.	24 LD, 24 high achieving elementary age	LD elementary age	After 6 weeks of tutoring test results showed that tutoring did not have a significant effect on any of the dependent measures.
Top (1984)	Cross-age reverse-role tutoring to improve reading skills of tutors and tutees.	Pre-post, control. Classes and students randomly assigned.	39 LD and BD elementary age	39 non-handicapped younger elementary age	After 14 weeks of tutoring (four 20-minute sessions per week) tutors and tutees both performed significantly better than controls on criterion and standardized reading tests. Tutors also improved more in their attitude toward school than did nontutors.
Truesdale (1976)	Peer tutoring to improve spelling skills of tutors and tutees.	Pre-post, control. Students randomly assigned.	17 mildly MR adolescents	17 mildly MR adolescents	After 4 weeks of 15-minute daily sessions tutors and tutees performed significantly better than controls on spelling measures.

made significant gains over nontutored LD students. Swenson (1975) reported one of the rare cases in which achievement of tutees did not improve relative to a no-treatment control group. Mellberg (1980), however, did report mathematics as well as reading achievement gains for students tutored by LD and EMR students in summer programmes.

Behaviourally disordered students as tutors

Investigations primarily involving behaviourally disordered (BD) students as tutors have generally supported the investigations involving LD tutors with respect to tutee academic gain. Maher (1982, 1984), in two investigations, found that BD students could function effectively as tutors of younger EMR students in a variety of content areas. Maher (1984) indicated that amount of completed academic work increased, as did weekly test scores of the tutees. Csapo (1976) and Lane, Pollack, and Sher (1972), using pre-post designs, concluded that BD students could effectively tutor younger, lower academically functioning students in reading, in that reading achievement of tutees increased over expected levels. Top (1984) also found that when tutored by BD students, first-grade academically delayed tutees performed significantly better than controls on both criterion and normed reading tests.

Franca (1983) and Gable and Kerr (1979) using single subject methodology and criterion-referenced measures, presented data indicating that BD tutees gained math skills from older BD tutors. In a similar investigation, Stowitschek, Hecimovic, Stowitschek, and Shores (1982) provided evidence that BD adolescents could effectively tutor each other in spelling.

Mentally retarded students as tutors

In addition to the Mellberg (1980) study cited above, researchers have recently indicated that educable mentally retarded (EMR) students can function effectively as tutors of spelling (Truesdale, 1976) and sign language (Custer and Osguthorpe, 1983; Eiserman and Osguthorpe, 1985). In addition, reports by Brown, Fenrick, and Klemme (1971) and Snell (1979) have indicated that lower functioning retarded students can effectively serve as tutors of word recognition and language skills.

In a series of studies investigating the effects of 'reverse-role tutoring', mentally retarded students taught sign language to same-age peers from the regular classroom (Custer and Osguthorpe, 1983; Osguthorpe, Eiserman, Shisler, Top and Scruggs, 1985). The results of these studies showed that in addition to learning basic sign language, regular class tutees interacted significantly more often with their tutors during non-tutoring time, as measured through direct observation.

Finally, Lombardo (1976) examined the relative performance of graduate students, average fourth-graders, and retarded students as tutors of younger retarded students on an associative learning task, as assessed by tutee gain. While Lombardo tended to discount his findings because there was 'no significant difference' among groups, the results are extremely supportive of the effectiveness of mentally retarded tutors. Comparing the Lombardo study with Mellberg's (1980) study (described earlier), it can be seen that the designs differed in one critical aspect, the inclusion of a 'no treatment' control group. Because Mellberg included such a group in his study, he concluded that tutoring had positively affected tutee performance, while Lombardo concluded that there was no difference among tutee groups. However, closer analysis of Lombardo's results would indicate that a more appropriate conclusion would have focused on the surprising result that tutees learned as much from mentally retarded tutors as they did from adult special education graduate students.

Conclusion

From the studies reviewed to this point it can be concluded that tutees receive specific academic benefits when they are tutored by special education students. The handicapping condition of neither the tutor nor the tutee appear to be critical factors in how much the tutee benefits from the tutoring. Additionally, special education students can be effective tutors in a variety of academic content areas from language arts to quantitative skills.

When considering the effects of tutoring on tutees the interesting question that arises is: How effective is tutoring compared with other specific instructional procedures? Most of the studies cited compared tutee performance with age mates who were not tutored. One criticism that might be levied against the research regarding tutee performance is that few researchers attend to how non-tutees spend their time during the tutoring sessions. The most common description is that non-tutees: 'received no treatment other than their normal classroom activities ... [which] included traditional independent seatwork language arts activities' (Carlton, Litton and Zinkgraf, 1985, p.75). What researchers often fail to document is how these classroom activities vary from one class to another. This becomes especially critical in the intra-class tutoring research in which classes must be assigned at random. Is there a tendency, for example, for teachers to reinforce throughout the day the topics being tutored? And would it be logical to assume that the amount of time spent on language arts (if that is the tutoring topic) is constant for all teachers?

In fairness to researchers cited in this section, it should be stated that in most cases the problem of no-treatment control conditions was recognised. In no case did researchers simply add on to the instructional time of tutees by conducting tutoring after school hours or during non-instructional time. And in certain cases, the problem was addressed openly by creating alternative treatments in addition to a no-treatment control. For example, tutees in Epstein's (1978) study performed better on criterion reading tests than did those who had received small group instruction by the teacher. But the tutored group did not do better than those who received 'self-instruction'. The tutees in Top's (1984) study performed significantly better on both criterion and normed reading tests when compared with controls who received equal amounts of reading instruction from their teacher or non-handicapped tutor. However, a recent study comparing tutoring with small group teacher-led instruction has shown that tutoring is sometimes less effective than the teacher-led treatment (Scruggs and Richter, in press)

The ultimate question regarding these data, then, is: Can tutoring be justified as an instructional alternative solely on the basis of tutee benefits? If those benefits are restricted to academic growth, alone, the answer is probably 'no'. But most researchers believe that personal/social benefits accrue to the tutee, even though most have not attempted to measure such growth. In addition, most researchers in the field also believe that benefits come to *tutors* as well as to the *tutees*. Therefore, let us consider the data that have been gathered regarding the effects on tutors. After these data have been presented, the issue of costs versus the benefits of tutoring will be discussed in more depth.

Tutor benefits

While a large segment of tutoring research conducted with non-handicapped tutors focused exclusively on the tutee, studies cited in this article have generally emphasised benefits to be derived by the handicapped *tutor*. As seen in Table 12.1, Snell (1979) was the only researcher who did not attempt to measure tutor growth. In a sense, most researchers in the area are hypothesising that special education students may learn more about a topic by teaching it to someone else than they would if they were to learn it from a teacher or a text. These researchers are often also interested in the personal/social effects that tutoring may have on the tutor. While most fail to measure such effects on the tutee, several have attempted such measures on tutors, even though the central purpose of the study was to improve some academic skill. This is a critical point because it signals a qualitatively different approach to social skills training. In other words, not one of the studies that focused on personal/social growth employed personal/social skills as the tutoring topic. Rather, researchers conjectured that the act of tutoring, itself, regardless of the topic, would enhance personal/social development of the tutors.

As in the first section, research regarding tutor benefits will be organised according to the handicapping condition of the tutor.

Learning disabled or academically delayed tutors

The 'Tutee benefits' section has suggested that LD (as well as BD and MR) students have functioned effectively as tutors. These students have often, themselves, also benefited from assuming the role of tutor. Mellberg (1980) suggested that LD (and EMR) tutors made greater gains in reading and arithmetic than control students during the course of a summer tutoring programme. LD tutors in the Singh (1982) investigation made significant gains in mathematics concepts/applications subtests over non-tutor LD students, but did not gain computational skills, as had their respective tutees. Likewise, Scruggs (1985, Experiment 1) reported that cross-age LD tutors scored significantly higher than control students on word-attack skills, but did not gain relative to controls on a criterion-referenced measure. These tutors did not report more positive attitudes toward school. However, Top (1984) found both criterion and standardised reading gains for LD tutors over LD control students. The results also showed that LD tutors' attitudes toward academic skills improved significantly more than those of LD students who did not tutor. Lamport (1982) reported that reading disabled tutors out-performed control students in decoding skills after a tutoring intervention. In addition, the tutors reported more positive attitudes toward school than control students. Landrum and Martin (1970), using a pre/post design, reported that tutors had gained nearly twice as much as tutees had, with both groups gaining well over expected levels.

When tutors and tutees alternated roles (Epstein, 1978; Higgins, 1982; Scruggs, 1985, Experiment 2), all students gained in the content area tutored. In the Scruggs (1985, Experiment 2) investigation, attitude changes were not observed, while Epstein (1978) and Higgins (1982) did not investigate potential social benefits.

Behaviourally disordered students as tutors

Social benefits
Social benefits to BD tutors have been more systematically evaluated than social benefits to LD tutors, perhaps because such potential benefits have more often served as the major research question (Scruggs, Mastropieri and Richter, in press). Csapo (1976) and Lane, Pollack, and Sher (1972) reported that BD students employed as tutors evidenced improvement in social functioning during the course of the tutoring experience. Lane et al (1972) reported that tutors' disruptive behaviour decreased, and that tutors

reported more self-confidence and more responsibility and expressed less anger than they had prior to the tutoring intervention. Csapo (1976) reported that tutors

a) increased in number of positive remarks to tutee and other tutors
b) came home earlier at night
c) decreased in number of adjudicated delinquencies, with respect to their performance prior to 10 weeks of daily tutoring.

Interpretation of these highly positive findings as well as those of Lane et al. (1972), must be tempered by the fact that both investigations employed pre/post designs with no control group. The absence of a control group in both of these studies opens up the possibility that some of these reported benefits may be attributable to other concurrent interventions in the school or home environments.

Maher (1982, 1984), in two separate investigations designed to investigate social benefits to BD tutors, reported decreases in disciplinary referrals of tutors in both investigations. The interesting finding in Maher's (1982) first study was the relative performance of the role of tutee versus that of tutor. As seen in Table 12.1, Maher found that the behaviour of the BD tutor improved more than that of the BD tutee or the BD student receiving group counselling. This is an important finding because it suggests that there is something inherent in the act of teaching someone else that exceeds the more passive role of learner.

Top (1984) reported that BD students employed as tutors demonstrated an improved perception of their own abilities as compared with controls. These findings are somewhat stronger than some other investigations in that the Maher (1982), Top (1984), and Osguthorpe (1984) investigations employed control groups, whereas in the Maher (1984) investigation, students served as their own controls.

Franca (1983) employed a single-subject design to investigate tutor benefits and reported that few and inconsistent changes in social behaviour occurred as a result of the tutoring experience. It was found, however, that both tutors and tutees reported more positive attitudes toward the subject tutored (maths).

Academic benefits

All the above investigations in which BD students were employed as tutors, reported that the tutors had evidenced academic gain as a result of the tutoring experience. However, with the exception of the Top (1984) investigation, none of these investigations employed both objective achievement test scores and appropriate control groups so further research is necessary to confirm these findings. There is on the other hand at least one investigation in which tutor academic benefits were not realized. Gable and Kerr (1979) trained BD adolescents and tutors of younger BD students and reported that, although tutee gains were observed on criterion-referenced tests, similar gains were not observed on the part of tutors, for which ceiling performance on those measures had already been observed at pre-testing. Their finding supports the hypothesis of Scruggs, Mastropieri and Richter (in press) that tutor academic gains are most likely to be evidenced when students are tutoring in an area in which they have attained accuracy, but are in need of fluency-building activities.

Mentally retarded students as tutors

Often, investigations employing mentally retarded students as tutors have addressed the 'can it be done?' issue and assessed effectiveness by assessment of tutee gain (eg, Brown et al 1971; Lombardo 1976; Snell 1979). Some researchers, however, have investigated the issue of social and academic benefits of mentally retarded students as tutors. Mellberg (1980) and Truesdale (1976) indicated that mentally retarded students evidenced academic gains when employed as tutors of younger or lower functioning students.

In a more unusual manipulation of the tutoring paradigm, several studies have employed EMR students as tutors of similarly aged, non-handicapped students in sign language (Custer and Osguthorpe, 1983; Eiserman and Osguthorpe, 1985; Osguthorpe et al, 1985). Unlike previous studies, the primary aim of this research has been to improve the social acceptance of handicapped tutors. Results of these studies have shown that handicapped tutors experience significantly more positive social interaction from non-handicapped students as a result of the tutoring. This increase in social acceptance has also been shown to be an enduring effect in multiyear studies (Osguthorpe et al, 1985).

Summary and conclusions

From the research reported in this review, it can be concluded that:

a) Special education students can function effectively as tutors if they are trained and supervised appropriately,

b) these students experience academic and social benefits by functioning as either a tutor or a tutee.

There is no question that methodological weaknesses inherent in conducting *in vitro* research (Scruggs and Richter in press) add scepticism to the results of some studies, but many of the studies employed more defensible designs. As seen in Table 12.1 of the 26 studies reported, five used a pre-post (no control group) design; five used a single-subject or multiple-baseline design; five used a pre-post (control group) with *classes* randomly assigned to treatment conditions and 11 used a pre-post (control group) with *students* randomly assigned to treatment conditions. Of these 26 studies, a total of 23 reported that tutors and/or tutees performed better on outcome measures as a result of the tutoring experience, while only three studies reported finding no treatment effects. It is important to remember that fully half (13) of the studies were unpublished manuscripts (usually dissertations), this discounting to some degree the criticism that review articles are often biased toward the treatment because journals are more prone to accept articles reporting significant treatment effects.

Although the academic and social effects are quite convincing, there are some areas in which tutoring does not seem to be beneficial. Many investigators have attempted to demonstrate the effectiveness of tutoring to improve 'self-esteem' on the part of the tutor. Generally, such attempts have been unsuccessful (Cohen et al 1982; Franca, 1983; Kreutzer, 1973; Lazerson, 1980; Sharpley, Irvine and Sharpley, 1983). It is difficult to ascertain at this point whether such failures are due to the weaknesses of the measures used, or to the fact that tutoring is not by itself an intervention of sufficient intensity to affect perceptibly such global aspects of a child's social or emotional functioning.

It is also possible, however, that some of the self-esteem research has suffered from the same measurement problems associated with certain studies assessing academic growth. For example, Top (1984) concluded that one of the reasons his LD and BD tutors did not experience growth in self-esteem was because their pre-test data were generally so positive that they had little room for improvement. This conclusion is close to that of Gable and Kerr (1979) when they noted that their tutors had no room to grow in the tutoring topic as measured by their criterion test. In other words, while parents and professionals may view self-esteem as one of the most serious problems faced by special education students, the students themselves often appear (at least on written tests) to possess a healthy self-concept. Interestingly, even though Top (1984) did not find differences on self-esteem between tutors and non-tutors, parents of tutors believed that the tutoring caused substantial growth in their child's self-esteem, consistently reporting it as one of the most important benefits of the programme. Such findings suggest that teachers or parents may perceive an increase in 'self-esteem' when, in fact, no such increase has been perceived by the student. It does seem, however, that tangible social benefits can accrue to the tutor, specifically in areas closely related to the tutoring process. Whether tutoring can influence broader areas of student functioning remains to be documented.

Given the generally positive nature of tutoring research one wonders why more teachers do not employ it in their classrooms. Although it is beyond the scope of this paper to present a complete cost-benefit analysis, teachers clearly need to know how much time and expertise is required to implement a tutoring programme before they can decide whether to begin such a programme with their own students. The main issues a teacher must face in making such a decision are:

a)   the specific needs of both tutors and tutees;
b)   the time and effort required to train tutors;
c)   the time and effort required for the actual tutoring.

It is clear that in certain studies more attention could have been paid to the specific needs of both tutors and tutees. In order to justify the additional time spent by students who function as tutors, teachers must tailor the tutoring topic to the needs of those students, as well as thinking of the tutee's needs. Krouse, Gerber, and Kauffman (1981) cautioned 'Although it has been demonstrated that academic and social gains are frequently obtained by the tutor, this in itself is not sufficient justification for the child to be a tutor. Instead it must be shown that by being a tutor specific needs are being met' (p.112). The most convincing justification, then, for using students as tutors is to tailor the programme to meet more than one need. Maher (1982), for example, reported that his BD student tutors experienced both academic *and* social/behavioural growth. This positive result occurred probably because BD students who had advanced academic skills were not selected as tutors. Other researchers attained similar dual effects with LD students, reporting growth in both reading skills and attitudinal measures (Lamport, 1982; Top, 1984). Lazerson (1980), on the other hand, apparently did not pay such close attention to the needs of both tutors and tutees, allowing tutors to select the content they preferred to teach, rather than pre-assessing student needs.

Once a teacher has determined whether a tutoring programme could meet certain student needs, the question of training time must be addressed. Tutoring research with both handicapped and non-handicapped students has shown repeatedly that training and supervision are essential components of effective tutoring programmes (see Osguthorpe, 1984, for further information on training procedures). Teachers cannot assume that they will have more free time because students are taking over an instructional task. The training time reported in the studies included in this review varied substantially, sometimes exceeding that of the tutoring time itself (Brown et al, 1971) but in most cases requiring only one to three hours. Most of these shorter training sessions focused on the actual tutoring skills that students would later be asked to use with their tutees. Studies employing longer training periods usually included time required to teach prospective tutors the actual content they would be tutoring (Brown et al, 1971; Custer and Osguthorpe, 1983; Eiserman and Osguthorpe, 1985). Tutors' handicapping conditions also probably had an effect on training time, with mentally retarded students requiring the most time and BD students the least. In each case, role-playing the part of tutor was the most common training activity reported by researchers. Teachers, then, must look at the purpose of the tutoring programme and weigh the time required to train the tutors against the expected benefits to be derived by tutors and tutees. The final step in the decision process is to determine the length of tutoring time needed. Before discussing the treatment times reported in Table 12.1, it should be noted that total tutor-tutee contact time is the most accurate way to view length of treatment. Some researchers, unfortunately, did not report the frequency and/or length of tutoring sessions, while others were quite specific. For those who did give these data, the average treatment time was 14 hours, but varied widely from a low of four total hours over eight weeks (Custer and Osguthorpe, 1983) to a high of 75 hours over five months (Kreutzer, 1973). Interestingly, treatment time appears to have no correlation with effectiveness of a tutoring programme (although there is likely a minimum time below which effects would be negligible). For example, of the studies that reported no effects of tutoring, two had relatively short treatments (Lazerson, 1980; Swenson, 1975), while the other had the longest treatment (Kreutzer, 1973). In her discussion section, Kreutzer conjectured that the reason her treatment produced no effect was due to the short treatment-time and recommended that future researchers extend the tutoring period to at least two years. However, from the majority of studies, it would appear that an effective tutoring programme will show positive results with as little as 10 total hours of tutor-tutee contact over a seven-week period.

Future research

Although current research has shown that tutoring often benefits both tutors and tutees academically, further research is necessary to determine the ultimate effectiveness of tutoring as compared with specific competing educational interventions intended to influence the same outcomes. For example, more research such as that recommended by Scruggs et al (in press) should be completed in which teacher-led instructional treatments are compared with tutoring. In such research, care should be taken to include multiple outcome measures, such as normed tests designed to assess academic growth, as well as instruments designed to measure attitude toward school. In other words, researchers must be careful not to make the mistake of assuming that tutoring is undesirable simply because a trained teacher may be more effective than a cross-age tutor at imparting information. As mentioned earlier, multiple benefits may have occurred in many tutoring studies that only attempted to measure academic growth.

In addition to refining the tutoring research focused on academic achievement, further research is critically needed that addresses the concomitant personal/social outcomes. This type of research may even be more important than further validating the effects of tutoring on academic achievement, because if tutoring only affects cognitive growth, the additional time and effort required for training and implementation may not warrant its use. One study attempting to document the benefits of tutoring on mentally retarded students' social skills is currently in progress (Whited, 1985). Unlike previous research, this study is attempting to measure tutors' social skills through multiple direct observation each time the tutors meet a new set of tutees. But in addition to more defensible measures of social benefits, future studies should be designed to allow comparison of these effects with alternative treatments, for academic effects. In this way research could be conducted in which students would be randomly assigned to receive either a teacher-led social skills training programme or to tutor other students in an academic subject. In such a study outcome measures would need to be carefully selected to ensure against bias for one treatment or the other. In other words, it would be inappropriate to use as the sole-dependent measure a criterion test designed to assess mastery of either the social skills associated with the training programme or the tutoring. Multiple measures, including direct observation, would be preferable to traditional criterion tests.

Research emphasising social benefits should also address the question of whether it is more effective to function as a tutor or as a tutee. Do special education students who serve as tutees receive as much personal/social benefit as those who serve as tutors? This is an important question if teachers are to design the most useful programmes for their students (see Eiserman, 1985, for a description of research intended to address this question).

Future studies should also address the question of the relationship between type of tutoring and expected outcomes. For example, is cross-age tutoring more likely to result in personal/social benefits than peer tutoring, or is the opposite true? Cross-age tutoring has been the most common type of tutoring used in special education research, accounting for 14 of the 26 studies reported in Table 12.1, with intra-class peer tutoring being used in eight of the studies and reverse-role (handicapped tutoring nonhandicapped) in four of the studies. However, it would appear from the data that different types of tutoring offer differing potential for specific outcomes. Cross-age tutoring is probably the most obvious choice for emphasising academic growth of tutees, while intra-class peer may be the best type for effecting academic growth in both tutors and tutees. Reverse-role tutoring, finally, is probably the most logical choice, if social acceptance and tutee attitudes are emphasised as desired outcomes. And these are not the only types of tutoring available to teachers. Osguthorpe (1985) has described several variations on these types, none of which have yet been formally tested.

In addition to further research data, efforts should be made to develop more effective materials to be used by special education tutors. From the descriptions of most of the studies reported in this article, researchers have usually been required to develop their own instructional materials before implementing the tutoring programme. This factor alone is a strong enough deterrent to keep most teachers from considering tutoring as an instructional option. There is also good reason to believe that the training time of tutors can be reduced significantly when appropriate materials are employed. Given the fact that most special education students have difficulty with reading, these materials will need to contain clear cues that allow the tutor to direct the tutee without relying on reading skills to do it.

Correspondence

Professor R T Osguthorpe, Office of the Dean, College of Education, Brigham Young University, Provo, UTAH 84602, USA.

13 The Exploratory pilot, a peer tutor? – the interpreter's role in an interactive service and technology centre

Melanie Quin

National and local organisations have been promoting science to the British public for many years. There has been a considerable upsurge of activity in the last five years. One of the most striking recent developments is the growth of interactive science and technology centres – exciting places where you can touch and play with the exhibits and experience scientific phenomena for yourself.

All interactive centres provide an informal environment and enthusiastic interpreters to welcome, discuss the exhibits and help if required. The interpreter's precise role varies from centre to centre – both in the UK and overseas. And within any one institution they must be adaptable beings: a visit to an interactive centre can be many things, from a family outing to an essential part of the term's science teaching, and the interpreter's task is to make the visit enlightening as well as entertaining.

Introduction

I propose to start by answering the question: Just what is an interactive science and technology centre? I shall then explore the role of interpreters, looking at the UK experience over the last 18 months and drawing on examples from science and technology centres overseas. (In case the title has you baffled, the Exploratory is in Bristol where the interpreters are known as 'pilots'.)

Context

The essence of a science and technology centre is interactive exploration of scientific phenomena. Fragments of the interactive approach have existed in major museums for some time: the handles and buttons in the Science Museum's Children's Gallery (South Kensington); the chemical demonstrations at the Palais de la Decouverte (Paris); and industrial engines, in action, at the Deutsches Museum (Munich). Significantly, at the Deutsches Museum, guides explain the engines' operation and visitors are encouraged to learn more about the principles involved. The Museum's founders intended not only to preserve technological artifacts, but to enhance respect for innovation and to improve vocational training through practical experience.

The South Kensington and Deutsches museums inspired Frank Oppenheimer. But the Exploratorium he founded in San Francisco in 1969 was the first of a completely new kind of institution with a truly hands-on approach. The Exploratorium has been the catalyst for many groups throughout the world that have since produced demonstrations and exhibits which have an open-ended outcome dependent on the visitors' input. The excellent 'Cookbooks' published by the Exploratorium provide details on how to make a large number of their exhibits, and have given many groups and individuals the confidence and know-how to get started.

Despite the considerable variety, interactive centres have several characteristics in common. They are:

- largely devoted to science and technology (including engineering and industrial processes);
- contemporary rather than historic;
- interactive ('hands-on'), with specially constructed exhibits that encourage visitor participation;
- informal – 'explainers', 'guides' or 'pilots' are always on hand to welcome, discuss the exhibits and help if required;
- publicly and educationally oriented – the idea is that you can best learn about scientific and technological phenomena if you try them out and experiment with them yourself.

The participatory approach to exhibitions, pioneered by the interactive science and technology centres, is now spreading to zoos, aquaria, and to the traditional science and natural history museums.

A typical science-technology centre offers exhibits on mechanics, electricity, optics, perception, health and transport that can appeal to children as well as their parents (Grinell, 1988). For example, an exhibit called 'Air Power' is motor given by compressed air from a blower. Air has to be let into the cylinder in bursts, at just the right moments, to push the piston and make the motor run smoothly. The cylinder is made of transparent perspex, so visitors can see exactly what is going on.

Hands-on science in the UK

At this point I should introduce myself and the Interactive Science and Technology Project of the Nuffield Foundation.

As part of a general programme of support for the public understanding of science, the Trustees of the Nuffield Foundation are keen both to help the development of science centres themselves, and to ensure that the ideas and methods that the centres pioneer should be exploited as widely as possible.

The Interactive Science and Technology Project was established in October 1987. It aimed to provide a focus for information exchange and to promote the development of hands-on ideas and expertise. The Project is funded jointly by the Nuffield Foundation and the Industry/Education Unit of the Department of Trade and Industry.

The Interactive Science and Technology Project has three broad objectives:

1   To establish a 'facts and resources' centre for schools, industry and the general public, providing information about interactive science and science centres both in the UK and overseas.
2   To pool experience and information, and so act as a resource for the science centres themselves and as a reference point for international exchange.
3   To liaise with COPUS and other bodies interested in the public understanding of science.

When I attended my first ASTC (Association of Science-Technology Centers) conference in Seattle, the Project was described as 'an information exchange on roller skates'. What follows is therefore a report from first-hand experience – from the centre of what might be seen as a spider's-web communications network.

There are 12 interactive science and technology centres in the UK. Five are linked to existing science museums, one to the Jodrell Bank Observatory, and one to a working windmill. The others are totally new institutions. There are plans for at least another six. One day, maybe, every city will have an interactive science and technology centre, just as today most cities have a library, art gallery, theatre and sports centre.

The centres will never be clones – their diversity and individuality are part of their excitement. However, they all share a common aim: to help young people, their parents and teachers discover the fascination of science and technology through hands-on exploration and fun. Oppenheimer took the university science laboratory, restructured it, and made it accessible to the general public. His Exploratorium became the first 'science-technology centre' — its style that of a public science lab. Others, since, have designed centres in which science becomes as 'easy' as drama or music, and the setting resembles an enticing department store more closely than a laboratory. Yet an essential element of all hands-on centres is the personal contact with interpreters – those members of the science-centre staff who might best be described as hosts at a scientific cocktail party.

The interpreter's role

Chambers Dictionary defines 'interpreter' as 'one who translates orally for the benefit of two or more parties speaking different languages'. In the terms of an interactive science and technology centre, this means one who bridges the gulf between the scientist/exhibit developer and the visitor. These people are given a number of different names:

- *Pilots* at The Exploratory (Bristol)
- *Gallery assistants* at Launch Pad (Science Museum, South Kensington)
- *Auxiliaries* at the Natural History Museum (South Kensington)
- *Hosts* at the Ontario Science Centre (Toronto)
- *Enablers* at Light on Science (Museum of Science and Industry, Birmingham)
- *Demonstrators* at Technology Testbed (Large Objects Collection, Liverpool)
- *Helpers* at TECHNIQUEST (Cardiff)
- *Explainers* at the Exploratorium (San Francisco) and Questacon (Canberra)

This variety reflects the subtly different roles they play in the different institutions. I will describe four specific examples to give you a feel for the range.

1 Technology Testbed (permanently closed in autumn 1989)

There are 80 ruggedly-constructed hands-on exhibits at Technology Testbed in the Large Objects Collection (Princes Dock, Liverpool). They illustrate basic engineering principles and demystify the science and technology of the museum objects nearby – rockets, tram cars and lorries, amongst others. Responsibility for training and organising the demonstrator staff rests with the Keeper of Educational Services, Paul Rees, and colleagues in the Department of Social and Industrial History at the main museum building in the centre of Liverpool.

At Technology Testbed, eight 'demonstrators', a team leader and senior demonstrator help run the exhibition (open daily from Easter to mid-autumn). They act as guides, take advance bookings from school groups, and demonstrate some of the large objects in action. Each demonstrator takes charge of a dozen children and guides them round Testbed and the other exhibits, encouraging visitors to experiment and learn as they play. The whole tour takes about an hour and a half (information supplied by Anne Pennington in a personal communication.)

The contrasts in scale and the attraction of the hands-on approach provided inspiration for the producers of the BBC series *Science in Action*. The TV crew filmed on location at Technology Testbed (also at The Exploratory, Launch Pad, and at the New York Hall of Science) and made ten programmes for 14–16 year olds. In each case the idea is to make science so exciting on screen that, at the end of the programme, viewers will turn off the TV and get involved in scientific activities themselves.

2   The Exploratory

Exhibits (known at The Exploratory as 'plores' for exploring) introduce visitors to structures, sound, electricity and magnetism, mechanics, light and optical illusions. 'Plores' on chemistry and earth sciences (among others) are in the pipeline.

The Exploratory is the brainchild of Professor Richard Gregory. He conceived of a place where active exploration would suggest interesting questions to investigate, and would perhaps inspire discovery and invention – 'hands-on' leading to 'brains-on'.

The 'Pilots' work part time and stay, on average, a year with The Exploratory. Training is informal and combines:

* 'shadowing' an experienced Pilot;
* reading specially-prepared science-behind-the-plore information sheets;
* dipping into a collection of physics books, from first-year secondary school to first-year undergraduate level;
* watching and discussing pilot training videos. These consist of 30-minute presentations by a scientist, demonstrating the use and explaining the science involved in a plore or group of related plores.

From day to day, the exhibition and Pilots are coordinated by Richard Spalding who sketched the following six Pilot profiles to give a feel for the range of people involved: Mrs Y: 70 years old. An arts graduate of many years' standing! Works on a totally flexible shift system: when we need her, she comes to work. Mr X : Retired science teacher. Works part-time, one day per week. Has participated in teacher workshops (evenings) and is a brilliant guide with teenage school groups. Ms A : 22 years old. Physiology graduate. Currently looking for a permanent job. Working two days a week. Mrs B: Mother of two children. Works two days per week and is available to work on a rota system in The Exploratory science shop. She has little formal education but is a great communicator. Mr Q : 40 years old. Married and currently doing an Open University science course. Reliable.

He needed to get out of the house for two half-days per week. Ms T : Three days per week. Does voluntary work in her non-Exploratory time. Her hours are leading to excessive tiredness and burn out. She is well aware of this – and indeed it highlights the specific problems of work in an interactive science centre.

3 Questacon

Questacon was established as a testbed for the Australian National Science and Technology Centre. As such, a mobile component – the Questacon Science Circus – was operated. This visited towns and cities throughout Australia, typically spending three or four days at each venue. The NSTC opened in Canberra in November 1988, catching the bicentenary celebrations. The Science Circus itself has attracted major corporate sponsorship, and for the next five years will tour as the 'Shell Questacon Science Circus'.

Michael Gore, director of the NSTC, describes the role of Questacon's 'explainers' as follows:

The Explainers proved to be one of the most important ingredients of the Questacon. They promote a very friendly atmosphere and make it much more 'user friendly'. In addition, the younger Explainers derive a tremendous benefit from the experience. As any teacher knows, the very fact of geting over a wide range of scientific concepts to an even wider-ranging audience has meant their own understanding has increased. But, perhaps even more importantly, it was fascinating to see how the experience enhanced their overall confidence and poise.

The Explainers move informally around the interactive exhibits, talking with the visitors and telling them something of their background. In addition the Explainers stage a series of 20-minute science demonstration shows. Most of the demonstration shows concentrate on a single scientific theme (eg the Pressure Show, the Liquid Nitrogen Show, the Structures Show) and involve a continuous series of demonstrations, carried out using the simplest of equipment. Unless it is absolutely essential, conventional scientific-laboratory equipment is not employed. This keeps production costs down and makes the task of replacing items relatively simple. More importantly, by using 'props' which can be readily recognised, the audience tends not to be blinded by science, and because the various items are readily available there is a good chance that some people will try the experiments themselves later, at home or in the classroom.

The shows are not scripted in the normal theatrical sense but each one is based on a set of written guidelines. These help ensure that the content of the show is accurate and each Explainer then injects their own style and personality into the presentation.

For the first two years that the Science Circus was on the road it was staffed by specially selected and trained students from the Australian National University (Canberra). When the Science Circus became part of the NSTC, it was decided that the team of young students who ran it should be selected on a national basis.

Thus in autumn 1987 the Australian National University established a one-year postgraduate programe in science communication – the first of its kind in Australia. Its aim is to provide a practical means by which science students can develop communication skills, and at the same time communicate and promote science to the general public. The applicants therefore had to present themselves for an audition. Simply having a good science degree was not sufficient, it was also necessary to possess an engaging personality and the ability to speak well. (Gore, 1988)

4 Inventorium

The Inventorium is just part of the vast Cité des Sciences et de l'Industrie at la Villette, Paris. The Inventorium is specifically designed for children up to the age of 12, and the presence of 'helpers' is an essential element of the children's space. But the observations of Gillian Thomas (head of the Inventorium until November 1989, now Director of the Halifax Children's Museum Project) are relevant to any interactive exhibition, and to anyone dealing with a mixture of paid and voluntary staff.

The necessity for helpers may seem less evident during the weekends and school holidays when the children are part of family groups. However, they help to reassure adults and enable them to make sense of the scientific content, both for themselves and for their children. With school groups they help teachers to make use of the resources and reduce anxiety about the group behaviour.

The precise role of these helpers needs to be clear, both to them and to the public. Some of their tasks include checking the working order of the exhibits, carrying out minor maintenance, controlling access to popular exhibits, asking questions to encourage children in their investigations, answering questions, doing small demonstrations and controlling entrances and exits – the tasks are not all carried out by the same person – volunteers generally have a different role from paid staff.

The number of helpers necessary depends on the type of activity involved. Some kinds of hands-on exhibits work with very little need for outside help. Other activities, such as handling live animals and collections (eg boxes or drawers where a selection of objects is presented for the child to look at and handle, accompanied by a small amount of written information), require a considerable degree of attention if the collections are to last and the animals not suffer from nervous breakdowns.

The numbers vary from about one helper for every 300m^2 for free-access exhibits, to one helper for every five children for some discovery room type exhibits – a clear estimation of the resources in personnel needs to be made before deciding on the kind of exhibit or activity to be offered. It is important to have sufficient staff present so that they do not feel threatened or overwhelmed either by the numbers of children or the amount of jobs to be done. Some things always go wrong in a children's space; exhibits break, children are sick, they lose their parents, fall over or swallow bubble mixture. The presence of a smiling adult is remembered more than the exhibit that did not work. (Thomas, 1987)

How long is a piece of string?

Despite the enthusiastic response of schoolchildren, their teachers and family groups alike, and the growing numbers of visitors to science-technology centres around the country, suspicion remains: 'Is it science? They may be enjoying themselves, but what are they learning'?

There is some consensus in the museum field (*Communicating science to the public*, Ciba Foundation conference, 1987) and amongst the hands-on profession (J Beetlestone, M Gore, RL Gregory, A Tomei, M Williams, 1988, personal conversations) that science centres are not good at teaching. They are about *inspiration*.

Interactive exhibits present scientific phenomena and aspects of technology in ways that encourage investigation and experiment. But the emphasis is on the phenomena. The exhibits whet the appetite. To build a deeper understanding, that interest – once aroused – must be taken advantage of. This, traditionally, has been the role of the teacher and of books.

However, as interactive centres become firmly established they are discovering a new area for growth – their relationship with teachers and schools.

During the last 18 months, I have heard interpreters defined as anyone from a superfluous being who could easily be dispensed with if exhibit designers, fabricators and caption writers got their collective act together, to a super-teacher who reaches the parts classroom teachers do not even aspire to. In most cases, reality falls somewhere between the two extremes, as the four brief case studies have shown.

In the growth area of the relationship between informal learning and formal science education, the interpreter has an extra role to play – that of diplomatic signpost – pointing interested visitors to available books, follow-up materials and the science centre's education contact.

'Science is boring' is often camouflage for 'I hate chalk-and-talk school science', or 'I'm scared of the complex technology all around me'. It is therefore essential that a visit to a science centre should be enjoyable and that exhibits should, like the best cocktail canapes, be attractive, stimulating and 'moreish'.

Different visitors will then find satisfaction through

- activities suggested by a book or kit they buy at the science-centre shop;
- a leisurely return visit;
- workshop or laboratory-type experiments in an area separate from the hands-on gallery;
- outreach programmes and formal lessons at school;
- a local BAYS (British Association Young Scientists) group or science inventors' club;
- a TV *Horizon* or *QED* programme on a related subject;

and so on – the range of possible follow-up activities is immense. Many are already run successfully at science-technology centers (sic) in the US. Others are now being pioneered in the UK, India and the Nordic countries (NCSM, 1988).

Pimlico Perspective

I was a Pimlico Connection tutor myself in 77/78 (Goodlad and Hirst, 1989, Chapter 5). When I first dicovered the interactive science and technology centre interpreter, he/she appeared quite familiar! The best of both species have so much in common: they are articulate young scientists, concerned to stimulate questions and help search for answers rather than to inform. Some of the most effective are also great actors.

In the informal atmosphere of a hands-on exhibition, the interpreter combines explanation with entertainment. The science-technology centre becomes a stage, the exhibits props, and the visitors take active roles in creating their own learning experience (Sondra Quinn, Orlando Science Centre, and Aubrey Tulley, Science Museum, South Kensington, personal communications).

Correspondence:
Dr Melanie Quin, 5 Milford Street, Cambridge, CB1 2LP

14 Peer tutoring, peer collaboration and the development of a memorisation strategy

David A Kellett

What experiences should peer tutoring and peer collaboration include? Should children's interaction be regulated by an adult? Does peer collaboration result in greater cognitive benefits for the tutor than peer tutoring? These are some of the questions addressed in the empirical study which is summarised in this chapter.

The empirical study investigated the cognitive benefits for children who used superior (tutors) and inferior (tutees) memorisation strategies. Children's interaction involved either peer tutoring or peer collaboration, and peer collaboration was either regulated by an adult or left relatively unregulated. Cognitive development was measured in terms of the development of a more effective memorisation strategy. The adult regulated peer collaboration was designed to include several experiences which have been identified by the neo-Piagetian theorists as important for cognitive development.

Children gained greatest cognitive benefits in the regulated peer collaboration condition. Greatest generalisation of the more effective memorisation strategy was also made by children in the regulated peer collaboration condition. This pattern of results indicates that an imaginative application of a theory of development to the design of peer interaction styles can result in profitable suggestions for how teachers can design and regulate peer interaction in a way which produces cognitive benefits.

Introduction

There have been many claims, in both the education and psychology literatures, for the so-called 'tutoring effect': that an individual 'tutor' may benefit through tutoring another individual 'tutee', perhaps even more than the tutee. For example in an early book Gartner, Kohler, and Riessman (1971) claimed that tutors can develop greater intellectual competence in the tutored domain through tutoring peer tutees who have less initial competence than themselves. They claimed further that the intellectual benefits to the tutor can be greater than the benefits to the tutee he or she tutors. If this effect can be found to occur in peer tutoring interactions, it must have enormous implications for any theories of development and instruction as well as for educational practice. The voluminous research undertaken since the 1970s, however, can in general be criticised on several methodological grounds (Kellett, 1989) and has failed to justify the early claims for greater intellectual benefits for the tutor than the tutee. For example a recent meta-analysis of studies of achievement gains to tutors from peer tutoring revealed only moderate gains, which were actually smaller than the equivalent gains for tutees (Cohen, Kulik and Kulik, 1982).

One of the most significant criticisms of the peer tutoring literature is that empirical work has often failed to be tied closely to sound educational or psychological theory. Styles of tutoring have typically not been developed from theoretical work such as that of Vygotsky (1978), or Piaget (1932) or the findings of those working in the Vygotskian (eg Wood, Bruner and Ross, 1976) or neo-Piagetian traditions (eg Perret-Clermont, 1980). This not only makes it very difficult to explain the tutoring effect, if or when it does occur, but perhaps also partly explains why the literature reveals little evidence for the effect. Only through designing or encouraging styles of peer tutoring which are likely to produce a tutoring effect, and then being able to explain the effect, can its instructional potential be fully exploited. From a psychological theory of development or a theory of instruction it may be possible to make recommendations for how a style of peer tutoring should be designed: what experiences or events it should include and how it should be conducted. The theory should then help provide an explanation for the effect in terms of specific developmental or instructional mechanisms, for example 'cognitive conflict' in the case of Piagetian theory. If the mechanisms can be shown to be responsible for the effect, then a potentially profitable contribution to education has been made because the mechanisms can be included as component processes within styles of peer interaction. The study presented in this chapter was one attempt to bridge the gap between theory and practice.

Designing styles of peer interaction

Recent research in the area of peer collaboration has yielded some interesting results. Peer collaboration is similar to peer tutoring in that it can involve the pairing of two individuals with initially different 'levels' or 'degrees' of intellectual competence in a particular domain or with a particular task. However, the individuals are not assigned to the roles of tutor and tutee with a definite teaching relationship; rather they cooperate to solve a problem. Perret-Clermont (1980), for example, found that a child can become more competent at a task involving spatial and motor coordination as a result of working cooperatively with an individual who initially had lower competence than him or herself. Similarly, Doise and Mugny (1984) found evidence that an individual with a more advanced cognitive strategy may develop an even more advanced strategy through collaborating with an individual who had an initially less advanced strategy. They also found evidence that when children with the same cognitive strategy interact there may be the development of a more advanced strategy than either of them initially performed if the strategies or centrations were expressed from a different perspective. Perret-Clermont, Doise and Mugny have sought to explain this effect, which they perceive as a kind of 'tutoring effect', with reference to neo-Piagetian theory of socio-cognitive conflict.

What is the neo-Piagetian theory of socio-cognitive conflict? The theory states that the conflict between individuals who use different cognitive strategies to solve the same problem, followed by the resolution of conflict in terms of a joint effort to determine a more effective strategy, can be a powerful mechanism of cognitive development (Doise and Mugny, 1984) According to the theory, if two children have two fundamentally different methods of solving a problem (neither of which is necessarily the best) a more effective or cognitively advanced strategy may develop. However, the interaction between the collaborators should involve the following processes:

First, when two individuals attempt to solve a problem, a difference between their methods of solving it should occur, and the difference should be noticed by the individuals. For example, according to Piaget's theory (1932) a child at the formal operations stage of cognitive development should solve a problem involving the conservation of an object's mass in a different way from a child who is still at the concrete operations stage of development.

Second, there should be an attempt to coordinate their action or points of view. That is, they should be able to test the strengths and weaknesses of each others' strategies.

Third, there should be an attempt to resolve the conflict through collaborative social interaction with the task or problem as the focus of attention. More mature 'centrations' or strategies will develop in this context if the results of action with the task or problem are considered in relation to their strategies and where each participant considers each others' utterances and actions as meaningful and important (Mugny, De Paolis and Carugati, 1984). Hence, although the child who uses an inferior strategy may not provide the correct answer, he or she may suggest to the child who employs the superior strategy 'some relevant dimension for the progressive elaboration of a cognitive mechanism new to him' (Doise, Mugny, and Perret-Clermont' 1981).

From the theoretical work of the neo-Piagetians it is possible to design a style of peer collaboration which includes, as far as possible, the processes identified as responsible for development. The study presented in this chapter had several explicit aims which are briefly summarised as follows:

1   To design a style of peer collaboration which includes the key social processes which have been identified by the neo-Piagetians as important components of socio-cognitive conflict. These processes have been mentioned briefly above.

2   To measure the relative cognitive benefits to pairs of peers who collaborate in the style recommended by the neo-Piagetians or who experience peer tutoring. In both styles of interaction a peer with a more effective cognitive strategy was paired with a peer who used a less effective strategy, but in peer tutoring there was an explicit tutor to tutee teaching relationship: the more effective strategy is transmitted to the tutee.

3   To determine the relative cognitive benefits to children whose collaboration was closely regulated by an adult or 'expert' or who were left alone to collaborate. If an intellectually beneficial style of peer interaction is to be developed, it is necessary to determine what role the teacher or 'expert' can usefully play. Therefore in the study summarised in this chapter the cognitive benefits to pairs of children whose interaction was regulated by an adult were compared to the benefits for children who were left alone to collaborate.

4   To improve on previous research by having a control group for each style of peer interaction. The children in the control groups enjoyed the same amount of time with the task and the same opportunity to interact as children in the experimental groups. However the content of the interaction was not designed to include the processes identified as important for development by the neo-Piagetians for example.

In order to meet these aims, a task was designed to measure the effectiveness of a child's memorisation strategy. Children of 14 years appear to memorise lists of words or pictures in a more effective way than younger children. Older children attempt to memorise cumulatively (Ornstein, Naus and Liberty, 1975; Kellett, 1989). That is, they will attempt to recall the previous items in a list each time they come to a new item. In contrast, young children of six and seven years will tend to rehearse non-cumulatively. They will rehearse each item in a list without attempting to recall the previous ones as they go along to each new item. As rehearsal strategies appear to follow a developmental path and are easily measurable, the task of memorisation was chosen for the study described below. Such a task may offer a means to make potentially powerful and easily justifiable recommendations for education. Socio-cognitive conflict requires the pairing of children with different cognitive strategies. Hence in the study reported below children were chosen to participate who showed non-cumulative rehearsal. The 'tutor' was then taught a 'partial' cumulative rehearsal strategy where he or she attempted to recall the first item in a list as he she rehearsed the second, but then continued to rehearse the rest of the items in the list in a non-cumulative way. Hence 'cognitive benefits' were defined as the development of a strategy which was more cumulative than either the non-cumulative rehearsal strategy the tutee began the study with, or the partial cumulative rehearsal strategy the tutor was taught. The way the task was used in the styles of peer tutoring and collaboration is described below.

Methodology

An abbreviated methodology is presented below. The full details are available in Kellett (1989)

Subjects
148 children were drawn from four primary schools in Nottingham. Ages ranged from 7 years 3 months to 9 years 7 months, with a mean age of 8 years 2 months. The children were 75 males and 73 females.

Materials
   1   *Task 1 (map task)* A simple road map was drawn on a piece of card 30 cm × 21cm. The map represented a journey from 'home' to 'school'. 23 hand-drawn pictures of objects which are common in street scenes, were made on 4 cm × 3.5 cm card. The name of the object was printed above each picture. This task was used during peer interaction, and was used with Task 2 for pre-and post-experiment assessment of memorisation strategy use.
   2   *Task 2 (shopping task)* 22 good – quality colour photographs of household and food objects were used. The pictures represented objects that the children would probably be familiar with buying in the shops. This task was designed and used to determine whether any strategy development made during peer interaction with Task 1 generalised to an analogous second task.
   3   *Interaction-style training task* A commercially-available bicycle lamp was used for the interaction style training procedure. The four main parts of the lamp had to be assembled in a particular sequence.
   4   *Video equipment* A video camera and recorder were placed several feet from the children, and in their full view.

Design
The experiment employed a 3 × 2 × 2 × 2 factorial design, with the following between–subject factors: tutoring style (peer tutoring, regulated socio-cognitive conflict, unregulated socio-cognitive conflict); treatment (experimental, control); and subject role (tutor, tutee). The one within-subject factor was post-test performance (Task 1, Task 2).

Procedure
Children experienced the different elements of the experimental procedure in the following order.

1 Pre-experiment assessment of rehearsal strategy use (tutors and tutees).
2 Partial cumulative rehearsal strategy training (for tutors only).
3 One of the peer interaction styles: peer tutoring, or either regulated or unregulated socio-cognitive conflict. The interaction styles were either 'experimental' or 'control'. Peer interaction with the memorisation task followed training in the appropriate style of interaction with a task which involved assembling a lamp (tutors with tutees).
4 Post-experiment assessment of the rehearsal strategy used to memorise a list of items (tutors and tutees).

The different stages of the experiment are described in more detail below.

1 Pre-experiment assessment of strategy use

Children's use of rehearsal strategy was assessed using Task 1. Children were taken individually from their main classroom and asked to learn six pictures which were placed face down on the map. They were informed that the pictures represented a journey that John took on his way from home to school one day, and that they could learn the pictures by turning them over, looking at them and turning them back. They could look through the pictures as many times as they wished until they could report all the things John went past on his journey without having to look at the pictures again. Only children who used a non-cumulative rehearsal strategy (see Ornstein, Naus and Liberty, 1975) were included in the experiment.

2 Cumulative rehearsal strategy training

Children were paired at random and randomly allocated to the roles of tutor or tutee. Tutors were then taught a partial cumulative rehearsal strategy with Task 1 as follows:

• Turn over the first picture, name it and turn it back.
• Turn over the second, name it and turn it back.
• Before you turn over the third picture, try to remember the first two.

- Then turn the third one over, name it and turn it back.
- Turn the fourth one over, name it and turn it back, then the fifth and then the sixth.

Pairs of children then experienced one of the following procedures.

3   Experimental procedures: peer social interaction

3.1   Peer tutoring experimental and control conditions
For subjects in the experimental and control conditions, the procedures for interaction style training were the same. Tutor and tutee were asked to take turns to assemble the lamp three times each. Tutors had been previously taught a correct method, tutees an incorrect method. For two of the assemblies, the tutor was asked to teach the tutee the correct method, and after all assemblies the pair were asked to to discuss what they enjoyed about fixing the lamp together.

Pairs of children in the experimental condition were then asked to take turns rehearsing six different sets of six pictures with Task 1, six times each. Following two learning trials, the tutors were asked to teach the tutees the partial cumulative rehearsal strategy they had been taught, and following all other learning trials pairs were asked to discuss what they enjoyed about learning the pictures. Pairs of children in the control condition took turns to rehearse six different sets of six pictures, six times each. Following the learning trials the pairs were asked to discuss what they enjoyed about learning the pictures.

3.2   Regulated conflict experimental and control conditions
For subjects in the experimental and control conditions, the procedures for interaction style training were the same. The tutor and tutee were asked to assemble the lamp three times each. The tutor had been taught a correct method, the tutee an incorrect method. Following the first assembly they were asked to discuss who fixed it together best. Following further attempts to assemble the lamp the pair were asked to describe to each other how they assembled the lamp and the similarities and differences between their memorisation strategies. Following a further assembly of the lamp, the pair were asked to discuss and reach agreement on the best assembly strategy. During all discussion periods the experimenter regulated the interactions. The regulation included prompts for subjects to ask and answer each others' questions.

Children in the experimental condition were asked to take turns to rehearse six different sets of six pictures, six times each. Following two learning trials, the pair were asked to decide who learned them the best way. After each of two further trials the subjects were asked to find out how the other person was trying to rehearse the information. Following further learning trials the subjects were asked to compare and contrast each others' learning strategy, and to talk until they could agree on the best way to learn the pictures. During each discussion period the experimenter regulated the interaction. The regulation included prompts to subjects to ask and answer each others' questions.

Pairs of children in the control condition followed a similiar procedure as children in the peer tutoring control condition described above. However, they were asked to describe to each other what they enjoyed about learning the pictures, what the similarities and differences were in what they enjoyed about learning the pictures, and to reach agreement as to what was the most enjoyable way of learning the pictures. The interaction was regulated in a similar way to the experimental condition, including prompts from the experimenter.

3.3   Unregulated conflict experimental and control conditions
For pairs of children in the experimental and control conditions, the interaction style training and the design of the style of peer interaction were similar to the regulated conflict conditions. However, during each discussion period, the pair were asked to reach their answers with no adult regulation of their interaction. The experimenter left the room for each discussion period.

4   Post-experiment assessment of strategy use

After peer interaction, the rehearsal strategy each child used to memorise a list of items was assessed individually with Task 1, then Task 2. For Task 1 the subjects were asked to show the experimenter the very best way of learning six pictures. Similar instructions were given for subjects to learn six pictures with Task 2.

From video recordings, the experimenter counted how many items had been rehearsed cumulatively on both tasks, the first time the subjects looked through the items. The number of cumulatively rehearsed items was summarised as two post-test scores, corresponding to the number of items which had been cumulatively rehearsed on both tasks. Two were subtracted from tutor Task 1 rehearsal scores because they had already been taught cumulative rehearsal on two items, ie partial cumulative rehearsal.

Results

The post-test scores for children in all social interaction conditions were calculated. A full statistical analysis of the results will not be presented here: such an analysis is available from the author, or in Kellett (1989). Instead a brief summary of the important aspects of the results will be presented.

An average (mean) post-test score was calculated for tutors and tutees who had experienced the different peer interaction styles. The means for each group of tutors are presented in Table 14.1. The post-test scores revealed that the development of the most cumulative rehearsal strategy was enjoyed by children in the socio-cognitive conflict experimental condition, and the least development was enjoyed by the children from the peer tutoring condition. In all styles of interaction the subjects in the experimental conditions enjoyed greater benefits than those in the control conditions, and this difference appeared particularly marked in the case of regulated socio-cognitive conflict. In summary, both styles of collaboration appeared to result in greater cognitive benefits than peer tutoring, though the difference between the benefits from regulated and unregulated socio-cognitive conflict appeared small.

Table 14.2 summarises the mean post-test scores for tutors in all conditions on the test of strategy generalisation, Task 2. On Task 2 the only style of peer interaction where there appeared to be a clear difference between experimental and control conditions was in regulated socio-cognitive conflict. In addition, scores of tutors in the regulated socio-cognitive conflict condition appeared clearly higher than those of other groups. In conclusion, both regulated and unregulated socio-cognitive conflict conditions led to fairly comparable developments of a cumulative rehearsal strategy. However, for the strategy to be effectively generalised to a second task it appeared more beneficial to have experienced regulated interaction.

The data in Tables 14.3 and 14.4 reveals that tutees in the regulated socio-cognitive conflict condition scored clearly higher on both tasks than the other tutee groups. Hence for tutees to develop and generalise a more cumulative rehearsal strategy than the one they used at the beginning of the experiment it was more advantageous for them to experience the regulated socio-cognitive conflict style of interaction than the unregulated collaborative interaction, or peer tutoring.

Table 14.1 Post test scores of Tutors in all conditions on Task 1.

child	group	N	Mean
pt	exp	13	1.9
pt	con	12	1.4
rc	exp	12	4.3
rc	con	13	1.4
uc	exp	12	3.8
uc	con	12	2.6

Note: 'pt' represents peer tutoring; 'rc' represents regulated conflict; and 'uc' represents unregulated conflict; 'exp' represents experimental condition, and 'con' represents control condition.

Table 14.2 Post test scores of tutors in all conditions on Task 2 (Abbreviations the same as in Table 14.1)

Child	group	N	Mean
pt	exp	13	1.8
pt	con	12	2.9
rc	exp	12	6.8
rc	con	13	0.7
uc	exp	12	3.4
uc	con	12	4.7

From the results there appeared to be little evidence of greater benefits to tutors than tutees from any of the styles of peer interaction. Hence the study found little justification for the claims of, for example, Gartner, Kohler and Riessman (1971) that tutors benefit more than tutees.

Table 14.3 Post test scores for tutees in all conditions on Task 1 (Abbreviations the same as in Table 14.1)

Child	group	N	Mean
pt	exp	13	2.3
pt	con	12	0.8
rc	exp	12	7.9
rc	con	13	0
uc	exp	12	1.25
uc	con	12	1.8

The results suggest quite strongly that peer collaboration may offer greater cognitive benefits than peer tutoring which involves the transmission of a cognitive strategy from one child to another.

Conclusions and recommendations for education

The results suggest that socio-cognitive conflict theory may offer a powerful mechanism of development and a useful starting point for the development of an effective style of peer interaction. However, several cautionary notes need to be offered. The neo-Piagetians have not, as yet, clearly demonstrated that socio-cognitive conflict has been responsible for the cognitive development enjoyed by children in their experiments.

Table 14.4 Post-test scores of tutees in all conditions on Task 2 (Abbreviations the same as in Table 14.1)

Child	group	N	Mean
pt	exp	13	3.1
pt	con	12	0.6
rc	exp	12	7.6
rc	con	13	0
uc	exp	12	0.6
uc	con	12	1.25

Indeed they have offered little means of examining and describing interaction in a way which points clearly to a role for their conflict mechanism. Similarly, although the socio-cognitive conflict style of collaboration proved to be most beneficial in the experiment described above, it is not clear whether the key processes identified by the neo-Piagetians were responsible for strategy development. A detailed analysis of the interaction (Kellett, 1989) revealed little clear evidence for the role of the conflict mechanism. Further research would have to be conducted to determine whether cognitive benefits resulted from a genuine elaboration of a cognitive strategy within socio-cognitive conflict, or whether a more cumulative rehearsal strategy developed spontaneously and was, for example, more effectively transmitted to the second child. The latter explanation would be favoured by, for example, Russell (1981). Hence the results should be of interest to researchers engaged in instructional design. However, as one of the themes of this chapter has been that the gap between theory and practice should be more effectively bridged, the results should be of equal interest, and for the same reasons, to teachers.

The results should be of interest to teachers who wish to experiment with different styles of peer tutoring and collaboration. To find a style of peer interaction which appears to 'work' may be beneficial for the children. However, it appears that experimentation with different styles of interaction in the same instructional domain or with the same task may in the longer term produce a more beneficial interaction style. The results should also be an encouragement to teachers to develop and evaluate their own styles of peer interaction. It is strongly recommended however that a starting point be made with sound psychological or educational theory. There are many theories which may be a rich source of ideas for what social processes effective styles of peer interaction should include and how they should be conducted.

Interestingly, the results point to a crucial role for the teacher or 'expert' if peer interaction is to be intellectually beneficial. This appears to confirm the findings of Glachan (1983) that the way an adult structures the interaction of a pair of collaborating peers can affect the cognitive benefits enjoyed by the peers. The nature of this role requires further investigation before clear recommendations can be made to teachers. In the study presented in this chapter, the adult regulation of the children's social interaction involved making sure that the child collaborators were clear about what they should be discussing at various points during the procedure. In this sense, the adult was a 'facilitator', though not explicitly a teacher in the sense of offering clues about the goal or appropriate 'correct answer' from the procedure, or clues about the way in which memorisation performance or the specific content of the interaction should be progressing. For example, the experimenter did not direct the children along relevant lines of discussion. Further research is required to determine the cognitive benefits to children of having an adult regulate their interaction who does not know the way the strategy should develop as a result of the experiment. Perhaps the study described above should be replicated with such a regulator. A replication would, it is hoped, confirm that cognitive benefits to the child collaborators did not develop as a result of a teaching effect from the experimenter.

Finally, although the intellectual benefit of peer tutoring and collaboration is by no means a new research area, there are many interesting and potentially useful project possibilities.

It is to be hoped that the application of tutoring and collaboration programmes in schools will not continue to progress more quickly than efforts to develop programmes of a high quality.

Correspondence:
Dr. D Kellett, The Post Office, Psychological Services, Fording House, 23 Glasshill Street, London SE1 0BQ.

15 Process and outcome in tuition for reading: the case of Paired Reading

Sam Winter

Paired Reading (PR) has been used with apparent success in a range of parent and peer tutor applications. Attempts to explain the effectiveness of PR projects fail to take into account findings which indicate:

a) the equivalent effectiveness of PR and a number of other oral-reading tutoring techniques;

b) the common failure of tutors to adhere to the PR techniques in which they have been trained.

A recent Hong Kong study suggests that the problem of aberrant tutors can be a very great one indeed. Interestingly, it is found that there is no link between tutor adherence to PR and tutee gains. There follows a discussion of why this may be. Reference is made to the Western Electric studies of the early 1930s. It is suggested that the organisational factors which are apparently important where there is innovation in the workplace are also important in PR (and possibly other tutoring) projects.

Introduction: Paired Reading

Since 1976, Paired Reading (PR) has been used with apparent success in the UK and elsewhere to encourage children's oral reading ability. Early projects involved parent tutors. Recently a number of apparently successful peer-tutored PR projects have been reported, the first being that of Winter and Low (1984).

PR may be summarised as follows. During *simultaneous reading*, the tutor and tutee read aloud together from reading material chosen by the tutee. If the tutee hesitates or fails to self-correct a mistake then the tutor models the word, the tutee repeats it, and the two continue to read together. The tutee signals if he/she wants to read independently. In the event of the tutor supplying a word during *independent reading* then the two subsequently read together until the tutee signals again. The tutor praises the tutee for signalling, self-correction and any other desirable reading behaviour.

Applications of PR

The PR literature relating to parent tutors suggests that

1   Low progress, 'dyslexic' and satisfactory readers, as well as ESL children, can benefit from PR.
2   The benefits encompass reading rate, accuracy and comprehension as well as improved attitudes towards reading.
3   Tutees from six years upwards into adulthood can benefit from PR.
4   Such benefits can be shown in projects as short as six weeks.

Many of the earlier studies are reviewed by Topping and McKnight (1984). For a more recent review, see Winter (1987). Reports of parent-tutored PR projects commonly indicate average gains in reading age which are several times greater than the actual duration of the project concerned; gains unmatched by 'no-treatment' groups where such comparison data is available.

Recent peer-tutored PR projects indicate that the technique can be taught to primary and secondary school children. These children can then act as successful tutors with partners who are the same age or younger, and they can sometimes make reading gains as great as those of the tutees. Early examples of peer-tutored PR projects are reported in Winter and Low (1984) and Limbrick, McNaughton and Glynn (1985). For recent reviews of similar research see Winter (1986) and Topping (1987).

A number of UK and Hong Kong research projects have shown that PR can improve the English reading ability of children for whom it is their second language. In a different vein, Chan (1987) has used the technique to improve the Chinese reading skills of pupils in Hong Kong. (For a fuller discussion of the ESL and Chinese language applications of PR see Winter, 1989.)

Why is PR effective?

Advocates of PR have offered a variety of explanations to account for its apparent effectiveness. Morgan and Lyon (1979) offered a broadly behavioural analysis, emphasising the participant – modelling and positive reinforcement components of PR. Bushell, Miller and Robson (1982), drew attention to other possible factors, arguing that PR provided opportunities for the development of prediction based on semantic and syntactic cues.

They also suggest that parent-tutored PR increases self-esteem by shifting parent attention towards correct reading performance and away from a primarily error-correcting emphasis, and providing the child with an unusual view of the parent as learner; a view which encourages the child to regard his/her own learning role in a more positive light.

Research calls these ideas into question and suggests that the apparent success of PR may not be so easily explained.

The problem of equivalent effectiveness

Swinson (1986a and b) and Pumfrey (1986) have drawn attention to the lack of any evidence showing PR to be any more effective than other tutoring techniques for improving oral reading. Indeed, research done to compare directly PR with other techniques such as Relaxed Reading (Lindsay, Evans and Jones, 1985) and Individualised Reading (Grigg, 1984; Burdett, 1986) fails to identify any as being clearly superior.

Other techniques not yet subjected to experimental comparison with PR also appear to work very well. Some appear to be variants of PR (eg Bryans, Kidd and Levey, 1985; Young and Tyre, 1983; Portsmouth, Wilkins and Airey, 1985). Other rather different approaches are Pause-Prompt-Praise (Glynn, 1981; Wheldall, Merrett and Colmar, 1987), Shared Reading (Greening and Spenceley, 1984, 1987), Read-Aloud methods (Wareing, 1985), and less structured approaches such as those of Tizard, Schofield and Hewison (1982); Widlake and Macleod (1985), Ashton, Stoney and Hannon (1986); Swinson (1985); and Sigston, Addington, Banks and Striesow (1984).

One reason why so many tutoring approaches seem to be effective may be that they share common features; the emphasis upon active engagement in reading; the presence of a tutor; and the emphasis upon positive reinforcement. However, in each case the evidence is not favourable.

The effect of active engagement in reading is questionable in view of evidence showing.

- no relationship between reading gains and time spent reading (Miller, Robson and Bushell, 1986) or amount read (Winter 1988);
- inferior gains for control groups which engage in private reading during tutoring projects, as in Wheldall and Mettem (1986);
- gains in reading in projects where active engagement in reading plays a lesser role, as in 'Prepared Reading' (Young and Tyre, 1983) and the 'Linguistic Method' (Wareing, 1985);
- reading gains in projects designed to improve social or emotional adjustment, and where little or no reading takes place, as in Wooster's (1986) work on social skills training and the work of Rocks, Baker and Guerney (1985) in the area of teacher-pupil relationship enhancement.

An effect of tutor presence upon tutees' interest, confidence and/or persistence when reading is contra-indicated by the common finding that untrained tutoring is less effective than trained tutoring. The work of Limbrick et al (1985) and Crombie and Low (1986) using PR, and of Wheldall and Mettem (1986) using Pause-Prompt-Praise, are cases in point.

The role of positive reinforcement of reading is questionable in view of the social skills training and relationship enhancement research already mentioned, in which there were few if any opportunities for such reinforcement to occur. Evidence from Heath (1981) suggests that massive amounts of positive reinforcement during a reading project can fail to produce the sorts of gains common under, for example, PR. There is also evidence that, despite the training given, tutors, at least those in PR projects, often fail to use positive reinforcement very much at all. This last matter – aberrant PR tutors – is an important one and deserves further attention.

The problem of aberrant tutors

It is quite clear from the PR literature that many tutors fail to employ the PR techniques in which they have been trained. Most of the evidence for this is anecdotal, derived from questionnaires completed by tutors or from checklists completed by observers during tutoring sessions. Until recently, only one study had reported direct and systematic measurement of tutor behaviour (Limbrick et al, 1985). The peer tutors in this study appeared, even after PR training, to employ little praise and to correct few errors.

No evidence has been presented, either in the above study or anywhere else in the PR literature, that aberrant tutors are less effective than others. The question regarding the link between tutoring process (what the tutor actually does during PR sessions) and tutee outcome (reading gains etc at project end) is a crucial one. As we have seen, advocates of PR have explained its effectiveness by drawing attention to aspects of the technique. If any of the technical aspects of PR do indeed account for its effectiveness then we should see an association between tutor adherence to PR and tutor effectiveness. If such a connection cannot be found than we should consider other factors which might account for the beneficial effects it has upon children.

The Hong Kong study

A recent Hong Kong peer-tutored PR project with which I was involved attempted to investigate the following issues;

1 The degree to which tutors trained to employ PR actually employ the technique during the course of a tutoring project.
2 The degree to which adherence to components of PR is associated with the reading age gains displayed by tutees.

A full account of the project is available in Winter (1988).

Method

Pupils from two English language primary schools in Hong Kong took part in concurrent peer tutor workshops involving the use of PR techniques.

Staff at School A invited pupils from four grade six classes to act as helpers (tutors) or readers (tutees). Tutees choose a tutor with whom they would like to work. 16 pairs resulted. Tutors and tutees were then taught how to use PR techniques by way of description, demonstration, practice and concurrent feedback. Tutor-tutee pairs worked for 10 minutes at the start of each school day for the six weeks the workshop lasted. During this time teachers associated with the project supervised the performance of tutors.

The workshop at school B differed from that at school A in so far as training preceded selection; that is, all pupils in two grade 6 classes were trained to use PR before being given the opportunity to volunteer to be tutors or tutees. Interestingly, a far greater proportion of pupils wanted involvement in the workshop; a total of 27 pairs were organised.

The reading ability of tutees was assessed at project start and end by way of the GAP Reading Comprehension Test. Each pupil was tested on Form B and R with order randomised.

Tape recordings of pre-project-selected tutoring sessions were analysed after the end of the project to provide information regarding tutor adherence to PR. 36 intact and audible recordings (accompanied by the text read) were analysed. Variables relating to tutor and tutee behaviour were scored for a period of five minutes from the beginning of the second minute of the tutoring session to the end of the sixth minute. Variables relating to tutor behaviour and found to be measured reliably were:

Number of errors corrected in any way by the tutor
Number of errors left uncorrected
Number of instances of positive reinforcement
Number of words modelled (short pause; under 2 secs)
Number of errors corrected in any other way
Correction rate in relation to number of errors
Words modelled during period analysed
Modelling rate in relation to number of errors
Praise rate in relation to number of words read
Modelling rate in relation to number of corrections made

Short-pause modelling rate in relation to corrections

Results

All tutors in some way failed during the project to follow the procedures for PR in which they had been trained and supposedly supervised. Basic data is summarised in Table 15.1.

Tutors were particularly negligent in regard to positive reinforcement. The highest rate of positive reinforcement in the sessions analysed stood at a level of one event per 38 seconds (or once in every 50 words read). Six tutors failed to use any reinforcement at all.

A large number of tutors observed failed to correct errors made by tutees. Errors left uncorrected outweighed errors corrected by a ratio of 4:1. Many errors left uncorrected were major; as in an extreme case in which a tutee turned over two pages without him or his tutor appearing to notice.

Where error correction occurred at all, tutors were quite conscientious in employing modelling (98% of error corrections). However there was a tendency for tutors to be careless about timing; about two out of every five words modelled were supplied after a pause substantially shorter than the four seconds which the tutors had been trained to use.

Tutors displayed consistent behaviour over the two sessions observed, despite a period of severals week between the two sessions which provided data. Tutors' failure to adhere to PR procedures therefore appears to have been persistent.

Despite all this, tutees in school A made an average gain of 0.29 years on the GAP test whilst those in school B averaged a statistically significant

Table 15.1   Tutor behaviour during paired reading sessions

Variable	MEAN	SD	MIN	MAX
Errors corrected in any way by tutor	2.97	2.88	0	15
Errors left uncorrected	15.25	8.08	0	42
Positive reinforcement	1.42	1.73	0	8
Words modelled; short pause	1.36	1.42	0	7
Errors corrected in any other way	0.19	0.82	0	6
Correction rate	0.19	0.16	0	1.00
Words modelled	2.78	2.34	0	11
Modelled words/errors	0.18	0.12	0	0.64
Pos. Rf. in relation to words read	0.00	0.00	0	0.02
Modelled words/corrections	0.98	0.08	0.70	1.00
Short pause models/corrections	0.43	0.33	0.00	1.00

Note: Figures relate to frequency during each five minute period analysed. Data for both schools is combined due to insignificant differences.

0.53 years. Furthermore, no relationship was found between tutor behaviour during PR and reading gains made by tutees at project end. The implication is that adherence to PR procedures (at least over the range observed in this study) has no impact whatsoever upon the effectiveness of tutoring, at least in regard to the tutor variables.

Critical note

It is important to note the following points: 1 The study described was a small one. 2 Only one measure of reading ability was employed. 3 A ceiling effect resulted in reading age data for some tutees being removed from the analysis. 4 Variables relating to tutor and tutee behaviour during PR sessions were based on a small sample of data. 5 Some possibly important PR variables (eg proportion of time spent in independent reading, specificity of positive reinforcement) were not measured. 6 Some of the variables that were measured displayed very narrow ranges, thereby making more difficult the task of locating relationships with other variables. Nevertheless, this study contributes further doubt regarding the claims made by Morgan and Lyon (1979) and Bushell et al. (1982) regarding the reasons for the effectiveness of PR.

Discussion

The several lines of evidence reviewed in this paper indicate that the success of PR projects may not result from any aspect of the PR technique itself. The equivalent effectiveness of other tutoring techniques, the apparent unimportance of amount of or time spent reading, the apparent importance of trained tutoring, and the apparent unimportance of adherence to tutoring guidelines, all suggest that PR projects are successful *not because of what technique is taught to tutors, how well it is used and how well tutees respond to it, but because of aspects of the project itself; what is organised, and how all concerned respond to being participants.*

It may seem that I am accounting for the success of PR by reference to a Hawthorne effect; that I am suggesting that the success of PR projects is a result of paying special attention to tutees and giving them special treatment that motivates them to higher levels of performance.

In fact, I am suggesting something both more sophisticated and more subtle. It may be helpful at this point to recall what actually happened in the 1920s and 30s studies at Western Electric's Hawthorne plant.

The telephone relay room studies

In one set of experiments, workers in the telephone relay room were subjected to changed working conditions in an attempt to study effects upon output. The workers were briefed at the start of the experiment and at various points thereafter regarding the proposed changes in working conditions, and the expected effects. Any changes of which the workers did not approve were abandoned. All workers were told they should work at a comfortable pace throughout the study. Researchers found that output rose slowly and steadily throughout the entire project, regardless of the changes in working conditions.

Owens (1987) draws attention to the following factors in the telephone relay room study. First, workers liked the experimental situation and considered it fun. Second, the new method of supervision, which stressed working at a comfortable pace, made it possible for the workers to work freely without anxiety. Third, workers knew that what they did was important and that results were expected. Fourth, workers were consulted about the projected changes. Lastly, the group of workers underwent change and development during the course of the experiment. It became more cohesive, developed a distinctive esprit and functioned at a more mature level than it had at the beginning.

Owens quotes Hersey and Blanchard's (1977) summary of this study:

> the (workers) were made to feel they were an important part of the company. They had become participating members of a congenial, cohesive work group that elicited feelings of affiliation, competence and achievement. These needs, which had long gone unsatisfied at work, were now being fulfilled. The women worked harder and more effectively than they had previously. (Owens p. 95–96)

To quote Owens again:

> *The higher productivity developed in the Western Electric research resulted from the fact that – under participative leadership – the groups of workers themselves developed cohesiveness, morale, and values that were highly motivating.* (p. 96, Owens' italics).

Simple substitution in the above paragraphs of 'pupils', for 'workers', 'school', for 'company' and 'work', 'tutoring', for 'supervision' and 'reading', 'for working' suggests factors which may account for the success of PR projects. Unfortunately, no research has been done which explicitly manipulates organisational and social psychological factors in PR projects in order to study effects on tutee gains. The consequence is that we have no positive evidence that the factors relevant in the telephone relay-room are also relevant in PR tutoring sessions. However, some of the evidence points that way. Some of it is mentioned below.

PR tutor gains

It is difficult to explain the gains made by *tutors* in PR projects; gains which are often greater than those of their tutees. Explanations in terms of the provision of positive reinforcement, modelling and semantic and syntactic cues are, as we saw earlier, inadequate as ways of accounting for tutee gains. In the case of tutor gains, such explanations are entirely inappropriate. It may be that concepts drawn from social psychology and the study of organisations (concepts such as expectations, commitment, participation, group cohesion, leadership etc) are of great value in explaining why so often a person who volunteers to help another learn to read ends up learning to read better himself.

The difference in tutee gains in schools A and B

Tutees in school B made reading gains superior to those in school A. This was despite equivalence in terms of pupil variables (SES, initial reading ages and chronological ages of the tutors and tutees) and in terms of observed tutoring behaviour. The major difference between the two PR workshops was the way in which they were organised. In school B, training preceded selection; all pupils were trained in the use of PR and were then allowed to make an informed choice regarding whether and in what role they would become involved in the project. In contrast, in school A selection preceded training; pupils had to decide whether to take part in the project and choose whether to be a tutor or tutee; only afterwards were they trained.

In the absence of any other features distinguishing the two workshops from each other, it seems plausible to suggest that the superior gains in school B may have been a result of the different consultation process, specifically the *informed choice* that pupils there enjoyed. Like the workers in the Western Electric studies they, more than their counterparts in school A, may have been made to feel an important part of their 'company', resulting in higher personal commitment by tutors and tutees alike. Such commitment is perhaps reflected in the higher proportion of pupils who volunteered to take part in the project at school B.

Conclusion

Experimental work is now needed to identify the role that social psychological and organisational factors might play in determining the effectiveness of PR. If such factors are really responsible for the tutee gains made under PR, then the task for researchers in this field should be to find out ways of incorporating them into our PR projects, perhaps by building in the types of participation, decision making, goal-setting, commitment building, and leadership strategies that will enhance the gains made by tutees.

Lastly, if such factors are responsible for the tutee gains made under PR, then perhaps they are responsible for those made under other oral reading tutoring techniques, if not other instruction strategies and educational interventions. If that is the case then the discussion presented in this paper may have relevance far beyond the rather esoteric topic of peer-tutored Paired Reading.

Correspondence:
Mr S Winter, Department of Education, Hong Kong University, Pokfulam Road, Hong Kong.

16 Issues and action: lines of development for peer tutoring

Sinclair Goodlad and Beverley Hirst

We trust that the preceding chapters have indicated both that enough is already known about peer tutoring for readers to be confident that they too can consider adopting and adapting it as a teaching strategy, and also that, although there are clear indications of what needs to be done to make peer tutoring both efficient and effective, much remains to be discovered by research. In this final chapter, we pull together a number of threads, drawing both on the chapters of this book and on ideas put forward in the final plenary session of the April 1989 conference on Peer Tutoring. We do so under two broad headings:

1 *Issues.* These are identified principally as obstacles which have to be overcome or strategic problems which need to be addressed if peer tutoring is to be made to work.

2 *Action.* This is analysed in terms of logistical matters corresponding to the level of tactics and questions to which we believe research needs to be addressed. To supplement our treatment of the issues and action, we offer in Appendix B a checklist of logistic details which anyone starting a peer tutoring scheme may wish to consider.

Issues

In our judgement, there is a large enough accumulation of evidence that peer tutoring can be of benefit to teachers, tutors, and tutees to suggest that it should without delay be promoted as a primary instructional technique at all levels of the educational system and beyond. Why, then, has progress been so relatively slow? What are the obstacles to be overcome?

There are three principal categories of obstacle: Political, Psychological, and Administrative.

Political

The obstacle here is not overt or explicit resistance but rather one of visibility in the avalanche of reforms with which educators are currently coping.

During the period (September 1987 to August 1989), of the UGC special initiatives project of which this book is one outcome, the 1989 Education Reform Act was passed. Local authorities and schools have been so absorbed with the National Curriculum and preparation for LMS (the Local Management of Schools), that they have had little time to consider anything else. Likewise, public sector higher education institutions (poly-technics, colleges and institutes of higher education) have been preparing for their new funding arrangements. Universities too have been so preoccupied with short-term measures to relieve financial pressures that we have found it hard to draw attention to peer tutoring as a teaching strategy.

Once (if ever?) the dust settles, it may be more timely for peer tutoring to be considered. We trust that the evidence accumulated here and in *Peer Tutoring* (Goodlad and Hirst, 1989) will serve its purpose then. But then a second category of obstacle will be encountered, namely, the psychological.

Psychological

As in the world of physical phenomena, so in the psychological, most systems settle into a state of equilibrium. However unsatisfactory prevailing circumstances may be, it is easy to fall into the way of thinking that anything different might be worse. In his slim but immortal volume *Microcosmographica Academica*. Francis Macdonald Cornford put it thus:

> Every public action which is not customary either is wrong or, if it is right, is a dangerous precedent. It follows that nothing should ever be done for the first time.

Teachers comtemplating the possibility of starting a tutoring scheme may fear that they would suffer a loss of authority, or that there would be negative reactions from parents, or that colleagues or superiors would be hostile, or that because it is manifestly cheap to organise, peer tutoring might be selling pupils short. Above all, the prospect of administrative hassle can put people off attempting an innovation. It is for this reason that we are devoting space in this chapter to spelling out what may seem painfully obvious - so that readers' sense of impossibility may be diminished.

Administrative

Participants in the 1989 conference confirmed what the literature suggests - namely that the three principal obstacles to running peer tutoring schemes are: the need for an initiator; timetabling; and resources.

Those who have had any part in the initiation or subsequent implementation of a peer tutoring scheme testify to the necessity of having one person who takes overall responsibility for the organisation of the scheme. The importance of the stabilising effect of such a key person is mentioned by Fresko and Carmeli (Chapter 4 above). As the PERACH scheme has expanded, it has no longer been expedient to use students as local managers: instead, individuals with management experience now fulfil this role – ensuring that there is at least one stable figure at each university experienced in the project's operation. Although this administrator (or coordinator) of a tutoring project has to deal with the logistics of the scheme (timetabling, tutor-training etc), the role is primarily that of a communicator. He or she must liaise with those sending tutors and those receiving them, ensure that necessary instructions are relayed to tutors and tutees, and keep significant others informed about the scheme.

Although it is relatively simple to outline the principal responsibilities of such a coordinator, it is not so easy to define who that person might be. Indeed, the most suitable candidate for the post may vary depending upon the particular features of a scheme. If a tutoring scheme is to be implemented within an institution, it is more than likely that a member of staff from that institution would be best suited to dealing with the organisation. However, as Fitz-Gibbon indicates (in Chapter 2 above), visiting researchers have also been successful at implementing tutoring projects. The initiator and ultimate coordinator of a programme need not, of course, be the same person. What does seem to be essential is that the person heading the scheme has the enthusiasm and 'belief' in tutoring to motivate others. In Chapter 5 above, Winter suggests that the organisation of a scheme can affect the attitudes of all participants to it and, therefore, the subsequent outcome. The influence of the coordinator's personality and commitment on this organisation cannot be ignored. In several instances, researchers interested in tutoring have initiated a tutoring programme within an institution; but once the scheme has been established and the positive benefits realised, an employee of the institution has been inspired to assume responsibility for maintaining the programme.

When schemes are instigated *between* institutions, it is probably preferable that the overall coordinator should come from the institution which has to organise the movement of tutors (although, of course, link persons are needed in both institutions). When students have to move from one institution to another, they need easy access to the coordinator who has information regarding placements, weekly variations in arrangements, changes to the timetabling, etc. Such a person could be a part-time member of staff able to devote a few hours a week to running this type of scheme: in higher education, a doctoral researcher might enjoy such a role.

We have suggested elsewhere (Goodlad and Hirst, 1989:138) that if tutoring is being offered to people of a distinctive neighbourhood or ethnic background, there is merit in the coordinator being a person of the same background as the participants. Such a person can interpret elements of the programme to those for whom it is designed, and is likely to have an appropriate appreciation of their needs. Some schemes, in particular American after-school programmes, have been coordinated by energetic para-professionals. Many of these were highly-educated women not currently in full-time employment (having taken time out for family reasons) who gained immense satisfaction from their involvement in tutoring schemes which served the community. Within schools, it is possible for a member of the PTA to take responsibility for sponsorship of a scheme (assisting with administration), but with the overall coordinator being a teacher with experience of the teaching/learning process, and familiar with the aims and objectives of the teaching staff.

One obvious concern of teachers restrained by rigid timetabling arrangements will be determining *when* tutoring might take place. In a survey of 82 peer tutoring projects, Fitz-Gibbon (1987:29) found that scheduling problems occurred in 52% of them. The possibilities, of course, are quite different depending upon whether a same-age or a cross-age programme is to be implemented. With a same-age, within-class scheme, it is relatively simple to devote a proportion of a timetabled lesson to tutoring, with little disruption to other school arrangements. Initiating a cross-age programme, however, means matching the timetables of those who do the tutoring and those to be tutored. This inevitably places restrictions upon which students can participate in a programme.

As Kennedy suggests (in Chapter 3 above), school registration periods (if of a suitable length) can be used as tutoring time, as can lunchtime sessions. However, to mount a peer tutoring programme in these times would effectively turn it into a voluntary scheme; it can be difficult to persuade tutors to work in registration periods of lunchtimes. Although many tutoring schemes are run as after-school activities, most workers in the field agree that it is best to schedule tutoring during class-time if possible. With a class-based scheme, uncooperative pupils who would not stay in school outside normal hours can be incorporated. If programmes are scheduled in the timetabled day, no pupils are deprived of their free time and fewer problems arise with school security personnel.

The financial cost of initiating a peer tutoring scheme is minimal. Learning materials are usually similar to those used in conventional classroom teaching and therefore cost little extra to produce. However, the time-commitment required to develop these materials, particularly at the start of a scheme, should not be ignored. The amount of time required to produce materials will be dictated largely by the degree of structure which is to be incorporated in the scheme – which, in turn, depends upon the age and ability of the tutors. Maheady et al found that in highly-structured schemes which involved some low-ability students in reciprocal peer tutoring, the biggest disadvantage to the scheme was the amount of time which was spent writing study-guides before the programmes could be implemented (Maheady et al, 1987a, 1987b, 1988a, 1988b).

People working with younger children who want to start a tutoring scheme in reading or arithmetic should be able to find commercial programmes to help them. However, secondary school teachers wishing to start tutoring schemes in, for example, third-year Science or GCSE French, will probably have to develop the tutoring materials themselves. In this case, two factors should be kept in mind: first, workloads to enable tutors to teach tutees will probably take longer to prepare than equivalent materials to be used for full-class teaching by the professional teacher, since written instructions need to be much more explicit. Second, once the work schemes have been produced, as with all teaching materials, subsequent changes and adaptations can be made for follow-on programmes in much shorter periods of time.

What is needed, therefore, is for those who are to become involved in organising peer tutoring to be released from other major extra-curricular responsibilities a number of months before the peer tutoring is due to begin, in order to develop these materials. (There is no reason why a working party should not be responsible for producing materials, although again an overall coordinator would be required.) It would, of course, be preferable for the coordinator to be granted extra periods of non-contact time to develop these materials within the timetabled day.

The other major resource which tutoring needs is space. If same-age, within-class tutoring is arranged, pupils will, of course, work in the allotted classroom as normal (although, it is to be hoped, sufficiently well spaced-out to facilitate tutor/tutee interaction without any disturbance to neighbouring pairs). Similarly the expedient of pairing classes makes it possible for half the class of tutors to go to the classroom of the tutees and vice versa, without additional demands being made on space. However, in some schemes this may not be possible and extra space will be needed. Occasionally, a special room can be set aside for tutoring, in which the dyads meet: in this case, it is relatively easy for the coordinator to supervise the tutoring. However, more generally out-of-the-way places have to be found (such as cloakrooms, dining-rooms, corridors, corners of the library). These arrangements increase the informality of tutor-tutee contacts, but they also expose the tutor-pairs to many interruptions and make supervision difficult.

Action

The notion of overcoming obstacles may seem too negative a way to conceive of promoting peer tutoring. We turn, therefore, to a number of actions which conference participants suggested – again classifying them as Political, Psychological, and Administrative.

Political

If new teaching strategies are to be given a high profile in schools and the necessary resource-provision made, some degree of LEA support is required. LEA personnel could help to ease the implementation of peer tutoring within schools in several ways. At present, they are the people in a position to grant money for centralised resource materials to support tutoring. County advisors and advisory teachers provide an information network between schools and offer in-service training. If these personnel are aware of the learning-possibilities which tutoring offers, the strategy of peer tutoring could be more easily disseminated to other schools and colleges, so building up a network of collaborators in the field. If schemes linking institutions are to be developed, advisors and advisory teachers are the people who will be aware of those schools in which teaching arrangements will lend themselves well to peer tutoring. Additionally, if an LEA will give its support to peer tutoring, then it is likely that the status of the strategy will be heightened in the eyes of headteachers and other school personnel, making it easier for those using the techniques to secure resources within their own institutions.

Another means by which the dissemination of information regarding tutoring is facilitated is by articles describing the technique being published in the popular press. Several newspapers have pages devoted to educational issues which are read not only by those involved in teaching but also by parents, pupils, industrialists, and school governors.

Informing industrialists of the potential of peer tutoring could lead to local sponsorship of peer tutoring. Peer tutoring offers benefits to participants of great value to industry. Industries might, therefore, be prepared to donate small sums of money to local schools for the implementation of peer tutoring programmes – if only in the hope of attracting recruits. The sums of money involved need not be large but could cover such things as the cost of resource materials, supply-cover so that teachers can be released from class-teaching to develop peer tutoring materials, photocopying, and any transport costs if schemes are to operate between institutions.

An additional benefit that might accrue from this sort of arrangement is the psychological boost to participants of involvement in a scheme deemed worthy of industrial sponsorship.

Psychological

If peer tutoring is to be used more extensively in schools, there needs to be a heightened awareness of the technique amongst teachers – not only of the logistics of such schemes, but also of the educational theories on which they are based. (It is, for example, important that teachers understand that the potential benefits to tutors are as great as those for tutees). Including tutoring as a possible teaching strategy to be studied by teachers-in-training is one means of getting tutoring more widely accepted as a legitimate teaching tool. However, it is unlikely that new teachers will have the influence (or indeed energy!) to implement a peer tutoring programme in a school early on in their careers (although there is no reason why they should not enjoy active involvement in one if a more senior colleague was coordinating the scheme).

If initial teacher training was the only vehicle for informing teachers about tutoring, it would take a long time for the strategy to infiltrate the school system. An alternative is to use INSET days to inform more senior teachers about the technique. There are now sufficient people who have tried tutoring (as the 1989 Peer Tutoring Conference revealed) to act as resource people for those organising in-service training. In light of the fact that almost all INSET days are currently devoted to some of the many aspects of the National Curriculum, it is worth noting that tutoring is a learning activity which fulfils criteria specified by the curricula in almost all subject areas: namely, that pupils should learn to work cooperatively rather than competitively; that group collaboration should be encouraged; and that pupils' communication and explanatory skills should be enhanced. Devoting an INSET training-day to the topic of peer tutoring could inspire teachers to adopt a whole-school policy of peer tutoring; alternatively, it could encourage individuals to incorporate tutoring within their teaching repertoire to be used in a more ad hoc fashion when considered appropriate.

Administrative

Apart from overcoming the administrative obstacles concerning the need for an initiator, the timetabling of peer tutoring and the provision of space, there are several other logistic matters that need to be attended to. We deal with them only briefly here because they are dealt with at length in the pre-conference book *Peer Tutoring* (Goodlad and Hirst, 1989, Chapter 7).

1 *Define aims.* It is important that all participants in a peer tutoring programme clearly understand the objectives of those implementing the scheme. Indeed, it is essential that administrators clarify for themselves what are their ultimate aims. For example, do they desire primarily academic gains or affective ones? Which group of students are intended to be the principal beneficiaries of the scheme? By taking time to ascertain their intentions they can more clearly define how these aims might be achieved and structure the programme accordingly.

In addition, only if the coordinator has clearly defined aims at the start of a programme can the subsequent success, or otherwise, of the scheme be evaluated. Regardless of the degree of academic rigour with which the programme is to be assessed, all people involved will wish to have some indication of whether or not their efforts have been worthwhile. As we suggest elsewhere (Goodlad and Hirst 1989:133), to maintain the morale of all concerned, the objectives of a peer tutoring scheme should be simple and readily achievable so that everyone may see how the scheme is working.

2   *Evaluate the tutoring* Almost everyone who takes part in a peer tutoring scheme likes to know 'how they have done.' Even though teachers overseeing the programme may see positive effects as a consequence of the peer tutoring, these may not be obvious to those actively participating unless there is some measurement of the outcome. That is not to suggest that highly-structured testing is always desirable: some teachers may feel that simple questionnaires or anecdotal reports satisfy their evaluation needs most appropriately. The evaluation methods used should be matched against the objectives of the scheme and all participants informed of the results of their work. Such evaluation is particularly valuable in formative evaluation when the effects of the intervention in the preceding year determine the structure of the programme in the forthcoming one. Equally, although a tutoring programme might be a 'one-off' intervention, much can be learnt form quite simple evaluation, adding to the body of knowledge already accumulated about tutoring and pointing the way to further research questions.

3   *Structure the content* The major decision for anyone running a tutoring scheme is the degree of structure to incorporate in the programme. Schemes can vary from those in which tutors work with highly-structured teaching materials with explicit instructions, to schemes in which tutors are given complete responsibility for choosing tutoring materials. The degree of structure which teachers employ is most likely to be determined by the age and ability of the tutors and whether the scheme is primarily intended to benefit tutors or tutees. The more structured a peer tutoring programme, the less likely tutors are to produce errors or display poor tutoring techniques. Less-structured schemes, by contrast, offer more possibilities for enhancing the learning of tutors, requiring them to reflect on the work they are teaching and formulate it into a coherent teaching programme. It is probable that most organisers will wish to strike a balance between the two extremes. Experience suggests that both tutors and tutees will feel at ease if there is some readily-apparent structure to the tutoring. Yet even with structured materials, time can be allowed for tutors to make a personal contribution to the tutoring material by building upon it, amplifying it and embellishing it.

4   *Define roles* When tutoring schemes have failed, this has often been due to two factors: a loss of initiative and impetus (nobody seemed to know who was responsible for what) or a lack of communication among those affected by the programme. The appointment of one overall coordinator (whose principal role is that of communicator), can alleviate these problems.

Communication is the most difficult single aspect of a tutoring scheme. In most secondary schools and colleges, few teachers are aware, in any detail, of what is happening in the classrooms of others. Although teachers are becoming more used to having other bodies in the classroom (special needs coordinators, advisory teachers, team teachers etc), many still resist open discussion of their teaching methods with colleagues. A tutoring scheme, which frequently involves inter-action between at least two groups of people, requires movement across boundaries and necessitates teachers having some appreciation of each others' aims and intentions.

The roles of all participants involved in a programme need to be clearly defined if it is to be successfully maintained. The coordinator of a tutoring programme might find it expedient to write down a list of the expected responsibilities of each party to the operation (following consultation with these parties) so that all participants (the sending-teacher, the receiving-teacher, school principal coordinator) know what is expected of them. Some possible task ascriptions for these key people are included in Goodlad and Hirst (1989:137).

5   *Train the tutors* Some form of training is needed for all tutors: the type and amount will, however, depend upon the age and ability of the tutors. Training need not take a long time. With highly-structured tutoring techniques (such as those employed in the Paired Reading and Companion Reading schemes described in Chapters 9 and 10 above) very young tutors have been trained in as little as two 20-minutes sessions. It is important to note, however, that the skills demanded of a good tutor require practice and cannot be acquired simply by tutors being told about the techniques. Tutor-training should allow tutors the opportunity to try out these techniques before the tutoring proper begins.

In less-structured schemes (such as those described by respectively Beardon and Jones in Chapters 5 and 6 above) a minimum half-day of tutor-training has been employed to orient students towards their task and educate them in good classroom-practice. Special techniques, such as role play and simulation exercises, have been found useful in giving tutors direct experience in exercising the skills they will need. Topics which have been included in training sessions cover such things as: how to start a tutoring session by establishing a friendly atmosphere; what to do when the tutee gives a correct/incorrect answer; how to vary the content of the tutoring sessions; how to end a tutoring session, etc. A more comprehensive list of tutoring skills which require special attention is given in Goodlad and Hirst (1989:139).

In addition to holding initial tutor-training days, many tutoring coordinators find regular debriefing sessions useful for enabling tutors to discuss any problems which have arisen. The need for such sessions with young children has been highlighted by Winter (Chapter 15 above) who found that although primary school tutors had been trained in Paired Reading techniques, a short time after training their incidence of using the specified responses was low. Those organising undergraduate tutoring schemes linking higher education establishments with schools have made use of the half-term weeks, in which tutors are not required in school to hold debriefing meetings.

6 *Support the tutors* Tutors, like all teachers, will need some reassurance that they are 'doing OK' and can rely on help from others if problems arise. Although tutors will probably find the whole tutoring experience enjoyable, most are likely to have some initial apprehension at being cast in this new role. The coordinator and other teachers involved can build the confidence of tutors by offering well-defined instructions for students to use during sessions and being available as consultants if tutors wish to discuss their experiences. (New tutors may need relatively frequent debriefing meetings early on in the scheme.) Schemes such as the Pimlico Connection undergraduate tutoring scheme, provide tutors with a quick-reference list of instructions to review between tutoring sessions (see Goodlad and Hirst, 1989: Appendix A).

7 *Documentation* Written information concerning a tutoring scheme need not be extensive but some record is needed of the activities in which tutors and tutees have engaged. Such record-keeping could involve a simple tick-list of exercises covered or books read. Alternatively, tutors could write a few lines describing what the tutoring session has involved. Information relating to the work covered by each tutee can be kept in a folder, enabling the teacher to review progress easily. The added advantage to such a system is that, if tutors are changed, a new tutor can pick up the work where the last tutor left off, without needing a great deal of guidance from the teacher.

It is also extremely useful if the coordinator of the scheme, or a group of those participating in the tutoring, writes a summary report at the conclusion of the tutoring for any one year. Such reports inform all of those involved in the scheme of its effects, and are useful sources of information for other teachers inspired by the programme who want to try tutoring for themselves. In the Pimlico Connection, annual reports have proved valuable documents (Goodlad and Hirst, 1989:97). Not only do they offer a tangible record for students of what they have done; they also serve as documents to be used in schools coming into the scheme for the first time. In addition, heads of department do not need to give an elaborate explanation of the aims, objects, procedures and so forth of the scheme each time a new teacher joins: they can pass on a copy of the most recent report.

Lines of development for peer tutoring

This volume should indicate to practitioners the enormous potential which tutoring offers for accelerating the learning of participants. The chapters of this volume have been written by those who have already been inspired by the strategy, and who are examining ways in which the tutoring model can be extended and adapted to meet the needs of educators working in many different contexts. There are still many questions which need to be answered concerning both logistics and educational theory before a cohesive body of knowledge about peer tutoring can be formed. We hope, however, that sufficient evidence has already been presented to demonstrate that peer tutoring is a viable teaching tool.

New educational strategies do, however, take time to infiltrate a system. If peer tutoring is to be used more comprehensively in the future, certain actions need to be taken by key persons.

Researchers should examine the effects on tutors and tutees of taking part in a tutoring programme *within the regular school context*. In particular, research should address the issue of which aspects of peer tutoring make it so successful as a strategy for learning.

Teachers already employing some form of peer tutoring should carry out evaluation of the programme (drawing on the expertise of researchers if necessary). Practising teachers can add much to the literature documenting the outcome of peer tutoring. In addition, they should document their schemes and publicise them (locally and nationally), so 'spreading the word' and informing others of the possibilities.

More information is also needed concerning the financial outlay and time-commitment necessary to initiate and maintain schemes. To date, much research on peer tutoring has been carried out by educational researchers who have perhaps concentrated more on the educational gains for tutors and tutees which are possible through peer tutoring and less on the practicalities of implementing strategies for the regular class teacher. Practitioners could contribute a great deal to the literature about peer tutoring by keeping careful records of the time necessary to prepare for, and conduct, tutoring. In addition, it is useful if those employing peer tutoring can communicate to others the cost 'per head' or 'per lesson' of the scheme. In these ways, practitioners can carry out quite simple evaluation invaluable to others considering using the strategy.

Principals and headteachers play an important role in informing parents, students, teachers and other school personnel of the aims of a tutoring scheme. In addition, they can make arrangements for INSET days or visits by staff from other schools to facilitate the dissemination of information about tutoring.

Principals can structure the timetable to maximise the use of tutoring, allocate room space, and allow teaching staff non-contact time in which to develop tutoring materials. Additionally, principals are the people who can best secure financial resources to implement a scheme, either by budgeting a proportion of the capitation for this use, or by liaising with local industry, the PTA and other sources of finance to raise the necessary funds.

Local Education Authorities should be responsible for organising INSET programmes informing teachers about tutoring as a learning strategy. School-based advisors and advisory teachers should be aware of the technique, so enabling them to demonstrate to teachers on their school visits how they could include tutoring in their teaching repertoire. A centralised bank of information and resource materials should be available in local teacher centres to aid those wishing to employ the technique.

LEA personnel who visit schools have a key role to play in bringing together teachers in the various school who are experimenting with (or wish to try) tutoring, so that a local network of collaborators in the field can be developed.

In conclusion

This book indicates the wide range of applications of peer tutoring and demonstrates that practitioners can, with confidence, adopt and adapt one or other of the tutoring models to meet their particular circumstances. We hope that the practical suggestions in this chapter will encourage educators to carry out their own explorations in peer tutoring.

Correspondence:
Dr. Sinclair Goodlad, Humanities Programme, ME Building, Imperial College of Science, Technology and Medicine, Exhibition Road, London SW7 2BX, UK.

Appendix A

Notes on the contributors

The biographical details are listed in alphabetical order of the first-named authors of the chapters. For those chapters where there is more than one author the biographical details of all contributors are listed alongside those of the first-named author.

Arblaster *Glynn Arblaster* is Headteacher, and Anne Taylor and Chris Butler are main professional grade teachers, at Castlefort Primary School, Walsall. They have been involved in peer tutoring for primary age children in reading since 1987.

Mick Pitchford is an Educational Psychologist with Walsall Education Department Psychological Services. He has been involved in the implementation of peer tutoring in reading in four schools in Walsall involving children as young as five. His other main interest is classroom management.

Beardon *Toni Beardon* is currently Coordinator of Mathematics Initiatives at the University of Cambridge Department of Education where she developed, and now teaches, a two-year PGCE course to train graduates in other subjects to teach Mathematics. She also organises the Cambridge STIMULUS project. Before taking up her current position in 1987, she taught in comprehensive schools for 12 years, and prior to that for 12 years in schools and colleges of education in this country and in the USA.

Button *Bryan Button* is Head of the Department of Mechanical Engineering and Dean of Engineering at Trent Polytechnic, Nottingham. Professor Button taught and carried our research in the USA and Hong Kong before returning to the UK as an engineer in the gas turbine industry. He later became Principal Lecturer in Thermodynamics and then Reader in Mechanical Engineering at Coventry

Polytechnic before taking up his current position. He has published widely on Heat Transfer and Engineering Education.

Ron Sims is Senior Lecturer at Trent Polytechnic, Nottingham with responsibility for Engineering Design. He is a chartered engineer and a member of the Institution of Mechanical Engineers and the Textile Institute. His special interest is in the design of high-speed computer-controlled machinery, especially associated with textile machines. He has published several papers on Engineering Design, in particular on Computer Controlled Mechanisms.

Laurie White is Senior Lecturer at Tent Polytechnic, Nottingham with special interest in Thermodynamics and Engineering Design. He is a Chartered engineer, a member of the Institution of Mechanical Engineers, a member of the Institution of Marine Engineers, and a fellow of the Institution of Plant Engineers. He has published several papers on Steam Turbine Applications and Thermal Power Plants as well as papers concerning Education and Professional Training.

Falchikov Having completed an undergradute degree in Psychology, *Nancy Falchikov* was awarded a PhD by Edinburgh University in 1982. She has worked in a variety of higher education establishments in Scotland and Australia, and is currently Lecturer at Napier Polytechnic, Edinburgh. She is interested in ways of increasing student self-reliance, competence and autonomy and has conducted research into self- and peer- assessment as well as into peer tutoring in higher education.

Fitz-Gibbon *Carol Fitz-Gibbon* is Senior Lecturer in the School of Education, Newcastle-upon-Tyne. Formerly a teacher of Physics and Mathematics, Dr Fitz-Gibbon has been conducting research into peer tutoring since 1971. From 1971–76 she was Co-director of a Summative Evaluation Project on Peer Tutoring at the Center for the Study of Evaluation, University of California, Los Angeles. Her other major research interests include performance indicators, meta-analysis experimentation, and evaluation.

Fresko *Barbara Fresko* is Lecturer in Statistics and Research Methods at Beit Berl College, and a member of the Department of Science Teaching at the Weizmann Institute of Science in Israel. She has conducted research primarily in the areas of tutoring, pre-service teacher training and INSET.

Amos Carmeli is the National Director of the PERACH tutorial scheme. He is involved in the planning and implementation of tutoring projects, including the educational, organisational, financial and social aspects of these projects.

Goodlad *Sinclair Goodlad* is Senior Lecturer in the Presentation of Technical Information at the Imperial College of Science and Technology, University of London. He founded the tutoring scheme known as 'The Pimlico Connection' and has written extensively on this and other projects in higher education designed to give students the opportunity to do work of direct practical value. He is editor of the journal *Studies in Higher Education*. He organises courses for lecturers at Imperial College and post-experience courses for scientists and engineers in industry, commerce, and the civil service who have to present very complex technical information to non-specialists.

Beverley Hirst took a degree in Physics at the Imperial College where she was a tutor in The Pimlico Connection. After taking a PGCE, she taught for two years in Cambridge before working for two years as Research and Project Development Officer on the UGC-funded initiative of which the conference reported in this book was a part. In September 1989, she resumed her teaching career as Head of Physics at the Hertfordshire and Essex High School, Bishop's Stortford.

Jones *John Jones* is head of the Higher Education Research Office at the University of Auckland, New Zealand. He is responsible for organising academic staff development programmes, as well as being involved in a range of research projects and teaching activities. Previously he held positions at the Universities of Malawi and Papua New Guinea.

Kellett *David Kellett* read Psychology at Nottingham University before conducting research there for his PhD. He was a research scholar at Purdue University before beginning work as a Psychologist for a major organisation in London.

Kennedy *Mary Kennedy* is Lecturer in Education at the Northern College of Education, Aberdeen. Dr Kennedy has been working as a teacher and educational researcher since 1979. Her PhD, from the Psychology Department of the University of Liverpool, involved her in investigating some aspects of peer tutoring in British junior schools. She conducted further experimental work on peer tutoring whilst teaching slow learners in the secondary school. In addition to peer tutoring, her work concerns the assessment of attainment, mathematical education, teacher education and research training.

Osguthorpe *Russell Osguthorpe* is currently an associate Dean in the College of Education at Brigham Young University. His research interests include tutoring with exceptional students, applications of technology in special education and instructional design.

Quin *Melanie Quin* currently directs the Nuffield Foundation's Interactive Science and Technology Project. After completing an undergraduate degree in Botany, she obtained an MSc in Environmental Technology, and a PhD in Atmospheric Physics from the Imperial College of Science, Technology and Medicine. More recently she has worked as science editor at Hobsons Publishing in Cambridge where projects included editing and coordinating production of the Launch Pad book for the London Science Museum. She continues to write and edit on a freelance basis.

Topping *Keith Topping* is an Educational Psychologist with Kirklees Psychological Services in Huddersfield. He is currently Director of the Kirklees Paired Learning Project and Chief Consultant to TEEMS (Training Education Evaluation and Management Systems) a private sector agency servicing the needs of education and industry. His main interests include: peer tutoring, instructional design, special educational needs, service delivery systems and community education.

Winter *Sam Winter* worked in the UK as a teacher of pupils with learning difficulties and as an educational psychologist before moving to Hong Kong University where he currently teaches Educational Psychology. His interests in peer tutoring focus on the teaching of reading. He is presently engaged in a series of studies which aim to isolate organisational factors which may underlie the success of peer tutoring.

Appendix B

Starting a peer tutoring project: matters to consider. A 12 Point Plan

1 Discuss your intentions with colleagues. Discussion will reveal which of your colleagues are interested in being involved in a tutoring scheme, and will inform others of your objects.

2 Decide who will be the tutors and who will be the tutees. (Ensure that timetabling arrangements make the pairing of the chosen tutors and tutees possible.

3 Decide *when* and *where* the tutoring is to take place.

4 Define the aims and objects of the tutoring scheme. Write a statement of intent to focus action, ie What benefits are intended for tutors/tutees?

5 Decide upon the degree of structure to be incorporated in the programme. If the tutoring is to be highly-structured, you will need to secure or develop materials well in advance of the start of the programme.

6 Decide how the tutoring scheme is to be evaluated. Educational researchers may be a useful resource for outlining the possibilities.

7 If extra resources/funding will be necessary to implement the programme, take steps to secure these. Local industries may help.

8 If the scheme is to involve several resource people (teachers, voluntary aides, researchers, or other personnel) define who is responsible for what.

9 Inform the intended tutors and tutees about the scheme, and contact any other people (eg parents) who should be aware of the aims of the programme.

10 Decide *when*, *where* and *how* tutors are to be trained. Arrangements also need to be made for de-briefing sessions and regular consultation between organisers and tutors.

11 Evaluate the tutoring using the criteria chosen. Inform all participants

and the other people you originally contacted of the results.

12   Document the scheme, outlining the logisitics of organisation and the subsequent outcome: This will help people in other places who may be thinking of starting a tutoring scheme – and will be essential for anyone who has to take over from you.

References

Ackerman, A.P. (1970) The effects of pupil tutors on arithmetic achievement of third grade students (Doctoral dissertation, University of Oregon, 1969) *Dissertation Abstracts International.* 31,918A (University Microfilms No. 75–15, 307)

Allen, V.L. & Feldman, R.S. (1973) Learning through Tutoring: low-achieving children as tutors *Journal of Experimental Education* 42,1–5

Allen, V.L. (ed) (1976) *Children as teachers: theory and research on tutoring* New York: Academic Press

Anderson, B.L., Licht, B.G., Ullman, R.K., Buck, S.T. & Redd, W.H. (1979) 'Paraprofessional reading tutors: assessment of the Edmark reading program and flexible teaching' *American Journal of Community Psychology* 7, 689–699

Argyle, M. (1976) 'Social Skills Theory'. In V L Allen (ed) *Children as teachers: theory and research on tutoring* New York: Academic Press

Asch, S.E. (1952) *Social Psychology* New Jersey: Prentice Hall

Ashton, C., Stoney, A. & Hannon, P. (1986) 'A Reading at Home Project in a first school' *Support for Learning* 1(1),43–49

Association of Graduate Careers Advisory Services (1988) *What do graduates do?* Cambridge: Hobsons

Bar-Eli, N. & Raviv, A. (1982) Underachievers as Tutors *Journal of Educational Research*, 75,3,139–143

Bell, A. (1797) *An experiment in education at the male asylum of Madras: suggesting a system by which a school or family may teach itself under the superintendence of the master or parent* London: Cadell and Davis

Bell, A. (1797) *Instructions for conducting schools through the agency of the scholars themselves: Comprising the analysis of an experiment in education, made at the male asylum, 1789–1796* London

Best, J.W. (1970) *Research in Education* New Jersey: Prentice Hall

Beuret, G. & Webb, A. (1983) *Goals for engineering education engineers – servants or saviours* London: Council for National Academic Awards

Bierman, K.L. & Furman, W. (1981) Effects of role and assignment rationale on attitudes formed during peer tutoring *Journal of Educational Psychology*, 73,1.33–40

Bloom, B.S. (ed) (1956) *Taxonomy of Educational Objectives, Handbook 1: Cognitive Domain* Ann Arbor, Michigan: Longmans

Bloom, B.S. (1980) 'The new direction in educational research: alterable variables' *Phi Delta Kappan* 61, 6, 382–385

Bloom, B.S. (1984) 'The 2-sigma problem: the search for methods of group instruction as effective as one-to-one tutoring' *Educational Researcher* 13,4–16

Bloom, S. (1975) *Peer and cross-age tutoring in the schools: an individualized supplement to group instruction* Washington DC: National Institute of Education

Boersma, F.J. & Chapman, J.W. (1978) 'Comparison of the Students Perception of Ability Scale with the Piers Harris Children's Self-concept Scale' *Perceptual and Motor Skills*, 47, 827–832

Boersma, F.J. & Chapman, J.W. (1979) *Students Perception of Ability Scale* Alberta: University of Alberta

Bohart, A.C. (1972) Role Playing and the reduction of interpersonal conflict. Unpublished doctoral dissertation, University of California, Los Angeles

Bremmer, B. (1972) *Students helping students Program*, Seattle Public Schools, Planning and Evaluation Department, August, ERIC No. ED 074 473

Bridge, W. (1975) *HELP Evaluation Report* University of Surrey: Higher Education Learning Project in Physics, Institute of Educational Technology

Brimer, A. (1969) *Bristol Achievement Test Mathematics* Middlex: Nelson

Bronfenbrenner, U. (1970) *Two worlds of childhood: US and USSR,* New York: Russell Sage Foundation

Brown, L., Fenrick, N. & Klemme, H. (1971) Trainable pupils learn to teach each other *Teaching Exceptional Children*, 4,18–24

Bruce, P. (1986) A peer tutoring project with a class of 9 & 10 year olds *Paired Reading Bulletin*, 2, 71–75

Bryans, T., Kidd, A. & Levey, M. (1985) The Kings Heath Project. Ch. 25 in *Parental Involvement in Children's Reading*, K.Topping & S.Wolfendale (eds) London: Croom Helm

Buckholdt, D.R. & Wodarski, J.S. (1978) The effects of different reinforcement systems on cooperative behaviours exhibited by children in contexts *Journal of Research and Development in Education*, 12,50–68

Burdett, L. (1986) 'Two effective approaches for helping poor readers' *British Journal of Special Education* 13,4,151–154

Bushell, R., Miller, A. & Robson, D. (1982) 'Parents as remedial teachers: an account of a Paired Reading project with junior school failing readers and their parents' *Journal of the Association of Educational Psychologists* 5,9,7–13

Button, B.L. (1985) *Learning methods for engineering courses: some thoughts for the future.* Paper presented at the European Society for Engineering Education annual conference, Patterns for the Future Madrid, Spain. 18–20 September: 611–615

Button, B.L. (1989) Cooperation between industry and higher education *International Conference on Engineering Technology Education,* Shanghai, People's Republic of China, 20–22 February, 56, 1–10

Button, B.L., Metcalfe, R. & White, L. (1987) 'Proctoring' *Engineering Design* Autumn, 4–8

Campbell, D.T. & Stanley, J.C. (1966) *Experimental and quasi-experimental designs for research* Chicago: Rand McNally

Carlton, M.B., Litton, F.W. & Zinkgraf, S.A. (1985) The effects of an intraclass peer tutoring program on the sight-word recognition ability of students who are mildly mentally retarded *Mental Retardation,* 23,2,74–78

Carnine, D. & Silbert, J. (1979) *Direct Instruction Reading* Boston: Charles. E. Merrill

Carsrud, A.L. (1984) Graduate student supervision of undergraduate research: increasing research opportunities *Teaching of Psychology,* 11,4,203–205

Cawood, S. & Lee, A. (1985) Paired Reading at Colne Valley High School *Paired Reading Bulletin,* 1,46–50

Center for the Study of Evaluation (1978) *Reports on Tutoring*: A; No. 116; No. 117; No. 118; No. 121; No. 122 Los Angeles: University of California

Chalip, P. & Chalip, L. (1978) Interaction between cooperative and individual learning *New Zealand Journal of Educational Studies,* 13,2

Chan Kong Chuk-Ling, S. (1987) Paired Reading: a comparison of the effectiveness of student teachers and peers in the tutoring of poor Chinese readers in a primary school in Hong Kong. Hong Kong University. Unpublished MEd. thesis

Clare, J. (1988) 'Job prospects for graduates have never been better' *Daily Telegraph,* 2 December

Clark, M. & Vere-Jones, D. (1986) *Science education in New Zealand: present facts and future problems* Wellington: Victoria University

Cloward, R.D. (1967) 'Studies in Tutoring' *Journal of Experiential Education* 36, 1, 14–25

Cloward, R.D. (1976) 'Teenagers as tutors of academically low-achieving children: impact on tutors and tutees' in V.L. Allen (ed) *Children as teachers: theory and research on tutoring* New York: Academic Press

Cohen, P.A., Kulik, J.A. & Kulik, C.L. (1982) 'Educational outcomes of tutoring: a meta analysis of findings' *American Educational Research Journal* 19, 237–248

Collier, G. (1980) Peer-group learning in higher education: the development of higher order skills *Studies in Higher Education,* 5,1,55–61

Collins, B.E. & Hoyt, M.F. (1972) 'Personal responsibility for consequences: an integration and extension of the 'forced compliance' literature' *Journal of Experimental Social Psychology* 8, 558-593

Conrad, E. (1976) *Effects of tutor training, achievement and expectancies on process and product peer tutoring variables. Research summary* Tucsan, Arizona: Arizona University Center for Educational Research and Development

Cook, T.D. & Campbell, D.T. (1979) *Quasi-Experimentation: Design and Analysis Issues for Field Settings* Chicago: Rand McNally College Publishing

Cook, S.B., Scrugs, T.E., Mastropieri, M.A. & Casto, G.C. (1986) 'Handicapped students as tutors' *Journal of Special Education* 19,4,483-492

Coopersmith, S. (1967) *The antecedents of self-esteem* San Fransisco, California: W.H. Freeman

Cornwall, M.G. (1979) *Students as teachers: peer tutoring in higher education* Centrum voor Odwrzoek van het Wetenschappelijik Onderwijs No. 7906-01 (Univeriteit van Amsterdam)

Crombie, R. & Low, A. (1986) 'Using a Paired Reading technique in cross-age tutoring' *Paired Reading Bulletin* No. 2, Spring UK: Kirklees Psychological Service

Crothers, C. & Jones, J. (1987) *Educational and vocational aspirations of Auckland school students* Tertiary Review Project Team, Dept of Education, Wellington

Csapo, M. (1976) If you don't know it, teach it! *Clearinghouse,* 12,49,365-367

Custer, J.D. & Osguthorpe, (1983) Improving social acceptance by training handicapped students to tutor their nonhandicapped peers *Exceptional Children,* 50,2,175

Daniels, J.C. & Diack, H. (1985) *The standard reading tests* St Albans: Hart-Davis

Davis, D., Snapiri, T. & Golan, P. (1984) *A survey of tutoring activities in Israel and associated evaluation studies* Jerusalem: NCJW Research Institute for Innovation in Education, Hebrew University

Deering, A.R. (1975) *Factsheet: High School Peer Tutoring (Homework Helpers) Program 1974-5.* New York: Board of Education of the City of New York

Devin-Sheehan, L., Feldman, R.S. & Allen, V.L. (1976) 'Research on children tutoring children: a critical review' *Review of Educational Research* 46, 355-385

Diamond, J.D., Cleary, M.J. & Librero, D. (1987) The Exploratorium's Explainer Program: The Long-Term Impacts on Teenagers of Teaching Science to the Public *Science Education,* 71,5,643-656

Diener, E., Fraser, S.C., Beamer, A.C. & Kelem, R.T. (1976) 'Effects of de-individuation variables in stealing among Halloween trick-or-treaters *Journal of Personality and Social Psychology* 33, 178-183

Doise, W. & Mugny, G. (1984) *The Social Development of the Intellect* London: Pergamon Press

Duff, R.E & Swick, K. (1974) 'Primary level tutors as an instructional resource' *Reading Improvement* 11,3,39–44

Dures, A. (1971) *Schools* London: Batsford

Edwards, J., Pitchford, M. & Story, R. (1988) 'Group instruction and peer tutoring' (in press)

Ehly, S. (1987) 'The present and future of peer tutoring: some implications for special education' *Techniques: A Journal for Remedial Education and Counseling* 3(3) 205–21

Eisenberg, T., Fresko, B. & Carmeli, M. (1980) *A tutorial project for disadvantaged children: an evaluation of the PERACH project* Rehovot, Israel: The Weizmann Institute of Science

Eisenberg, T., Fresko, B. & Carmeli, M. (1981) 'An assessment of cognitive change in socially disadvantaged children as a result of a one-to-one tutoring program' *Journal of Educational Research* 74,311–314

Eisenberg, T., Fresko, B. & Carmeli, M. (1982a) *A follow-up study of PERACH children two years after tutoring* Rehovot: The Weizmann Institute of Science

Eisenberg, T., Fresko, B. & Carmeli, M. (1982b) 'Affective changes in socially disadvantaged children as a result of one-to-one tutoring' *Studies in Educational Evaluation* 8,141–151

Eisenberg, T., Fresko, B. & Carmeli, M. (1983a) *The effects at different grade levels of one and two years of tutoring* Rehovot: The Weizmann Institute of Science

Eisenberg, T., Fresko, B. & Carmeli, M. (1983b) 'A follow-up study of disadvantaged children two years after being tutored' *Journal of Educational Research* 76,302–306

Eiserman, W.D. (1985) *Reciprocal, reverse-role, and traditional tutoring with learning disabled students* Provo, Utah: Brigham Young University

Eiserman, W.D. & Osguthorpe, R.T. (1985) *Increasing social acceptance: Mentally retarded students tutoring regular class peers* Paper presented at the annual meeting of the Council for Exceptional Children, Anaheim, California

Elashoff, J.D. & Snow, R.E. (1971) *Pygmalion Reconsidered* New York: Wandsworth Publishing Company

Ellson, D.G., Harris, P.L. & Barber, L. (1968) A field test of programmed and directed tutoring *Reading Research Quarterly*, 3,3, Spring, 307–67

Epstein, L. (1978) The effects of intraclass peer tutoring on the development of learning disabled children *Journal of Learning Disabilities*, 11,63–66

Eysenck, S.B.G. (1965) *The Junior Eysenck Personality Inventory* London: University of London Press

Falchikov, N. & Fitzgibbon, C.T. (1989) 'Peer tutoring in higher education: an experiment' in C. Bell, J. Davies & R. Winders (eds) *Promoting learning. Aspects of Educational and Training Technology XX11* London: Kogan Page

Feldman, R.S., Devin-Sheehan, L. & Allen, V.L. (1976) 'Children tutoring children: a critical review of research' in V.L. Allen (ed) *Children as teachers: theory and research on tutoring* New York: Academic Press

Fenrick, N.J. & Peterson, T.K. (1984) Developing positive changes in attitudes towards moderately/severely handicapped students through a peer tutoring program *Education and Training of the Mentally Retarded,* 19,2,83–90

Fitz-Gibbon, C.T. (1975) *The Role Change Intervention: an experiment in cross-age tutoring* Los Angeles: UCLA Graduate School of Education PhD dissertation

Fitz-Gibbon, C.T. (1977) *Tutoring and ESEA Title 1. CSE Report on Tutoring No. 2.,* California University, Center for the Study of Evaluation

Fitz-Gibbon, C.T. (1978) *A Survey of Tutoring Projects.* CSE Report on Tutoring No 118, California University, Los Angeles, Center for the Study of Evaluation

Fitz-Gibbon, C.T. (1980) *Measuring Time Use and Evaluating Peer Tutoring in Urban Secondary Schools* SSRC End of Grant Report 6570/2

Fitz-Gibbon, C.T. (1981) *Time-use and peer tutoring in urban secondary schools* Final report to Social Science Research Council

Fitz-Gibbon, C.T. & Reay, D.G. (1982) Peer Tutoring: brightening up FL teaching in an urban comprehensive school *British Journal of Language Teaching* XX(1), Spring, 39–46

Flavell, J.H. (1968) *The development of role-taking and communication skills in children* New York: Wiley

Fox, D. (1983) 'Personal theories of teaching' *Studies in Higher Education,* 8,151–163

Franca, V.M. (1983) Peer tutoring among behaviourally disordered students: Academic and social benefits to tutor and tutee *Dissertation Abstracts International,* 44,459–A

Free, L., Harris, C., Martin, J., Morris, S. & Topping, K.J. (1985) Parent, peer and cross-age tutors *Paired Reading Bulletin,* 1,59–64

French, D.C., Brownell, C.A., Graziano, W.G. & Hartup, W.W. (1977) Effects of cooperative competitive and individualistic sets on performance in children's groups *Journal of Experimental Child Psychology,* 24,1–10

Fresko, B. (1988) 'Reward salience, assessment of success and critical attitudes among tutors' *Journal of Educational Research* 81,341–346

Fresko, B. & Chen, M. (1989) 'Ethnic similarity, tutor expertise and tutor satisfaction in cross-age tutoring' *American Educational Research Journal 26(1), 122–140*

Fresko, B. & Eisenberg, T. (1985) 'The effects of two years of tutoring on mathematics and reading achievement' *Journal of Experimental Education* 55,193–201

Gable, R.V. & Kerr, M.M. (1979) Behaviourally disordered adolescents as academic change agents. In *Severe behaviour disorders of children and youth* (Vol. 4,117–124), R.B. Rutherford, A.G. Prieto & J.E. McGlothlin (eds) Reston VA: Council for Children with Behavior Disorders

Gale, I. & Kendall, D. (1985) 'Working together': the Marsden Junior School peer tutor project *Paired Reading Bulletin*, 1,59–64

Garbarino, J. (1975) 'The impact of anticipated reward on cross-age tutoring' *Journal of Personality and Social Psychology*, 32,3,421–428

Gardner, W. (1978) 'Compeer assistance through tutoring and group guidance activities' *Urban Review* 10,1,45–54

Gartner, A., Kohler, M. & Riessman, F. (1971) *Children teach children: learning by teaching* London: Harper and Row

Gerber, M. & Kauffman, J. (1981) Peer tutoring in academic settings. In P. Strain (ed) *Utilization of classroom peers as behavior change agents* (155–187) New York: Plenum

Glachan, P. (1983) Peer interaction: its role in cognitive development. Unpublished doctoral dissertation, University of Southampton

Glynn, E. (1981) 'Behavioural research in remedial education: more power to the parents' Ch.7 in *The behaviourist in the classroom: aspects of applied behavioural analysis in British educational contexts* K.Wheldall (ed). Educational Review Offset Publications No. 1, University of Birmingham.

Goldschmid, M.L. (1970a) Instructional options: adapting the large university course to individual differences *Learning and Development*, 1, February, 5

Goldschmid, M.L. (1970b) Instructional options: adapting the large university course to individual differences, *Learning and Development*, Centre for Learning and Development, McGill University

Goldschmid, B. & Goldschmid, M.L. (1976) 'Peer teaching in higher education: a review *Higher Education* 5,9-33

Goodlad, S. (1977) *Socio-technical projects in engineering education* University of Stirling: General Education in Engineering (GEE) Project

Goodlad, S. (1979) *Learning by teaching* London: Community Service Volunteers

Goodlad, S. (ed) (1982) *Study Service: An examination of community service as a method of study in higher education* Windsor: NFER-Nelson

Goodlad, S. (1985) Putting science into context *Educational Research* 27,1,61-67.

Goodlad, S., Abidi, A., Anslow, P. & Harris, J. (1979) 'The Pimlico Connection: undergraduates as tutors in schools' *Studies in Higher Education* 4,191-201

Goodlad, S. & Hirst, B. (1989) *Peer Tutoring: A Guide to Learning by Teaching* London: Kogan Page

Gore, M. (1988) *The Shell Questacon Travelling Science Circus.* Paper presented at Museums Without Walls Conference, National Council of Science Museums, India

Greening, M. & Spenceley, J. (1984) *Paired Reading made easy* Cleveland County Psychological Services, Cleveland LEA

Greening, M. & Spenceley, J. (1987) 'Shared Reading: support for inexperienced readers' *Educational Psychology in Practice* 3(1), 31-37

Grigg, S. (1984) Parental involvement with reading: an experimental comparison of Paired Reading and Listening to Children Read. Unpublished MSc. dissertation, University of Newcastle

Grinell, S. (1988) 'Science centers come of age' *Issues in Science and Technology* IV, 3, 70-75

Gross, S.C. (1975) Behavioral engineering procedures in a self-feeding maintenance program for institutionalized severely mentally retarded children in higher functioning institutionalized maintenance tutors. Unpublished doctoral dissertation, New Mexico State University, Las Cruces

Guarnaccia, V.J. (1973) Pupil-tutoring in elementary school arithmetic instruction (Doctoral dissertation, Columbia University) *Dissertation Abstracts International,* 33, 32838 (University Microfilms No. 72-33,422)

Harris, G. & Bland, M. (1988) 'Chemical reactions at school' *Special Children* 20, 7-8

Harris, J. (1987) 'Using three students to enhance learning in peer tutoring groups' *Techniques: A Journal for Remedial Education and Counseling* 3(2)125-127

Harris, P.L. (1968) Experimental comparison of two methods of tutoring-programmed versus directed *Dissertation Abstracts,* 28,8-A,3072, University Microfilms No. 67-16, 405, EdD Indiana University

Harrison, G.V. (1983) *Companion Reading Program: a systems approach to reading instruction* Utah: Metra Summerhays

Harrison, G.V. & Gottfredson, C. (1983) *Companion Reading Program: a systems approach to reading construction* Blanding, Utah: Metra Summerhays

Hartup, W.W. (1976) 'Cross-age versus same-age interaction: ethological and cross-cultural perspectives' in V. L. Allen (ed) *Children as teachers: theory and research on tutoring* New York: Academic Press

Hawke, G. (1988) *Report of the committee to review post compulsory education and training* Wellington: Government Printer

Heath, A. (1981) ILEA Project – A Paired Reading Programme. Edition 2,22-31, ILEA

Hedin, D. (1987) 'Students as teachers: a tool for improving school' *Social Policy* Winter, 42-47

Hendelman, W.J. & Boss, M. (1986) Reciprocal peer teaching by medical students in the gross anatomy laboratory *Journal of Medical Education,* 61,8,674–680

Hendrickson, J.M. (1982) *Using low achievers to tutor reading and mathematics.* Paper presented at the International Reading Association Conference, Gatlinberg, Dec 1982

Hersey, P. & Blanchard, K. (1977) *Management of organizational behavior: utilizing human resources* Third edition Englewood Cliffs: Prentice-Hall

Higgins, T.S. (1982) A comparison of two methods of practice on the spelling performance of learning disabled adolescents *Dissertation Abstracts International,* 43 (8–A), 1926

Hill, A. & Helburn, N. (1981) Two modes of peer teaching in introductry college geography *Journal of Geography in Higher Education,* 5,2,145–154

Hobfall, S.E. (1980) 'Inter-racial commitment and involvement in under-graduate tutors in an inner-city preschool' *Journal of Community Psychology* 8,80–87

Howes, D. Potter, M. & Pitchford, M. (1989) 'An evaluation of Compan-ion Reading' *Educational Psychology in Practice* 5,.1.,34–41.

Isaacs, L.M. & Stennet, R.G. (1979) *Increasing 'Time on Task' Through a Multi-Method Approach to Reading Instruction* Educational Research Services Research Report, Ontario, Canada: London Board of Educa-tion

Jenkins, J.R. & Jenkins, L.M. (1982) *Cross-age and peer tutoring* Reston, VA: Council for Exceptional Children

Johnson, D.W. (1971) 'Role reversal: a summary and review of research' *International Journal of Group Tensions* 1,318–334

Johnson, D.W. (1975) 'Co-operativeness and social perspective taking' *Journal of Personality and Social Psychology* 31,241–244

Jones, J. (1982) 'Access to university education in New Zealand' *Studies in Higher Education* 7,159–168

Jones, J. (1985) *Opinions of recent Commerce Graduates: A report to the faculty of Commerce* University of Auckland: HERO

Jones, J. & Bates, J. (1987) *University Students as Tutors in Secondary Schools* Wellington: Dept of Education

Jones, J. & Jones, A. (1987) *Spreading the word: university students in school classrooms* Paper presented at the 13th annual HERDSA conference, Perth

Kammer, C.H. (1982) 'Using peer groups in nursing education' *Nurse Educator* 7(6) 17–21

Keller, F.S. (1986) Goodbye, teacher ...! *Journal of Applied Behavior Analysis,* 1,79–89

Keller, F.S. & Sherman, J. (1974) *The Keller Plan Handbook* Menlo Park, California: W.A.Benjamin

Kellett, D.A. (1989) The cognitive benefits of peer tutoring and peer collaboration. Doctoral dissertation, University of Nottingham

Kennedy, M.H. (1985) An empirical and theoretical evaluation of some aspects of peer tutoring in British Junior Schools. Doctoral Dissertation, University of Liverpool

King, R.T. (1982) 'Learning from a PAL' *The Reading Teacher* 35,6,682–685

Klaus, D.J. (1975) *Patterns of peer tutoring: Final Report* Washington: American Institutes for Research in the Behavioural Sciences

Kohlberg, L. (1968) 'The child as a moral philosopher' *Psychology Today* 2,4,24–30

Kounin, J. (1970) *Discipline and Group Management in Classrooms* New York: Holt, Rinehart and Winston

Kreutzer, V.O. (1973) A study of the use of underachieving students as tutors for emotionally disturbed children *Dissertation Abstracts International,* 34 (06–A),3145

Krouse, J., Gerber, M.M. & Kauffman, J.M. (1981) Peer tutoring: Procedures, promises, and unresolved issues *Exceptional Education Quarterly,* 1(4),107–115

Kuhn, T.S. (1970) *The structure of scientific revolutions* (1962) Chicago: University of Chicago Press

Laetsch, W.M. (1987) Chairman's summary, CIBA Foundation Conference *Communicating science to the public* Chichester: Wiley

Lakin, D.S. (1972) Cross-age tutoring with Mexican-American pupils (Doctoral dissertation, University of California) *Dissertation Abstracts International,* 32,3561A. (University Microfilms No. 72–2847)

Lamport, K.C. (1982) The effects of inverse tutoring on reading disabled students in a public school setting *Dissertation Abstracts International,* 44,(03–A), 729

Lancaster, J. (1803) *Improvements in education as it respects the industrious classes of the community* London: Darton and Harvey National Foundation for Educational Research

Landrum, L.W. & Martin, J. (1970) When students teach others *Educational Leadership,* 27, 446–448

Lane, P., Pollack, C. & Sher, N. (1972) Remotivation of disruptive adolescents *Journal of Reading,* 15,351–354

Lazerson, D.B. (1980) I must be good if I can teach! – Peer tutoring with aggressive and withdrawn children *Journal of Learning Disabilities,* 13,152–157

Le Compte de Laborde, A. (1815) *Plan d'education pour les enfantes pauvres, d'apres les deux methodes combines du docteur Bell et M. Lancaster* Paris: H. Nichole

Lee, A. (1986) A study of the longer term effects of Paired Reading *Paired Reading Bulletin,* 2,36–43

Levin, H.M., Glass, G.V. & Meister, G.R. (1987) Cost-effectiveness of computer-assisted instruction *Evaluation Review,* 7,1, February, 50–72

Levin, H.M. (1988) 'Cost effectiveness and educational policy' *Educational Evaluation and Policy Analysis* 10,1,51–69

Levine, K.P. (1976) The effect of an elementary mathematics tutoring programme upon the arithmetic achievement, attitude towards mathematics, and the self-concept of fifth-grade low-achievers when placed in the role of student tutors, *Dissertation Abstracts,* 37,4,2039A

Lewy, A. & Chen, M. (1977) 'Differences in achievement: a comparison over time of the ethnic group achievement in the Israeli elementary school' *Evaluation in Education: International Progress* 1,1–72

Liette, E.E. (1970) *Tutoring: Its effects on reading achievement, standard setting and affect mediating self evaluation for black male underachievers in reading.* Cleveland: Case Western Reserve University (ERIC No. ED 059020)

Limbrick, E., McNaughton, S. & Glynn, T. (1985) 'Reading gains for underachieving tutors and tutees in a cross-age tutoring programme' *Journal of Child Psychology and Psychiatry* 26(6), 939–953

Lindsay, G., Evans, A. & Jones, B. (1985) 'Paired Reading versus Relaxed Reading: a comparison' *British Journal of Educational Psychology* 55,304–309

Lohnes, P.R. (1972) Statistical Descriptors of School Classes *American Educational Research Journal,* 9,4,547–556

Lombardo, V.S. (1976) The effectiveness of retarded and nonretarded tutors for educable mentally retarded children. Unpublished doctoral dissertation, University of Missouri, Columbia

Longeran, N. & Andresen, L. (1988) 'Field-based education: some theoretical considerations' *Higher Education Research and Development* 7,63–77

Madden, N.A. & Slavin, R.E. (1983) Effects of cooperative learning on the social acceptance of mainstreamed academically handicapped students *Journal of Special Education,* 17,171–182

Maheady, L. & Harper, G.F. (1987a) A class-wide peer tutoring program to improve the spelling test performance of low-income third and fourth grade students *Education and Treatment of Children,* 10,2,120–133

Maheady, L., Sacca, M.K. & Harper, G.F. (1987b) Classwide student tutoring teams: The effects of peer-mediated instruction of the academic performance of secondary mainstreamed pupils *The Journal of Special Education,* 21,3

Maheady, L., Harper, G.F. & Sacca, K. (1988a) A classwide peer tutoring system in a secondary resource room program for the mildly handicapped *Journal of Research and Development in Education,* 21,3

Maheady, L., Sacca, M.K. & Harper, G.F. (1988b) Classwide peer tutoring with mildly handicapped high school students *Exceptional Children,* 5,1,52–59

Maher, C.A. (1982) Behavioral effects of using conduct problem adolescents as cross-age tutors *Psychology in the Schools*, 19,360–364

Maher, C.A. (1984) Handicapped adolescents as cross-age tutors: Program description and evaluation *Exceptional Children*, 51,56–63

Mainiero, J., Gillogly, B., Neese, O., Sheretz, D. & Wilkinson, P. (1971) *A Cross-age Teaching Resource Manual,* California: Ontario-Montclair School District, Montario

Malamuth, N.M. & Fitz-Gibbon, C.T. (1978) *Tutoring and Social Psychology: a theoretical analysis* CSE Report No. 116 Los Angeles: Center for the Study of Evaluation, UCLA, Graduate School of Education

Mathematical Association (1979) *Report of the Assessment Sub-committee of Teaching Committee on Standardised and Other Tests* Leicester: Mathematical Association

Medland, M. & Vitale, M. (1984) *Management of Classrooms* New York: Holt Rinehart and Winston

Meiklejohn, J.M.D. (1882) *Dr Andrew Bell: An old educational reformer* London: Blackwood

Mellberg, D.B. (1980) The effect of the handicapped and nonhandicapped tutor on the academic achievement of the economically disadvantaged adolescent tutor and the elementary age tutees Unpublished doctoral dissertation, University of Wisconsin, Madison

Meyers, P.C. (1972) Effects of tutorial relationships on adjustments of fifth-grade pupils *Dissertation Abstracts,* 33,3–B, University Microfilms No. 72-22,845, PhD Illinois Institute of Technology

Miller, A., Robson, D. & Bushell, R. (1986) 'Parental participation in Paired Reading': a controlled study *Educational Psychology* 6,3,277–284

Miller, R.L., Brickman, P. & Bolen, D. (1975) 'Attribution vs persuasion as a means of modifying behaviour' *Journal of Personality and Social Psychology* 31,430–441

Mohan, M. (1972) *Peer Tutoring as a technique for teaching the unmotivated,* State University of New York, Teacher Education Research Center, January, ERIC No. ED 061 154

Monk, M. (1988) 'Bowed heads, long silences: on the challenges and surprises of working with Japanese students' *Times Educational Supplement* 17/6/88

Moon, M. & Wilson, D. (1970) Teacher counsellor cooperation: building self-concepts and confidence in children *School Counsellor,* 17,5,364–66

Morgan, R.F. & Toy, T.B. (1970) 'Learning by teaching: a student-to-student tutoring program in a rural school system and its relevance to the educational cooperative' *The Psychological Record* 20,159–169

Morgan, R.T.T. (1976) 'Paired Reading tuition: a preliminary report on a technique for cases of reading deficit *Child Care Health and Development,* 2,13–28

Morgan, R.T.T. & Lyon, E. (1979) 'Paired Reading: a preliminary report on a technique for parental tuition of reading retarded children' *Journal of Child Psychology and Psychiatry* 20,151–160

Morris, R.J. & Dolker, M. (1974) Developing cooperative play in socially withdrawn retarded children *Mental Retardation,* 12,24–27

Mouly, G.J. (1978) *Educational research; the art and science of investigation* Boston: Allyn and Bacon Inc

Mugny, G., De Paolis, P. & Carugati, F. (1984) 'Social regulations in cognitive development' in W. Doise & A. Palmonari (eds) *Social Interaction in Individual Development* Cambridge: Cambridge University Press

National Council of Science Museums (in press) *Museums Without Walls* National Council of Science Museums: India Conference 1988

National Foundation for Educational Research (1967) Reading Test DE; Reading Test BD: London: Ginn and Co.

Neale, M.D. (1966) *Neale Analysis of Reading Ability* London: Macmillan Education Ltd

Niedermeyer, F.C. (1970) 'Effects of training on the instructional behaviours of student tutors' *Journal of Educational Research* 64,119–123

Notz, W.W. (1975) 'Work motivation and the negative effects of extrinsic rewards' *American Psychologist* 30,884–891

Nunally, J.C. (1975) 'Study of change in evaluation research' in E.L. Struening & M. Guttentag (eds) *Handbook of Evaluation Research Volume 1* Beverley Hills, California: Sage Publications

Ornstein, P.A., Naus, M.J. & Liberty, C. (1975) 'Rehearsal and organisational processes in children's memory' *Child Development* 46,818–830

Osguthorpe, R.T. (1984) Handicapped students as tutors for nonhandicapped peers *Academic Therapy,* 19,4,474–483

Osguthorpe, R.T. (1985) Trading places: Why disabled students should tutor nondisabled students *The Exceptional Parent,* 15,5,41–48

Osguthorpe, R.T., Eiserman, W., Shisler, L., Top, B.L. & Scruggs, T.E. (1985) *Final report (1984–5):Handicapped children as tutors* Provo, Utah: Brigham Young University

Owens, R. (1987) *Organizational behavior in education* Third edition Prentice-Hall

Page, I.A. (1975) The effects of tutoring on the sight word gains of some primary pupils. Unpublished doctoral dissertation. Graduate College of the University of Illinois at Urbana, Champaign

Paolitto, D.P. (1976) The effect of cross-age tutoring on adolescence: An inquiry into theoretical assumptions *Review of Educational Research,* 46,215–238

Perret-Clermont A.N. (1980) 'Social interaction and cognitive development in children' *European monographs in Social Psychology* 19

Piaget, J. (1932) *The Moral Judgement of the Child* London: Routledge and Kegan Paul

Piaget, J. (1948) *The moral judgement of the child* Glencoe, Illinois: Free Press

Piaget, J. (1950) *The psychology of intelligence* New York: Harcourt Brace Jovanovich

Pigott, H.E., Fantuzzo, J.W. & Clement, P.W. (1986) 'The effects of reciprocal peer tutoring and group contingencies on the academic performance of elementary school children' *Journal of Applied Behaviour Analysis* 19,1,93–98

Pindar, S. (1988) Personal communication with authors

Pitchford, M. (1983) Paired reading and same age peer tutoring. Unpublished report

Pitchford, M. & Story, R. (1988) *Companion Reading: group instruction, peer tutoring and in-service for teachers.* Occasional papers of the DECP, British Psychological Society

Polya, G. (1945) *How to Solve it* Princetown: Paperback Printing

Portsmouth, R., Wilkins, J. & Airey, J. (1985) 'Home based reading for special school pupils' *Educational Psychology in Practice* 1,2,52–58

Pumfrey, P. (1986) 'Paired Reading: promise and pitfalls' *Educational Research* 28,2,89–93

Pumfrey, P.D. (1987) A critique of Paired Reading *Paired Reading Bulletin*, 3,62–66

Putt, G.D., Kibblewhite, A.C., Stamp, A.P. & Tindle, C.T. (1985) *A study of university bursary awards and entrance standards* University of Auckland

Quin, M. (1989) *So, just what are interactive science and technology centres?* London: Nuffield Foundation

Quinn, S. & Bedworth. J. (1987) Science theatre: an effective interpretive technique in museums, CIBA Foundation Conference *Communicating science to the public* Chichester: Wiley

Ramig, L.N. & Ramig, C. (1976) *Cross-age tutoring: a study of achievement and attitudes at grades 3–5.* Paper presented at the Annual Convention of the International Reading Association, Anaheim, California

Ramsden, P. (1985) 'Student learning research: retrospect and prospect' *Higher Education Research and Development* 4,51–69

Raven, J.C. (1958) *Standard Progressive Matrices* London: H.K. Lewis and Company Limited

Raven, B.H. (1965) 'Social influence and power' in I.O. Steiner & M. Fishbein, (eds) *Readings in Contemporary Social Psychology* 371–382 New York: Holt, Rinehart and Winston

Riley, R.D. & Huffman, M. (1980) *Peer Support during Student Teaching: A Shared Relationship,* North Carolina, USA, ERIC No. ED 194 468

Roach, J.C. et al (1983) The comparative effects of peer tutoring in math by and for secondary special needs students *Pointer,* 27,4, Summer, 20–24

Robertson, D.J. (1971) *The Effects of an Intergrade Tutoring Experience on Tutor Self-concept.* Paper presented at the Annual Conference of the California Educational Research Association, April, ERIC No. ED 059 769

Rocks, T., Baker, S. & Guerney, B. (1985) 'Effects of counselor-directed relationship enhancement training on under-achieving, poorly communicating students and their teachers' *School Counselor,* January, 231–238

Rogers, M.S. (1970a) A study of an experimental tutorial reading program in which sixth grade underachievers tutored third grade children who were experiencing difficulty in reading. *Dissertation Abstracts,* 30, 11–A (University Microfilms No. 70–9381)

Rogers, V.R. (ed) (1970b) *Teaching in British Primary Schools* London: Macmillan

Rosenthal, R. & Jacobsen, L. (1968) *Pygmalion in the Classroom: Teacher Expectations and Pupils' Intellectual Development* New York: Holt, Rinehart and Winston Inc.

Rosner, H. (1970) *Facets of a cross-age tutorial program.* Paper presented to the International Reading Association, Anaheim, California

Royal Society (1986) *Girls and Mathematics* A report of the Mathematics Education Committee of the Royal Society and the Institute of Mathematics and its Appreciation. Para. 44

Russell, J. (1981) 'Why 'socio-cognitive conflict' may be impossible: the status of egocentric errors in the dyadic performance of a spatial task' *Educational Psychology* 1,2, 159–169

Rust, S.P. Jnr (1970) The effect of tutoring on the tutor's behaviour, academic achievement and social status (Doctoral dissertation, University of Oregon, 1969). *Dissertation Abstracts International,* 30,4682A (University Microfilms No. 70–9469)

Ruthven, K. (1987) *STIMULUS: a report on the feasibility study* Cambridge: Cambridge University, Dept of Education

Sarbin, T.R, (1976) 'Cross-age tutoring and social identity' in V.L. Allen (ed) *Children as Teachers: theory and research on tutoring* New York: Academic Press

Schenkat, R. (1987) Report of a study of high ability students and the effects of using Companion Reading. Unpublished study. District 861, Winona, Minnesota

Scruggs, T.E. (1985) *Tutoring within special education settings* Paper presented at the annual meeting of the Council for Exceptional Children, Anaheim

Scruggs, T.E., Mastropieri, M.A. & Richter, L. (1985) 'Peer tutoring with behaviorally disordered students: social and academic benefits' *Behavioral Disorders* 10,4,283–294

Scruggs, T.E., Mastropieri, M.A. & Richter, L. (in press) 'Peer tutoring with behaviorally-disordered students: social and academic benefits' *Behavioral Disorders*

Scruggs, T.E., & Richter, L. (in press) Tutoring interventions with learning disabled students: A critical review *Learning Disability Quarterly*

Selig, S.M. & Perlstadt, H. (1985) An instructional method for mixed medical sociology classes: paired observations of practitioner-patient interactions *Teaching Sociology*, 12,4

Sharpley, A.M., Irvine, J.W. & Sharpley, C.F. (1983) An examination of the effectiveness of a cross-age tutoring program in mathematics for elementary school children *American Educational Research Journal*, 20,103–111

Sharpley, A.M., & Sharpley, C.F. (1981) Peer tutoring: a review of the literature *CORE Collected Original Resources in Education*, 5,3,7–11

Shaver, J.P. & Nuhn, D. (1968) Underachievers in reading and writing respond to a tutoring program *The Clearinghouse*, 4,3,236–239

Sherif, M. & Sherif, C.W. (1969) *Social Psychology* New York: Harper and Row

Sherman, J.A. & Harris, V.M. (1975) Effects of peer tutoring and homework assignments on classroom performance, in *Applications of Behaviour Modification* P. Thompson & W.S. Dockens (eds) New York: Academic Press

Shisler, L., Top, B.L. & Osguthorpe, R.T. (1986) Behaviorally disordered students as reverse-role tutors: increasing social acceptance and reading skills *BC Journal of Special Education*, 10,2,101–119

Sigston, A., Addington, J., Banks, V. & Striesow, M. (1984) 'Progress with parents: an account and evaluation of a home reading project for poor readers' *Remedial Education* 19,4,170–173

Singh, R.K. (1982) Peer tutoring: Its effects on the maths skills of students designated as learning disabled *Dissertation Abstracts International*, 42,4793–A

Slavin, R.E. Madden, N.A. & Leavey, M. (1984) Effects of cooperative learning and individualized instruction on mainstreamed students *Exceptional Children*, 50,434–443

Smith, C. (1977) 'Partner learning: peer tutoring can help individualization' *Educational Leadership* 361

Snell, M.E. (1979) Higher functioning residents as language trainers of the mentally retarded *Education and Training of the Mentally Retarded*, 14,2,77–84

Soar, R. (1972) An empirical analysis of selected Follow Through programs: an example of a process approach to evaluation. In *Seventy-First Yearbook of the National Society for the Study of Education, part II* Chicago: University of Chicago Press

Stallings, J.A. & Kaskowitz, D.H. (1974) *Follow Through Classroom Observation Evaluation 1972–73* Menlo Park, California: Stanford Research Institute

Stander, A. (1973) Peer tutoring and reading achievement of seventh and eighth grade students *Dissertation Abstracts*, 33,11–A (University Microfilms No. 73–11,266)

Stotland, E., Sherman. E.S. & Shaver, K.G. (1971) *Empathy and birth order: some experimental explorations* Lincoln: University of Nebraska Press

Stowitschek, C.E., Hecimovic, A., Stowitschek, J.J. & Shores R.E. (1982) Behaviorally disordered adolescents as peer tutors: Immediate and generative effects on instructional performance and spelling achievement *Behavioral Disorders*, 7,136–148

Strain, P. (1981) *The utilization of classroom peers as behavior change agents* New York: Plenum

Strodtbeck, F.L. Ranchi, S. & Hansell, S. (1976) 'Tutoring and psychological growth' in V.L. Allen (ed) *Children as Teachers: theory and research on tutoring* New York: Academic Press

Swenson, S.H. (1975) Effects of peer tutoring in regular elementary classrooms on sociometric status, self-concept and arithmetic achievement of slow learning tutors and learners in a special education resource program. *Dissertation Abstracts International*, 36(09–A),6003

Swinson, J. (1985) 'Encouraging parents to listen to their children read' Ch. 6 in *Parental Involvement in Children's Reading* K. Topping & S. Wolfendale (eds) London: Croom Helm

Swinson, J. (1986a) 'Paired Reading: a critique' *Support for Learning* 1,2,29–32

Swinson, J. (1986b) 'Paired Reading: why all the fuss?' *Special Children*, July, 24–25

Thelen, H. (1969) 'Tutoring by students' *School Review* 77,229–244

Thomas, G. (1985) 'Room management in mainstream education' *Educational Research*, 27,3

Thomas, G. (1986) 'Integrating personnel in order to integrate children' *Support for Learning*, 1,1

Thomas, G. (1987) 'The Inventorium', in S. Pizzey (ed) *Interactive Science and Technology Centres* London: Science Projects Publishing

Tizard, J., Schofield, W. & Hewison, J. (1982) 'Collaboration between teachers and parents in assisting children's reading' *British Journal of Educational Psychology* 52,1–15

Top, B.L. (1984) Handicapped children as tutors: The effects of cross-age, reverse-role tutoring on self-esteem and reading achievement. Unpublished doctoral dissertation, Brigham Young University, Provo, Utah

Topping, K.J. (1986a) *Paired Reading training pack, 2nd edn* Huddersfield: Kirklees Psychological Service

Topping, K.J. (1986b) Effective service delivery: training parents as reading tutors *School Psychology International*, 7,231–236

Topping, K.J. (1986c) *Parents as Educators,* London: Croom Helm

Topping, K. (1987) 'Peer tutored Paired Reading: outcome data from ten projects' *Educational Psychology* 7,2,133–145

Topping, K.J. (1988) *The peer tutoring handbook: promoting co-operative learning* Beckenham: Croom Helm

Topping, K. & McKnight, G. (1984) 'Paired Reading – and Parent Power' *Special Education – Forward Trends* 11,3,12–15

Topping, K.J. & Whiteley, M. (1990) Participant Evaluation of Parent-tutored Projects in Reading *Journal of Educational Research* 31.3

Topping, K.J. & Wolfendale, S. (eds) (1985) *Parental involvement in children's reading* Beckenham: Croom Helm

Townsend, J. & Topping, K.J. (1986) An experiment using Paired Reading with peer tutors versus parent tutors *Paired Reading Bulletin*, 2,26–31

Trimbur, J. (1987) 'Peer tutoring: a contradiction in terms?' *The Writing Center Journal* 7,2,21–28

Trovato, J. (1978) Peer tutoring with or without home-based reinforcement Unpublished Masters thesis, University of Western Ontario, London, Ontario

Truesdale, E.L. (1976) The effects of assigned tutorial responsibilities on mildly retarded students *Dissertation Abstracts International*, 37(06–A),3556

Tudge, J. (1986) *Collaboration, conflict and cognitive development: The efficacy of joint problem solving* Paper presented at the annual meeting of the Eastern Psychological Association, New York City

Tudge, J. (1987) Peer collaboration and cognitive development. *Paper presented at the biennial meeting of the Society for Research in Child Development*, Baltimore

Verma, G.K. & Beard, R.M. (1981) *What is educational research?* Guildford: Gower Publishing Company

Vygotsky, L.S. (1978) *Mind in Society* Cambridge, Mass: Harvard University Press

Wareing, L. (1985) 'A comparative study of three methods of parental involvement in reading' Ch. 26 in *Parental involvement in children's reading* K. Topping & S. Wolfendale (eds) London: Croom Helm

Watts, R.L. (1987) *Report of the Universities Review Committee to the New Zealand Vice-Chancellors' Committee* Wellington: NZVCC

Whalen, C.K. & Henker, B.A. (1969) Creating therapeutic pyramids using mentally retarded patients *American Journal of Mental Deficiency*, 74,331–337

Wheldall, K., Merrett, F. & Colmar, S. (1987) 'Pause, Prompt and Praise' for parents and peers: effective tutoring of low progress readers *Support for Learning* 2,1,5–12

Wheldall, K. & Mettem, P. (1986) 'Behavioural peer tutoring: training 16 year old tutors to employ the 'pause, prompt and praise' technique with 12 year old remedial readers' 199–216 in *Behaviour analysis in educational psychology* K.Wheldall, F.Merrett & E.Glynn (eds) London: Croom Helm

Whited, S.G. (1985) *The effects on attitudes and social skills of reverse role tutoring with mentally retarded students* Provo, Utah: Brigham Young University

Widlake, P. & Macleod. F. (1985) 'Parental involvement programmes and the literacy performance of children' Ch. 9 in *Parental involvement in children's reading* K.Topping & S.Wolfendale (eds) London: Croom Helm

Wilkes, R. (1975) *Peer and cross-age tutoring and related topics: an annotated bibliography.* Theoretical Paper 53 Wisconsin: Wisconsin Research and Development Center for Cognitive Learning

Winter, S. (1986) 'Peers as Paired Reading tutors' *British Journal of Special Education* 13,3,103–106

Winter, S. (1987) 'Parents and pupils as remedial tutors' *Bulletin of Hong Kong Psychological Society* 18, 15–31

Winter, S. (1988) 'Paired Reading: a study of process and outcome' *Educational Psychology* 8,3, 135–151

Winter, S. (1989) 'Paired Reading in Hong Kong: second and Chinese language applications *School Psychology International* 10, 25–35

Winter, S. & Low, A. (1984) 'The Rossmere Peer Tutor Project' *Behavioural Approaches with Children* 8,2,62–65

Wood, D., Bruner, J. & Ross, G. (1976) 'The role of tutoring in problem solving' *Journal of Child Psychology and Psychiatry*, 17,2,89–100

Wood, E.L. (1976) Cross-age tutoring; a strategy for increasing reading achievement and improving self-concept for elementary school children. Unpublished doctoral dissertation Hofstra University

Wooster, A. (1986) 'Social skills training and reading gain' *Educational Research* 28,1,68–71

Young, C.C. & Kerr, M.M. (1979) The effects of a retarded child's social initiations on the behavior of severely retarded school-aged peers *Education and Training of the Mentally Retarded*, 14,185–191

Young, P. & Tyre, C. (1983) *Dyslexia or illiteracy? Realizing the right to read* Milton Keynes: Open University Press

Index